W9-CPG-549

Sonia Gandhi

AN EXTRAORDINARY LIFE, AN INDIAN DESTINY

RANI SINGH

Foreword by Mikhail S. Gorbachev,
Former President of the Soviet Union

palgrave
macmillan

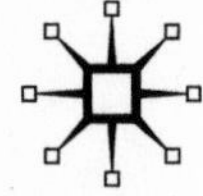

First published in 2011 by PALGRAVE MACMILLAN® in the United States–a division of St. Martin's Press LLC, 175 Fifth Avenue, New York, NY 10010.

Where this book is distributed in the UK, Europe and the rest of the world, this is by Palgrave Macmillan, a division of Macmillan Publishers Limited, registered in England, company number 785998, of Houndmills, Basingstoke, Hampshire RG21 6XS.

Palgrave Macmillan is the global academic imprint of the above companies and has companies and representatives throughout the world.

Palgrave® and Macmillan® are registered trademarks in the United States, the United Kingdom, Europe and other countries.

ISBN 978-0-230-10441-9

Library of Congress Cataloging-in-Publication Data
Singh, Rani (Rani Gagan Deep)
Sonia Gandhi : an extraordinary life, an Indian destiny / Rani Singh.
p. cm.
ISBN 978-0-230-10441-9 (hardcover)
1. Gandhi, Sonia, 1946– 2. Politicians—India—Biography. 3. Prime minister's spouses—India—Biography. 4. India—Politics and government—1977– I. Title.
DS481.G325S56 2011
954.05'2092—dc22
[B]

2011005255

A catalogue record of the book is available from the British Library.

Design by Letra Libre, Inc.

First edition: September 2011

10 9 8 7 6 5 4 3 2 1

Printed in the United States of America.

To Jairaj and Sukhraj, for sharing the journey.

CONTENTS

PART IV
A BROKEN DYNASTY

PART V
SONIA'S REBIRTH

PART VI
CONSOLIDATING POWER

Photographs appear between pages 148 and 149.

PREFACE

One evening in the East Indian state of Uttar Pradesh I was visiting the village of Samra in the constituency of Amethi, whence Sonia Gandhi was elected as a member of parliament, and which is now represented by her son Rahul. A couple of five- and six-year-olds, still in their school uniforms, were cleaning steel dishes with mud and grass by the light of a kerosene glass lamp. A boy scampered along with an improvised toy, a stick and a cycle tire. A man who used to mix potions for a doctor had set himself up as a pharmaceutical dispenser and was selling medicines for common ailments; he said he was practicing *"doctori,"* the art of being a doctor. To his right, past the village hand pump, there was a large space where Rahul Gandhi brought a British foreign secretary to talk to village women and hear them sing. That night they slept on *charpoys* (wooden frames on four legs strung with rope) in separate small, thatched-roof mud homes until around 4:30 AM. In Samra, there are self-help groups of women who spin thread on manually operated spinning wheels, as advocated by Mahatma Gandhi—a focused task that has lifted them out of poverty and created a sense of community. Once a month they clean the entire village themselves. For me, it was an illuminating visit to an outreach program in the heartland of Amethi, which is indelibly identified with the Nehru family. It gave me insight into how Sonia's son is continuing the family desire to effect change; this was just one of the many voyages of discovery I made during my research for this book.

The idea of a biography of Sonia Gandhi was originally Palgrave Macmillan's. They approached me and a couple of other journalists, searching for a suitable writer. The editor liked my approach and sometime later we signed a contract. An up-to-date story of one of the most powerful people in the world had not been told in depth; for it appeared that no major international house outside India had published an English-language biography on Sonia Gandhi. I prepared a list of essential questions, which expanded indefinitely as time went on, and set off for Delhi with two voice recorders. During my research trip in India, which lasted more than three months, and then later back in Great Britain, I collected over a hundred interviews. All, except for four, were recorded. All interviews were manually transcribed by me, word for word, and time-coded. The four untaped interviewees spoke deliberately enough for me to write down their answers verbatim. Most of my interviewees were prepared to be identified, though information on some episodes of Sonia Gandhi's life was provided by people who were recorded but asked to remain anonymous, and their wishes have been respected. Some of the interviews were conducted in two or three sessions, occasionally covering different continents.

Immersing myself in the Indian political arena, it was fascinating to observe Mrs. Sonia Gandhi in a formal setting in New Delhi, as she sat on the front bench of the Lower House of parliament. Back in London, I sat in the second row when she gave the fourteenth Commonwealth Lecture for the Commonwealth Foundation on March 17, 2011, called "Women as Agents of Change."

During my stay in India to research this book, I traveled to the southern state of Tamil Nadu. Getting away from cities showed me the challenges that politicians face in addressing the needs of the majority: Some 180 or so miles south of the city of Chennai, after driving past tractors and motorcycles on a dusty road along the east coast of India abutting the Bay of Bengal, I witnessed a villager from a low caste complaining to a politician about his lack of access to proper drinking water. For a long time, the overhead tank in the village had not been cleaned, he said, and one day when he opened a tap, to his astonishment a fish plopped out. He kept the fish and took it to show to the head man of his village council as evidence, but no one was interested in the problem. He told the politician that, apart from water needs, his village of fisher folk needed more homes and more money. An aide took notes while the politician listened. It was a small example of the problems faced by ordinary marginalized Indians, at a time when the gap between rich and poor is widening.

As is often the case with significant figures on the world stage, this biography is not an authorized work. The information and episodes covering Sonia Gandhi's life come from primary and secondary sources. My purpose in writing this book was *not* to provide a definitive political critique—with a scorecard of achievements and mistakes—of any of the main players involved; rather, I sought to tell the story of Sonia Gandhi using research and interviews with those who know or have known her. I have tried to provide an easy to understand account of the complex historical events surrounding her extraordinary life. Given that there were and are more than one person in political circles named Mrs. Gandhi, I have mostly referred to Indira and her daughters-in-law, Sonia and Maneka, by their first names. This is to avoid confusion, and no disrespect or attempt at familiarity is intended.

This undertaking has been the toughest challenge of my career, but I gave it my all, and learned much from having to deal with the various hurdles along the way. It has been a privilege to work on a project of this significance—India is at a very exciting point in its contemporary life, and the Gandhi family looks set to be at the center of the political arena for the years to come—which is why I was asked to look at the part that Rahul Gandhi has played and is likely to play in the future.

—Rani Singh
London, May 2011

ACKNOWLEDGMENTS

Another Palgrave Macmillan author once commented that it takes a village to write a book. I agree. I have included here, as many as possible, those who made the biography "Sonia Gandhi" happen.

My primary debt of thanks is due to my sons, Jairaj and Sukhraj. They always encouraged and kept me going through the challenges with huge emotional support in London and in India. They read and gave me valuable feedback on the whole book.

In Moscow, the former president of the Soviet Union, Mikhail S. Gorbachev, wrote a personal, illuminating foreword for which I am very grateful. I also thank Pavel Palazhchenko, President Gorbachev's Adviser for International and Media Relations; Vladimir Grigoriev, Deputy Head of the Federal Agency for Press and Mass Communication; and Mr. Grigoriev's assistant, Marina Savusya, for their excellent cooperation.

In London, James Brewer, senior international business journalist and former editor of global insurance at *Lloyd's List,* devoted many hours to a meticulous reading on virtually every chapter at each draft, as well as ancillaries.

In India, Romila Sharma, the former business head of television networks ETC Punjabi and Zee Punjabi, coordinated the Uttar Pradesh trip and did what no one else could or would do so that I could get to my goal. On March 31, 2010, with Romila's help we were admitted to a meeting at Fursatganj airport, where a small number of local Congress leaders had gathered to interact with Sonia Gandhi.

In New Delhi, Archana Datta, officer on Special Duty (PR) to the President, organized an interview with President Pratibha Devisingh Patil. Frank Christopher, the former director of the Lok Sabha (lower house) Secretariat (the Parliament Library, and also his origination, the Hi-Tech Museum), provided resource material including practically the only library copy in Delhi of the June 8, 1991, issue of *Frontline* magazine. Thanks also to the director of the Photo Division of the Ministry of Information and Broadcasting, Debatosh Sengupta, and in the Nehru Memorial Museum and Library, Academic Coordinator Dr. Bhashyam Kasturi. Neena and Ashok Vasudeva and All India Congress Committee National Secretary Major Dalbir Singh were also supportive.

Former Indian Youth Congress General Secretary Vikram Malhotra, YC Secretary Netta D'Souza and YC National Coordinator Szarita Laitflang facilitated my talks with ministers, including Arun Yadav and C. P. Joshi, upper house MP Professor Saifuddin Soz, and cricketer-turned-lower house MP Mohammed Azharuddin. I also met lower house MP Vijay Inder Singla.

India Today senior editors Sandeep Unnithan and Priya Sahgal were great on security and politics respectively. Sonia Gandhi biographer and journalist with Kolkata's *The Telegraph* Rasheed Kidwai was always helpful. Veteran television journalist Madhu Trehan organized research in the *TV Today Network* library. Adviser to *The Hindustan Times,* Vir Sanghvi, provided access to footage and records of all *The Hindustan Times* summits, and *Outlook* group editor in chief Vinod Mehta opened up his organization's library. I thank author and *The Times of India* consulting editor Dileep Padgaonkar for his macro and micro theories on the Nehru–Gandhi family. I am grateful to the former editor of *The Times of India* and author of "Indira Gandhi," Inder Malhotra for providing much insight and for leading me to the highly experienced and geopolitically wise Pranay Gupte, the editor in chief at *Al Aribiya English* and author of *Mother India,* a political biography of Indira Gandhi. I am grateful to Pranay for his extraordinary generosity I thank Kuldip Nayar, author and human rights activist, former BBC Delhi chief of bureau Mark Tully, and television correspondent Jabaakhi Borthakur. Rajiv Gandhi Foundation archivist Sourabh Dubey gave his first-ever interview to me. Krishna Rao, former media relations officer with the RGF, was educational. Those who gave interviews/briefings include: Special Commissioner to the Supreme Court of India and National Advisory Council member Harsh Mander (in the interests of full disclosure, my first cousin), *Cobra Post*'s Aniruddha Bahal, Suhel Seth, Managing Partner of Counselage India, and *The Hindustan Times*'s Pankaj Vohra.

In London, author and former Channel 4 commissioning editor Farrukh Dhondy helped with the narrative arc and nodal points. Author Ziauddin Sardar gave practical research advice.

Friends and family who hosted and supported were mainly: Sarwandeep Singh and wife Neerja Handa (who also generously provided staff and an office), Jeetinder and Harpreet Sindhu, Mrs. Harinder Matai and family; artist-teacher Sujata Singh and husband Harrie, Captain Tajinder and Meeta Bakshi, Professor (Doctor) Updesh Bevli, Poonam Bevli Sahi (who designed a special contribution), and family. In Uttar Pradesh, Romila Sharma arranged for Mukesh Srivastav to host us.

In Turin, Sister Maria Angela Gribaudo of the Salesian Order translated and clarified events. I acknowledge Sister Margaret and Sister Geraldine of the Little Company of Mary. Talal Karim was informative on Bangladesh, as was Romulo Bruni on Italy. David Ayrton looked out for me. I was photographed by John Dawson, MD of Imagethirst Ltd.

When I was young, my parents, Harbans (High Commission of India, retired) and Parsan Singh imbued me with a deep fascination and visceral love for the many parts of the undivided land of my forefathers.

Palgrave Macmillan team members to mention are senior vice president and publisher Airié Stuart and senior production manager Donna Cherry. Henry Kaufman in New York City oversaw the legal review process.

Some of my interviews did not form part of the final narrative and I apologize for the omission, but I want to assure those concerned that all their words deeply enriched my understanding. I am grateful to *all* those who spoke to me; especially as many of them had never spoken of their experiences before.

—Rani Singh, May 2011

FOREWORD

Rani Singh's comprehensive biography of Sonia Gandhi gives me a welcome opportunity to share some memories of how our relationship with Rajiv and Sonia Gandhi developed.

It began in May 1985, when Rajiv Gandhi came to Moscow on his first official trip abroad. It was some six months after he became prime minister and a little over two months after my election as general secretary. The meeting marked a change of generations, this alone making it a major political event. As leaders of two major powers with shared responsibility for maintaining world peace, we understood the need to consult closely on the issues confronting the world. There was also something else that our countries had in common: In spite of all the differences, the Soviet Union and India faced problems of modernization, renewal, and radical reform.

It was at that meeting that I established a warm personal rapport with Rajiv Gandhi. Our thoughts went along the same lines, and our conversations ranged far beyond the formal agenda of the negotiations. I was deeply impressed by the way he organically combined the profound philosophical tradition of India and the East with wide-ranging knowledge and comprehension of current political issues.

During that visit, my wife Raisa spent many hours together with Sonia Gandhi. The relationship that she and my wife established was warm and heartfelt. I knew that it was the beginning of friendship between our families.

Indeed, our Indian guests were an extraordinary couple. Rajiv followed in the footsteps of his grandfather, Jawaharlal Nehru, and his mother, Indira Gandhi. Sonia came from a little village in Italy. They were very private people and at first they had no plans to enter politics. Eventually, however, they had to, and both did so with great dignity.

We knew the dangers that the Gandhi family was facing and Raisa and I felt that it would be appropriate to offer hospitality to their children, Rahul and Priyanka. They spent some time in the Soviet Union and appreciated the opportunity to travel here and learn more about our country and its people.

After our first meeting with Rajiv and Sonia, we met on several other occasions, including the unforgettable visit I paid to India in November 1986, right after the summit meeting with Ronald Reagan in Reykjavik. The idea of a nuclear-weapon-free world, inscribed on the international agenda in Reykjavik, became the keynote of that visit. We signed the Delhi Declaration on the principles of a world without violence and nuclear weapons.

Raisa and I had been looking forward to that visit. Rajiv and Sonia invited us to their house. Among the guests were prominent scientists and artists, and we discussed long-term prospects for our nations' cooperation. But what I remember most about that evening was the remarkable atmosphere of warmth and hospitality, sincere and without any ostentation, that Sonia created in their home.

Rajiv's tragic death in a terrorist attack came as a shock to me and Raisa. We knew what it meant to India—the loss of a great leader—and to Sonia, whose love for her husband we admired.

I have been following the events in India during the years after my presidency. India's development has been impressive. The foundations of friendship between our countries, which Rajiv and I worked so hard to strengthen, are strong. I was glad to learn of Sonia's decision to enter politics to continue on the path of her husband, and I was happy to send her a letter of congratulations on her election success. With her wisdom, love of her adopted country, and concern and affection for ordinary people, she has a lot to contribute to India's development.

Sonia Gandhi has served India in many ways—as Rajiv's wife, as the mother of two remarkable children, as an example of dignity and strength, and as a political leader of high caliber. India must be proud of her. I am sure the readers of this book will agree.

—Mikhail Gorbachev
May 2011

PART I

ITALIAN GIRL TO INDIAN WOMAN

PROLOGUE

THE TIGERS' REVENGE

Not in my wildest dreams could I have imagined then the course my destiny would take.

—*Sonia Gandhi*

On May 21, 1991, at precisely 9:30 PM, the buck-toothed, 25-year-old female assassin, fully made up with flowers in her hair, was in disguise and in place. A belt bomb was strapped around her waist, hidden by loose green trousers and an orange overdress. A green scarf draped across her chest from shoulder to shoulder hung down her back, large glasses screened her eyes, and she carried a sandalwood garland to present to the dignitary. The bomber's alias was Dhanu. She stood between two innocents: a party worker and a 15-year-old girl preparing to read a poem to the politician. Her target was Rajiv Gandhi, India's leader of the opposition, who was on his way to a general election campaign rally deep in the south of India.

Seven years earlier, a considerable distance north of this assembly point, in a hospital in India's capital, Delhi, the body of his mother, Prime Minister Indira Gandhi, had been lying on an operating table. She was still warm. Hours earlier she had been assassinated by multiple gunshots; Rajiv Gandhi's wife, Sonia, shocked and terrified, had held her mother-in-law in her lap for the car ride to the hospital. Rajiv was Indira's only surviving son, and Indira's political party wanted a Gandhi at its head to lead the government. In a room next to Indira's now lifeless body, Sonia Gandhi had begged her husband to spurn those who were pushing him into assuming the leadership of his party and the premiership of India; she had just lost her mother-in-law and refused to allow her husband to walk into the line of fire. She pleaded with everyone around him to listen to her. In the hospital, Rajiv held Sonia's hands and explained his decision to accept the post of prime minister, telling her that "he had no choice" as "he would be killed anyway."[1]

During 1984, the Gandhi family had been the prime target for multiple terrorist groups. Rajiv remained prime minister for five years during which he was well guarded by an elite commando force, the Special Protection Group (SPG). There had been two attempts on Rajiv's life during this time, one in 1986 and the other in Sri Lanka in 1987. Sonia had been present at both.

Now, in 1991, the government had withdrawn the SPG from him, but the threats to his life remained as potent and as numerous as they had ever been. Sonia and their children, Rahul and Priyanka, were scared every time he went off to campaign. In March 1991, Rahul was so anxious about his father, he flew back to Delhi from America for his college spring break. Having spent his teenage years being home-schooled, surrounded by security on account of the threats to his family members' lives, he was shocked to see that Rajiv did not even have basic protection now that he was no longer prime minister. Rahul had told his mother that "[i]f something was not done about it, he knew he would soon come home for his father's funeral."[2]

Rajiv's one personal security officer, Pradip Kumar Gupta, a police subinspector who was at Rajiv's side the night of May 21, was loyal but not specifically trained in close protection work and was no match for determined hit squads. Sonia was usually at her husband's side as much as she could be, but this time, she remained in Delhi. Rajiv, a professional pilot, was flying himself and a copilot to the rally in a small plane, and there was not enough room for Sonia.[3] In any case, she thought that he would be back soon and was looking forward to the end of the campaign.

Dhanu and her assassination squad waited in dusty, sleepy Sriperumbudur, more than 1,864 miles south of Delhi. Their quarry, Rajiv, was a north Indian, aristocratic and tall. He had an open, honest face, with clear skin and liquid-brown eyes framed by thick black lashes. An easy, freewheeling style that he used for the election campaign, now in its final phase, allowed him to appear atop vehicles frequently to wave to the hordes who wanted to get close to him. Smiling broadly, he often plunged into the shouting, cheering throngs without any concern for his own safety; the enthusiastic crowds on his tours meant inevitable holdups.

Sonia and the children worried over any delay to Rajiv's schedule in these frightening times. Aware of impending doom, within a month of Indira Gandhi's murder Sonia and Rajiv had drafted together identical but separately signed instructions for their two children. Rajiv's said: "In the event of my death as well as that of my wife, Sonia, at or about the same time, at the same place or at different places, within or outside India, our bodies should be brought to Delhi and cremated together. . . ."[4] Sonia was ever conscious of the grim probabilities that lay in their path: "After my mother-in-law was killed, I knew that he too would be killed . . . it was just a question of when."[5]

The leader of the assassination squad was disguised as a journalist so that he had clear access to a special enclosure where Rajiv would pause before mounting the stage. From that vantage point, Dhanu's handler could supervise her and provide backup if needed. An expert in explosives, he wore thick photochromatic spectacles to hide his glass left eye, held a blank notepad, and had a hidden 9mm pistol. Indian Intelligence would call him "One-Eyed Jack." He wore a long, collarless white shirt and cotton trousers, carried a shoulder bag, and stood one person away from the human bomb, near the young girl eagerly waiting to deliver her poem.

The May 21 hit had been precisely planned, with dry runs performed at nighttime political events during the previous weeks. The whole squad had taken part; now a second bomber and an accomplice, Nalini Sriharan, who had provided them with safe accommodation, sat on the ground toward the back of the women's section of the audience. Sriharan looked anxious and tense.

Dhanu, along with the rest of the 10,000-strong crowd at the rally grounds in Sriperumbudur, was being entertained by a music troupe singing patriotic tunes and songs of welcome while they awaited Rajiv's arrival. Royal Demolition Explosive (RDX) was packed into the steel-ribbed denim belt around Dhanu's waist. Compartments in her belt bomb had been filled with 2mm round steel pellets. She was a human antipersonnel mine, capable of causing maximum damage within a 60-degree radius for more than 300 feet. The highly malleable bomb was invisible to metal detectors and had a two-switch triggering mechanism to prevent premature detonation.

During Rajiv's years as prime minister, India had sent a peacekeeping force to Sri Lanka to assist the island's government in its conflict with the Tamil community, which sought a separate state. A militant faction of the Tamils, known as the Tamil Tigers,[6] was engaged in armed conflict with the Sri Lankan authorities. Their leader had decided that Rajiv should be neutralized and worked with his lieutenants from the Black Tigers, their suicide wing, to formulate a plan. One of these lieutenants was One-Eyed Jack, who recruited Dhanu, the assassin, and the second bomber. They, along with some of the rest of the team, had been smuggled onto the mainland from Sri Lanka.

Rajiv Gandhi had already campaigned in two other Indian states that day, May 21. Finally, Rajiv flew to the nearest airport, Chennai (formerly Madras), in the state of Tamil Nadu, at 8:26 PM. He mixed ebulliently with throngs of well-wishers during the 24-mile drive to Sriperumpudur. Mark Tully, the BBC Delhi bureau chief for many years, remembers covering the first of Rajiv's large campaign outings of this election, some time before Rajiv's current visit to the south. On that occasion, just as was happening now, the crowds had slowed Rajiv's schedule, and Tully had to wait until 2 AM to start his long interview. "I said to him . . . you've got absolutely no security at all, you're wide open. . . . I remember he said to me, 'All of you journalists accused me of having too much security before, and now you're accusing me of not having enough security!' . . . He was mobbed so anyone could have stabbed him . . . he had zero security."[7]

At 10:10 PM this night, Rajiv Gandhi placed a garland on a statue of his assassinated mother en route to the election rally. He spent around five minutes meeting and greeting. Rajiv knew all about the protection issues, but he was less concerned about his personal safety than he was about doing his duty, which was to support the local candidate. In Sriperumbudur, around 300 to 400 people were slowly gathering around the stage area to see Rajiv, who was in a rush as he was behind schedule. His bulletproof car drew up and stopped by a red carpet that led to the stage. There was one wooden barricade, and as hands stretched forward to touch him, he responded by reaching out and smiling. Dressed in a white overshirt and trousers, he walked toward the customary line of party workers, who were waiting to place garlands around his neck or drape shawls around his shoulders in south Indian tradition.

Dr. Rema Devi, a senior state party functionary and medical practitioner with 35 years' experience, placed a handwoven cotton scarf in the party's orange, white, and green colors around Rajiv's neck. He appeared happy and relaxed, she remembers. She started to tell him about what the local party workers had been doing for the election, but he stopped her, asking her to talk to him about it later at the airport as they were running short on time. For Devi, most faces at party rallies were usually recognizable, but there was something different about this event. "We saw three women, all between 22 and 25, and a man we had not seen before." She noticed that "one girl was carrying a garland. Usually we don't carry garlands around. We keep them in one place. When the leader comes, we give them to him all in one go. But this girl, she was carrying the garland in her hand . . . so we were making fun of her. We thought she must be a new entrant to the party, wanting to show off . . . we had not seen any of them before. Rajiv arrived . . . we were waiting on both sides of the dais. Then one party worker's young daughter wanted to read a poem to Rajiv."[8]

As Rajiv Gandhi listened intently to the girl's recitation, he placed his left hand on her shoulder reassuringly. Like a shark homing in on its prey, Dhanu moved forward and stooped down, as if to touch Rajiv's feet in a mark of respect. As she bent low, she triggered the bomb with her right hand "and directed the force of the blow at Rajiv's unguarded face like a missile. . . . Rajiv Gandhi was scooped out from the front above his waist, but the shell of his back—including the back of his head—was relatively intact and recognizable, and so were his brand new walking shoes," Indian national magazine *Frontline* reported.[9]

General panic and confusion took over, and people scattered, running helter-skelter as a huge ball of fire erupted. The *Hindustan Times* said that hundreds of steel pellets tore into Rajiv from his face to his lower abdomen. The pellets "pierced his heart and lungs, causing instant clinical death."[10]

Rema Devi remembers the carnage vividly: "We heard a big noise. I was knocked to the ground for a moment. There was thick, black smoke rising. There were headless, armless, half-bodies, we all scattered, running, looking for Rajiv, he was not found. We thought he had escaped." Eyewitnesses described people falling backward like the slow-motion unfolding of the petals of a flower. Devi realized that Rajiv was on the ground, but it still took a few minutes to register. "There was nothing we could do. . . . Mr Gandhi's body was . . . disfigured and disintegrated. . . . There was no face, nothing, only his scalp. We could just see the back of his head. No part of his chest. His shoes, his clothes and the cotton cloth I had garlanded him with, a portion of it was hanging there. I started crying. In one second we lost him. There was lots of blood. My chest, my sari, was covered in pieces of flesh and blood."[11]

The Tamil Tigers had commissioned a 22-year-old freelance photographer, Haribabu, to record the whole sequence of steps. The photographer died in the blast, but his camera's color film survived to provide the most gruesome visual record ever of an assassination. There were two photographs of the human bomber alive and a shot of the explosion at 10:20 PM. The photographs, particularly one of the slain Rajiv, are so horrifying that they are rarely published.

Fifteen minutes after the bomb went off, a telephone call broke the news to Sonia at home in Delhi. There was no information at that point on Rajiv. Through an intercom, Sonia spoke urgently to his secretary, Vincent George, asking him to get proper intelligence as to what had happened. She waited anxiously while he spoke to the wife of a former minister who had sought information from a police director general; then the news was confirmed to Sonia. She went into shock and froze. Her worst nightmare had just come true. Rajiv had perished, along with his personal security officer, Pradip Kumar Gupta, and many others. Sonia later told a television interviewer, "Well I really sort of blanked out at that point, but later on my daughter told me that when she came in and told me I said, 'I wish I had gone to Madras with him.'"[12]

With her mother in a daze and Rahul back in America, 19-year-old Priyanka took charge of the situation and banned access to Sonia's room. She asked her father's former flying companion, Satish Sharma, and other aides who were present to arrange for her and her mother to fly to Chennai. A crying Sonia, dressed in white—the Hindu color for mourning—was driven to Delhi airport by an uncle of Rajiv and boarded a requisitioned air force plane at 1:40 AM. Sonia could be heard sobbing on the flight, which landed at 4:20 AM. Rajiv's body was lying in a guarded coffin in the cordoned-off terminal.[13] Sonia, inconsolable, laid a garland on her husband's casket before the plane took off. As news of the tragedy spread, crowds gathered in the south of the country as well as in Delhi. Sonia and Priyanka tearfully clung to each other as they sat by the body of the man they adored on the flight home. Priyanka put her arms across her father's coffin. Sonia, seeing Pradip Kumar Gupta's coffin unadorned, took some flowers from Rajiv's casket and placed them on top of his security officer's.[14]

Back in Delhi, Sonia, wearing dark glasses to hide her swollen eyes, descended the steps of the plane with Priyanka. They were met on the tarmac by a group that included the president of India, R. Venkataraman, and his wife, Janaki. Sonia seemed to be disoriented; she attempted to engage with them but turned this way and that, distraught. She put her left hand up to her mouth and leaned into her tall daughter for support.[15] Priyanka placed her arm around her mother's shoulder, and they accompanied her father's body in an ambulance to the All India Institute of Medical Sciences, the same large hospital that had received Indira's dying body seven years earlier. When the doors of the ambulance were opened, Sonia emerged with Priyanka. Crowds jostled and screamed, straining to catch a glimpse of them. Only some of the body was left for the embalming process. *Frontline* described what the doctors had to work with: "The neck and head was one mass. There was a bit of the mouth and an eye but no nose. The skull was cracked. The doctors from the anatomy section struggled to reconstruct the face. Though the legs and arms were intact, the chest had caved in."[16] It took hours for the doctors to complete their task, after which the body was draped in a white sheet.

Sonia and Priyanka escorted their departed loved one, who had been the center of their lives, back to Rajiv and Sonia's home in central New Delhi. There a room was cleared and white sheets spread over the floor, ready for prayers. Sonia, bathed and wearing a pure white sari, sat by the body. Then, ahead of Rajiv's final departure from the home in which they had shared so many happy times, the doors were closed and the curtains were drawn for Sonia and Priyanka to spend ten minutes alone with Rajiv. After that, draped in the Indian flag, his body was taken to Teen Murti Bhavan (Three Statues House), where it was mounted on a raised platform. While Rajiv Gandhi lay in state, Sonia and Priyanka kept vigil. Rahul arrived in India in the early hours of May 23. In the glare of the cameras and flashbulbs, Priyanka met him at the airport. They hugged before getting into the car, their arms around each other, and drove straight to Teen Murti, where Rahul broke down on seeing the mortal remains of his father.[17]

The Gandhis' hearts were broken. Sonia lost the man she had fallen in love with in England, where she had pursued her education after a secure and balanced childhood in Italy. Within the space of 11 years, two members of their family, including the man she loved with every fiber of her being, had been killed. It did not seem likely at the time that Sonia would eventually rise to become the most powerful politician in the largest democracy in the world, ruling without conquering, holding sway over one-sixth of humanity. Yet the tragedy marked the beginning of an intensely transformational journey.

1

FROM ITALY TO BRITAIN

It was very soon evident to both of us that we would spend our lives together.

—*Sonia Gandhi*

Sonia Gandhi was born Edvige Antonia Albina Maino[1] to Stefano and Paola Maino on December 9, 1946, in Lusiana, a tiny town of fewer than 3,000 inhabitants nestled quietly in the crisp air of the verdant lower Alps of northeast Italy. A smoker, Stefano Maino had a strong personality as deeply etched as the lines around his mouth and as defined as his square jaw. Along with many who fought for Mussolini's Italy with the Axis powers in the Second World War, he had been taken prisoner during the German invasion of Russia.[2] Having been helped by natives of that country before returning home, he apparently decided to give his daughters Russian pet names after three women who had aided him[3]—Sonia has an elder sister Anouchka, originally named Alessandra, and a younger sister called Nadia. Stefano became quite enamored of Russian culture, heritage, and language, which Sonia learned to speak at an early age. Known simply as Signor Maino, he owned a successful building firm, and the postwar construction industry was booming. Sonia described him in her first photo-memoir, *Rajiv,* as a "blunt" and "straightforward" man who worked hard; she clearly inherited his grit and no-nonsense approach to life. Like many provincial Italian fathers, he was strict and traditional, but he was self-made and progressive enough to want Sonia to have an education.

The quarter of Lusiana where the family lived—in a gray-fronted house with wooden shutters at the windows—was called Maini; people with the

Maino surname had been there for several generations. When Sonia was around the age of nine, Stefano and Paola (her maiden name was Predebon) decided to move their family to Orbassano in Piedmont, around nine miles southwest of the Fiat automobile capital of Turin. Orbassano was a typically neat, medium-sized town with a population of some 25,000, whose narrow sidewalks are punctuated with metal benches and iron lampposts. The Mainos lived in a detached two-story villa, proudly built by Stefano, with high iron gates and a sloping tiled roof. It remains the family home.

The Mainos had ambitions for their daughters. In those days, there was no *scuola media* (middle school) in many of the smaller towns, so young girls were sent to the Salesian boarding school, the Convent of Maria Ausiliatrice, some nine miles from Orbassano, in Giaveno. There, they could either take a special course of study to join the order or follow a separate curriculum. The Salesian Sisters of St. John Bosco, or Daughters of Mary Help of Christians, were founded in 1872 to work alongside St. John Bosco in his education projects in Turin, Italy. Essentially a teaching order, today they run youth clubs and boarding and primary schools for girls all over Italy and on five continents. Their constitution describes their spiritual heritage inspired by the charity of Christ and a "strong missionary impulse."

Sonia attended the school from around the age of 9 to 14,[4] wearing the uniform of black overalls with white collars, black stockings, and a black coat for outdoors. Many of those who taught Sonia have passed on, but a few contemporaries who chose to join the order at an early age do remember the Maino girls. Two types of three-year educational tracks were available when the girls attended school there—one was vocational and did not require an entrance exam, covering courses useful for working in an office as a secretary, for instance. The other, designed for those girls who would go on to study further, required an entrance test and was more academic, with subjects such as Latin and Italian literature. Sonia's older sister, Alessandra, was in the vocational training course while Sonia took the academic path. Sister Maria Angela Gribaudo, who still teaches in Turin, said that the choices would have been made by their parents based on personality and parental ambition. To prepare for the exam, Sonia was sent to Giaveno for the fifth elementary form (the last year of primary school), where she, along with another three or four girls, had daily private lessons with a retired teacher.[5]

Though Sonia was a year younger than Alessandra, Paola and Stefano decided that the girls should both start at the same time. Sister Maura Reissent, a contemporary, comments that Sonia "was not homesick firstly because there was her sister Alessandra with her and secondly because of the joyful atmosphere." Sister Domenica Macario, also now in her late sixties, knew the late Sister Adelaide Carle, who was one of Sonia's *assistenti* (an *assistente* in the Salesian order was a sister who took care of the girls outside school hours). Sister Adelaide was "intelligent, practical, intuitive, . . . able to sort out the personality of each of the girls entrusted to her. She was very understanding and had a lovely and maternal way of dealing with them." Sonia, according to the sisters' accounts, responded and was an affectionate child, very fond of her *assistente.* Sister Maura Reissent explains that Sonia's parents chose the boarding school "to avoid her traveling every day from Orbassano to Giaveno, above all in wintertime as she suffered from asthma."

There was a simplicity about this time; neither home nor school was ostentatious. The boarders had everything they needed in the large, modern dormitories—but no luxuries. The relationship between *assistenti* and pupils was caring but disciplined; after tea and "playful recreation" in the evenings, the girls settled down to homework in the study, supervised by teaching *assistenti.* All the sisters talk of a family ambience, a peaceful coexistence among different personalities. Sister Maura Reissent recalls Sonia being a bit more reticent, and definitely calmer, than her older, taller sister Alessandra, but not really shy. In fact, most remember Sonia as lively, cheerful, and talkative. Sister Maura remembers that Sonia liked acting and taking part in the frequently staged plays, seen by the school as a useful means of personal expression and education. Later on, only those close to Sonia would see this uninhibited side to her. And despite her asthmatic condition, the sisters do not remember her ever complaining: She was willing to take part in all the school activities, ball games, theater, and singing.

Although the Maino family did not live very far away, their daughters did not go home every weekend. The sisters say there would have been little reason to make an exception to the general practice of remaining at school seven days a week. Boarders went home mainly for major holidays: Christmas, Easter, and in the summer. The Maino parents, and perhaps other relations, visited the girls and brought them special treats every other weekend.[6] Sister Reissent described Paola and Stefano as "simple people . . . all our families wanted the best education for their children. Most of them made sacrifices with the purpose of finding a good, serious school for them." A notion that Sonia's asthma was worsened by the living conditions at the school was indignantly dismissed by the sisters as stuff and nonsense. Sister Domenica Macario says that the *assistente* was always careful and would not have allowed the girls to be exposed to *any* harmful conditions. In fact, Sister Adelaide was highly protective of Sonia. She worried at night if "Sonia was coughing more than usual because of her asthma . . . and went near her bed to make Sonia feel safe and cared for." Once, when Sonia was not too well, all the students and the *assistente* did a *novena* for her recovery.[7]

Sonia learned the value of honesty and community with the sisters. She grew up knowing what it was like to be on the receiving end of compassion, so it placed her in a strong position to show it when needed. It helped her form an inner core of stability. And though her parents had reared her in a middle-class environment, she was not cocooned, for she was made aware of the plight of those less fortunate than herself, the many who were suffering in postwar Italy, at quite an early stage. Later on she would tell an interviewer, "In Italy there is a lot of poverty,"[8] and when asked on television how she first came to be concerned about those on the margins of society, she replied: "This was something I learned through my parents."[9]

As good as her education was, it was narrow: "At school, I learned of the Risorgimento, of Mazzini and Garibaldi, and the unification of Italy. But of India, its great history, and its emergence as a modern nation-state, I was taught nothing."[10] When her time with the Salesian Sisters was over, Sonia took a three-year course in English and French at a Berlitz Language School (at the Istituto Santa Teresa, on the Via Santa Teresa in Turin),[11] which she finished in 1964. English was viewed as useful for the job market at the time. Although language schools were springing up in Italy, those who could afford to do so sent their progeny to England, her next destination.

On January 7, 1965, Sonia arrived in Cambridge, the vibrant, historic university town—popular with those from abroad as it was cleaner and safer than London—and enrolled at one of the two main language schools, which also assigned her a family to stay with. The Lennox Cook School, based in an attractive residential house at 75 Barton Road, had a relaxed family atmosphere, dynamic teaching methods, and was the cheaper and (by all accounts) better of the two institutions. It also had an impressive success rate for helping students achieve international qualifications in English as a foreign language.[12] Sonia's English was still far from perfect, and, separated from her homeland for the first time in her life, she found Cambridge depressing. "I had never eaten boiled cabbage and gooey spaghetti on toast, nor had I ever had to pay to have a bath every day. . . . I missed home terribly."[13] Nevertheless, it was in England that Sonia met the love of her life, Rajiv Gandhi, while he was studying at Trinity College, Cambridge University, just as his grandfather had done.

Rajiv (his name means lotus flower) was born in 1944 at Belle Vue Nursing Home in Bombay (now Mumbai), India's noisiest and most populous city. His education, though he also boarded in a single-sex school, was wide and cosmopolitan. His grandfather was the aristocrat Jawaharlal Nehru, the first prime minister of India, who had played a leading role in India's fight for independence from the British, so the boy was exposed to world leaders and international travel from an early age. In 1953, Rajiv, along with his brother, Sanjay, attended the *Ecole d'Humanité* in Goldern, Switzerland, for a short while as part of a trip to Europe with Indira for Queen Elizabeth II's coronation. Before coming to Cambridge, Rajiv had attended the exclusive Doon boarding school for boys in the Himalayan foothills. Upper-class parents from all over India, particularly those from Delhi and the north, strove to have their boys admitted into this establishment. In this fairly egalitarian environment (given that *nearly all* were from the upper strata), the boys placed academics and community spirit in high esteem. Doon alumni, known as Doscos, are found at the highest level in most professions across India. Some of Rajiv's school friends were among his inner circle in later years.

Nestled in the Doon valley, an ideal location for exploring the mountains, rivers, and forests on its doorstep, the school had a great deal of sports and trekking in its curriculum. But once Rajiv got to Cambridge, he was a lot freer to do as he pleased. He shared a house in Derwent Close with friends and was fully occupied with English life. He was interested in but not committed to his Engineering Tripos course, and he certainly did not appear to be using the university to develop any kind of political career as many others were doing. Kenneth Clarke, later British secretary of state for justice, for instance, was busy being president of the Cambridge Union, but, he states, "Rajiv—I do not recall doing *anything* political at Cambridge."[14]

Sonia's presence in Cambridge altered her life, for there her future was sealed in an instant. "I missed Italian cooking. I found out that the only place in Cambridge you could have something close to home food was a Greek restaurant called Varsity. . . ."[15] The eatery, owned by a Greek Cypriot, the late Charles Antoni, was popular as it served meals at student-friendly prices, and Sonia started to dine there on a regular basis. Rajiv, too, often went there with his friends, and it was in the Varsity that she first noticed Rajiv's striking looks and manners. He was quieter and less unruly than the others. One day, Sonia was having lunch when Christian Von Stieglitz, an Italian-speaking friend of hers, entered with Rajiv. "We greeted each other, and, as far as I was concerned, it was love at first sight. It was for him, too, as he later told me; he had in fact asked Christian earlier to introduce us."[16]

Rajiv's family enjoyed a tradition of letter-writing, a vital communication method during lengthy periods of separation. Jawaharlal and Indira exchanged letters throughout their lives, as did Indira and Rajiv. Rajiv wrote to his mother describing new experiences such as learning how to dance the Twist, attending concerts, being a traditional Cambridge student, punting and rowing, and enjoying life away from the attention and maelstrom of being the grandson of a prime minister—he was also getting used to living on a restricted allowance. Sonia soon started to feature in his letters. It was 1965, and the young couple was exploring a new, freer existence. Rajiv would cycle over to see his girlfriend every day. He had an old Volkswagen, and on holidays they would share the gas costs with friends and go for a drive.

One of Sonia's housemates was Karma Topden, who was from the kingdom of Sikkim, later annexed by India. His girlfriend, Cherry Yorke, who lived across the road, vividly remembers seeing Sonia in a ball gown and Rajiv in a dinner jacket seated in a red open-topped car, ready to go to the college's traditional May ball, which is held in June.[17] The gala was the biggest social event of the calendar, and Kenneth Clarke attended every year: "We all used to dress up, . . . you stayed up all night and saw the dawn and went on a punt," he recalls with nostalgia. But the "swinging sixties" had not quite arrived for this couple; the atmosphere was still quite strict. Rajiv would wait for his girlfriend in the communal family sitting room at her host family's house, 55 Tenison Road. The location was respectable but not particularly fashionable. On one side, where Sonia was living, there were large houses; on the other, there were two-story terraced buildings, mainly rooming houses. But it was near the station and very safe. The brick house had a small kitchen with a table, and its landlady was a lively, buxom, bottle-blonde Italian named Puccina[18] Norris, who lived there with her daughter and son. Sonia shared a room with a Swiss girl, Ruth,[19] and a common language—French.

Indians were not allowed to take much money out of the country, and foreign exchange was quite tight, so international students often took temporary jobs during school holidays. Karma Topden had finished university by this time, but he worked at the Cooperative bakery with Rajiv—Karma on cakes; Rajiv in the bread section.[20] A contemporary remembers Rajiv also selling ice cream—and not charging children.[21] Besides Karma, Ruth, and Sonia, the tenants of 55 Tenison Road were mostly language students, and others were at Cambridge University. At different periods, they included a South Asian mathematician, a young Cambridge-area girl named Christine, a German fellow called Thilo Dilthey,[22] and Hans Loeser, a German at the university who stayed for three months one summer. Loeser did not socialize with Sonia and Rajiv outside the house, but he did observe that Sonia was quite active: "Very often she was out of the house, she was not very sedentary . . . all of us were young and going out in the evenings." He remembers that various guests of different tenants, including young language teachers, would visit at Tenison Road, too. There was always something going on; Thilo Dilthey recalls going to Silverstone with Sonia and

Rajiv to watch some car racing. In Cambridge, just as in Giaveno, Sonia was not remembered as being at all retiring; that was a side to her character that would emerge later on in India. "I wouldn't describe her as being shy. Definitely not! She was very open-minded!" Loeser declares.

She also sometimes displayed a certain fiery Italian temper. One night, Loeser and another young man (possibly one of the language teachers) were in the communal kitchen. He remembers the incident because he saw a revealing aspect of Sonia's personality. She "was cooking spaghetti . . . she had done everything [to get it ready]." Behind her back, the young man added to the dish "some white powder used in cooking as a taste intensifier, sodium glutamate; if you take too much of it, it doesn't taste very well. He must have put in quite a dose. We—the young man and I—had been drinking, and we were giggling. Sonia must have noticed that he had prepared something to tease her, and she turned around quite suddenly, astonished, and without saying anything, put the hot spaghetti on his head. He was shouting, and finally, laughing; it was really quite funny."[23] Sonia clearly knew how to make a point in a memorable way.

According to Loeser, Sonia did not suffer any financial problems; she "obviously had enough money even by the end of the month" when he and his friends "sometimes ran out of pocket money." He believes the relationship between Sonia and her family was good because they were "in close contact," and Cherry Yorke describes Sonia then as "quite comfortably off." Another Cambridge friend of Rajiv's, Tahir Jahangir, remembers Sonia as always being "well dressed, well turned out."[24]

At the time, the Cambridge male-to-female ratio was 12 to 1, so naturally, with her long dark hair and slim figure, Sonia was one of the most beautiful women in town. Loeser and his friend Thilo Dilthey felt that she was aware of her striking good looks. He recalls Dilthey remarking to him once, "She's very pretty, but unfortunately, somebody must have told her." From being a playful child in Giaveno, Sonia had grown into a self-assured young woman. Rajiv was a keen photographer, and as the couple grew close, Sonia became his favorite subject.

This was an uplifting time for Sonia: Cambridge was now much more palatable; she had made many friends, and Rajiv was "a special one." The homesickness had gone. And as they got to know one another, she realized that although their families came from different worlds, they shared core values. The director of studies at the Lennox Cook School, Amorey Gethin, recalls that for many of the students, "and so perhaps for Sonia too, it was the happiest time of their lives. With nobody expecting anything of them, they were free and able to enjoy themselves in a way they never had done before or would do again."[25]

The relationship between Rajiv and Sonia was gathering momentum; he wrote to his mother quite soon after meeting Sonia that he had found a "special girl." The deepening bond with Sonia seems to have had a beneficial effect on Rajiv's level of communication with his own mother, too. Although there had been a slight distance between Rajiv and Indira during adolescence, he now felt more comfortable and at ease with her. Nevertheless, the first time that Rajiv arranged for Sonia to meet his mother, who was then the Indian minister for information and broadcasting, Sonia had an attack of nerves and canceled. The second time, however, she did meet with Indira at the Indian High Commissioner's Residence in Kensington Palace Gardens in London. Indira, herself shy when she was young, made an effort to relax the girl. She spoke to Sonia in French, knowing that the latter was more fluent in that language than English at that stage, and asked about her studies.

While Rajiv had been eager to introduce the two women he loved most, Sonia was more circumspect. It seemed that the relationship between Sonia and her parents was not quite as open as Rajiv's was with his mother, and that there was a little more going on than what appeared on the surface to Hans Loeser. In one of his letters to Indira, Rajiv puzzled over why Sonia seemed to be unable to talk to them. Sonia was nonetheless quite determined to marry Rajiv, and she implied in the photo-memoir that she later wrote for him that she went home to Orbassano to speak with them. The stark contrast between Rajiv's and Sonia's upbringing was clear to her: "Although we were a close-knit family, they were old-fashioned, and my father a patriarch of the old school. In my milieu, contact between boys and girls was strictly controlled. My parents were displeased by my departure from their norms . . . it took all my courage to get them to let me return to Cambridge."[26] Despite their reluctance, Sonia did return.

Rajiv left his Tripos program partway through, and by 1966 had moved to Imperial College London on a mechanical engineering course, so the two of them commuted between Cambridge and the capital, enjoying life together over weekends and holidays. They were sometimes joined in Cambridge by Rajiv's younger brother, Sanjay, who had started a three-year apprenticeship in Crewe with Rolls-Royce, to explore his passion for cars. But Sonia and her boyfriend were somewhat anxious about the future: She still feared her strict father. The young couple was determinedly making practical plans for their lives together, as it was clear that they intended to marry and to live in India. Sonia returned home to Italy in July 1966 while Rajiv worked on a building site to earn enough money to visit her family and seek Stefano's approval. They wrote to each other every day. Passionate about flying, Rajiv trained for a pilot's license, having now dropped out of the engineering program at Imperial College too.

In November 1966, Rajiv traveled to Italy. To Sonia's concerned parents, he earnestly explained that his plan was to go to India and get a commercial pilot's license so that he would be able to support her after they were married. Sonia's father believed Rajiv had good intentions: "'One look at his eyes and you know the boy,'" he said.[27] But he was skeptical about the seriousness of the relationship and his daughter's ability to settle in a foreign country. Though he had granted permission for Sonia to fly to England at 18, he would not entertain the thought of even a short holiday in India until Sonia was of legal age. "He did not like the thought of my marrying a foreigner. He thought if he agreed to my marriage, he would not be fulfilling his duties as a father. He did his best to dissuade me."[28] Stefano seemed to think that if he called a halt to proceedings, the relationship might dissipate. However, knowing that his daughter could not be coerced, he insisted that the young couple wait a year, and then, if they still felt the same, he would allow Sonia to go visit her boyfriend's country for herself so that he would not be blamed for "messing up" her life.

Sonia was resolute. She did not want to hurt her father, so she agreed to his request to wait for 12 months. Deploying her capacity to play the long game, she marked time to win what she held most dear—while making sure that those around her were caused the least fuss. Staying with her parents, she took on occasional interpreting assignments at conferences. Stefano, meanwhile, was convinced that the relationship would fizzle out very soon.

2

SAFDARJANG ROAD

Along with my husband, she guided me patiently through the confusions and hesitations of my early adjustments to India.

—*Sonia Gandhi*

On January 13, 1968, arriving in Delhi after a year away from the man she adored, Sonia felt a wave of relief when Rajiv met her at the airport along with his brother, Sanjay, and a close family friend of the Gandhis, Amitabh Bachchan. Grit, faith, and hope had helped Sonia to spend the time in Italy that she had promised her father, away from Rajiv. Stefano, Sonia's father, had been proved wrong; her feelings for Rajiv had simply strengthened and, though nothing looked familiar, she was happy just being on the same soil as her future husband. She had no fear of the new country: "I just wanted Rajiv. I could have gone to any part of the world for him. He was my biggest security."[1] It would have been inappropriate, protocol-wise, for Sonia to be staying in her future in-laws' home at this point. It was thus arranged for her to spend six weeks with Amitabh Bachchan's parents to familiarize herself with a new culture, a new language, and the new experience of living close to the most prominent family in India. She later told a television interviewer, "I came here because I was madly in love with my husband, and he was with me. So nothing else mattered."[2]

The center of New Delhi, where the Bachchans and the Gandhis lived, had been neatly laid out, like pieces on a chess board. The Lutyens zone, covering roughly 16 square miles, had always been where the Indian administration resided. Before India gained independence from its British colonial masters and became a democratic republic, that meant senior politicians and officials of the Raj; it still houses the rulers of independent India, the keepers of its constitution, today. British architect Edwin Lutyens designed the palace of the former viceroy of India, built between 1912 and 1931, that is now the presidential complex on top of Raisina Hill, and other monuments in which neoclassical features from Western architecture blend with Mughal or Buddhist forms and motifs. Mindful of the hot summer winds that engulf Delhi for nine months of the year, the team created broad, tree-lined avenues radiating from a series of roundabouts. Alongside occasional open green spaces, low bungalows can be glimpsed over walls bearing the name plaques of their residents. Within the palm of the city sat the center of power and everything needed to service it: shops, hotels, offices, transport hubs, museums, galleries, libraries, and members-only recreational facilities. The flying club and nearest airstrip were roughly a half-hour's drive away from the inner circles of roads.

The whitewashed colonial bungalows sat in two- and three-acre plots of land of spacious, manicured gardens. Driveways leading to walls with double gates fronted onto pathways raised roughly 10 inches from wide roads. Robert Tor-Russell, one of the less-known members of Lutyens's team, designed a series of homes and buildings, including that of Indira Gandhi.

When Rajiv's mother and Sonia first met in England, Indira was a cabinet minister living at 1 Safdarjang Road,[3] and she chose to continue living there when she became prime minister in 1966. Rajiv and Sanjay were now permanently back from Great Britain; Rajiv, a qualified commercial pilot flying Dakota aircraft, and Sanjay, having failed to complete his mechanical apprenticeship with Rolls-Royce, wanted to design and manufacture a homegrown Indian car.

When a bride joins an Indian household, the couple sometimes remains with the groom's relations and does not move away, as is the norm in the West (though this is changing in some urban areas with a slow shift toward nuclear families). Sonia was soon to be part of what Indians call a joint family, with everyone living under the same roof. That roof covered a one-story bungalow, probably the most startling prime minister's residence ever.

Sonia entered her new home, now preserved as the Indira Gandhi Memorial Museum, through a pillared, arched veranda. The house consisted of just a few bedrooms, a book-lined study with an anteroom, a large living room, a small prayer chamber, dining area, kitchen and pantry,[4] and other spaces. The terrazzo floor, the clean, dazzling white walls, the bedspreads made of hand-spun materials—all contributed to a surprising display of austerity. The home was comfortable but unostentatious, decorated sparingly with the crafts of India. When Indira lived there, regardless of the fact that it was the prime minister's house, the gates were left open except at night.[5] She went out of her way to be accessible and did not feel the need for high security at that point in her life. The atmosphere, though busy, was relaxed.

Indira had gone to university in Europe as had her father. She married outside her community of India's highest caste of Hindu Brahmins after she fell in love with a Parsi, Feroze Gandhi. The tiny Parsi community, followers of the Zoroastrian religion, landed on the coast of western India from Iran many centuries before and were concentrated around Mumbai, then known as Bombay.

Trading one famous surname for another, Indira Nehru became Indira Gandhi, but she was not related to Mahatma Gandhi, though the family was close to him. The Nehrus were from a small group known as Kashmiri pandits, who originated in the northern mountain state of Jammu and Kashmir. They were an aristocratic line of confident, Western-educated individuals with a strong sense of self-worth. Open to prevailing cultural winds, courtesy of the British, Indira's grandfather Motilal had studied law and built a highly successful practice. The Nehrus made extraordinary amounts of money and were wealthy enough to build a 42-room mansion with a swimming pool and tennis courts, give it to the country, and then build a slightly smaller one. They used the best bone china, employed European tutors and nannies, and wore the finest clothes. But they were progressive and always interested in new ideas.

The Nehrus still blend the traditional with the new and have a liberal outlook that rejects dogma, prejudice, and cant. Their attitude is highly inclusive in a country containing a huge number of class, caste, and religious divisions. So Indira did not resist her son's intercultural marriage, and, in keeping with the family's broad, flexible traditions, the ceremonies were low key and graceful. On January 26, 1968, thirteen days after Sonia's arrival in India, the engagement took place, and the wedding was scheduled for a month later. Sonia was immediately the focus of preparations. Although she had been happy taking part in stage plays as a child, under the intense scrutiny that India's first family is always subject to and removed from her own environment, she suddenly became quite self-conscious. Indians stare unashamedly, and they stared a lot at Sonia. She began to feel quite inhibited and to withdraw into herself.

But she still had to prepare for a big event: her wedding! She had to learn how to wear the formal and national dress of India, the sari—a length of material that is draped around the body in different ways and worn with a blouse. In the beginning, she was terrified that it would fall off each time she wore one. She also found it difficult to adjust to the unfamiliar pungent flavors of Indian food and would have Italian meals prepared for her. Gradually, she got used to the cuisine of her new homeland, even learning new recipes, such as those from Kashmir that one of Indira's aunts taught her.[6]

Indira's cosmopolitan father and grandfather had been part of the freedom movement that liberated India from the yolk of the British. As a consequence of this nationalistic political background, it was very important that the official language of India, Hindi, was spoken and understood in the household. Furthermore, Indira's grandfather had settled in the town of Allahabad in the state of Uttar Pradesh, part of the northern, Hindi-speaking belt of India, so the language was a key part of family culture. Sonia started studying it, and within six weeks, her mentors, the Bachchans, a very literary couple, had given her a good foundation in the language. During a prewedding ceremony in which flowers adorned her hair and decorative henna was applied to her hands, Sonia was asked by a guest, "'How do you feel?" to which she replied in Hindi with a broad grin, "I'm fine, I'm happy."[7] Author and publisher Malvika Singh remarks that a lot of upper-middle-class Indians were brought up with a preference for speaking English—a holdover from imperialism: Many private schools, based on British models, taught mostly in English. But, says Singh, by learning Hindi, Sonia demonstrated her "value system. She studied the language. Sonia reads and speaks Hindi better than I do. . . . I was brought up with English—I didn't learn Hindi."[8]

The wedding took place on February 25, 1968. The Gandhis, eschewing pomp and ceremony, had a civil function with just two traditional rituals: an exchange of jasmine flower garlands and the chanting of verse chosen by Indira, who translated it into English. Sonia's mother and sisters were "got up in frills and ruffles," according to the *Hindustan Times.* Sonia wore a pale-pink cotton sari made from cloth that had been hand-spun by Jawaharlal during one of his terms in a British jail. He had made it for his daughter's wedding, and Indira in turn had presented the sari to Sonia for hers. The bride's father, Stefano Maino, still seeking to demonstrate his disapproval of the union, did not travel to India for the formalities. Sonia's maternal uncle, Mario Predebon, gave her away.

The wedding at the prime minister's house made the front page of the *Hindustan Times,* which reported, "To the gentle dropping of rose petals and the sprinkling of rose water," roughly 100 guests, "mostly relations," witnessed the signing of the marriage register and an exchange of rings by Sonia and Rajiv in the festively decorated, Japanese-inspired garden with its plants and shrubs, the grass dotted with trees and a curved pond. Among the witnesses were the bride's uncle and aunt, Angelo and Anita Predebon.[9]

A photo showed the two mothers-in-law, sitting next to each other, smiling contentedly in similar poses, their hands clasped in their laps. Two different mothers united for one event that, neither then knew, would open a new chapter in Indian political history. The paper's *Onlooker* columnist described Sonia, with a barely disguised hint of superiority, as "a simple, straightforward girl from an unsophisticated family."[10] The columnist did note, though, that the bride was fond of the outdoor life, keen to adjust to her new surroundings, and charmed by her new environment.

The reception the next day was an altogether larger occasion, and again the *Hindustan Times* carried a front-page photograph of the president of India exchanging a folded hands greeting with Sonia while Rajiv looked on solicitously. The venue was Hyderabad House, often used by the Government of India for official banquets and meetings with foreign dignitaries. The imposing dusky-pink-and-cream building with its colonnades and pillars stands opposite India Gate, an arched war memorial whose environs form the background of a popular photograph of Sonia and Rajiv eating ice cream bought from a roadside vendor.

Though Sonia was part of a busy household, she and Rajiv were able to build a private life for themselves; she described it as "tranquil togetherness." The house was not large, but everyone had their own defined space and everyone gathered when they could at mealtimes in a much-photographed, simple, elegant dining room. New Delhi was resplendent with cultural offerings, among them live recitals, and the couple went to classical concerts of both Indian and Western music. Her in-laws did not force-feed India to her; they simply encouraged her and allowed her to remove her stabilizers in her own time. There was a sensitivity to the way Sonia was helped to settle in. When Sonia sadly said goodbye to her mother, Paola Maino, a month after the wedding and returned to an empty house, "feeling very depressed and lonely,"[11] Indira was at her office. She sent home an envelope with Sonia's name on it. "My mother-in-law sent a little note to me: 'Hi Sonia, this is just to tell you that we all love you.' And that totally melted me. It gave me a lot of strength, that I am loved and cared for."[12] Indira was relaxed about Sonia eating Indian food or wearing a sari if they were going to a wedding, which helped Sonia to feel more at ease.[13]

On the other hand, four thousand years of culture had ingrained certain habits in Indian society, and there were prescribed patterns of behavior for daughters-in-law. They were expected to be domesticated, to follow the rules, and to be subservient and compliant. Sonia fitted into the conventional norms. Even the most cosmopolitan and modern of Indians glowingly describe her as being "the perfect housewife/daughter-in-law!" delighting in the artificially constructed stereotype that she conformed to and that many Indians themselves find impossible to contend with. She would later say to a newspaper interviewer (causing some feminists to hyperventilate), "Since childhood, I had been told that girls could only do certain things and not others. But there was nothing a man could not do—that they were superior to women."[14] Underneath it all, however, she was not finding it *that* easy, and she let slip her difficulties to some. One of her late *assistenti* in Italy, Sister Adelaide Carla, told Sister Domenica Macario, "At the beginning Sonia suffered a lot in trying to adapt to the very strict and formal way of life, made up of protocols which did not allow her to see her husband when and as much as she would have liked."[15]

However, the young Italian buckled down. One of Indira's biographers described Sonia as "docile, accommodating and quietly affectionate. She was also intensely interested in the domestic arrangements of the household and an excellent cook."[16] Indira's position left her little time for domestic detail, so two personal assistants on rotation handled the residence. When Rajiv was on a two- or three-day shift for the airline, Sonia would spend time with one or the other of the assistants. She said later that she learned how to manage a home and some Indian culinary fare from them and pursued her duties assiduously: "When I got married I didn't know how to cook. I had to learn from books."[17]

In families from the subcontinent, the way progeny refer to their parents is adopted by their spouses, so for Sonia, Indira was *Mummy.* "Mummy depended on me to see to her clothes—so I used to go shopping for her and the house. Then, if we were having visitors or house guests, I would see to all the arrangements for them."[18] Sonia quickly got to know what Indira's domestic preferences were. Thus began an unconscious process of demarcation, for later Sonia would assume greater and greater responsibility over the household terrain and, in times of hardship or straitened circumstance for Indira, would become indispensible to the family. To a degree, the voluntary investment she made in this area also turned her into a stakeholder, a position she would carefully maintain. Indira was thrilled. She told fellow Kashmiri pandit and former cabinet minister Makhan Lal Fotedar that she had always wanted a Kashmiri girl for a daughter-in-law, but "Sonia is just like a Kashimiri girl; faithful to her husband, faithful to the family. I am satisfied."[19] The Nehru-Gandhis felt that having a Kashmiri pandit heritage was like being "top of the heap,"[20] though at the same time they were not at all arrogant or infected with hubris about it.

Each member of the household had a niche, and there was an easy atmosphere in which Sonia faced no competition—she was the only beloved daughter-in-law. Her social circle with Rajiv consisted mainly of old schoolmates, many of them also friends from Cambridge, and their wives, as well as continental Europeans—Delhi being the diplomatic capital of the country. There were long drives, movies, dances, and fun. While Sonia was adapting to Indian food and dress for her formal life, she also sometimes dressed in a late 1960s–early 1970s European fashion style: tall boots, short skirts, form-fitting trousers and jumpers, big earrings, and makeup, her long luxurious hair often worn down with a side part. She was striking in an unmanufactured, film-starry way and always turned heads.

All the while, she soaked up her mother-in-law's knowledge on India's incredible variety of fabric texture and design. She was also rapidly getting used to a life of meeting leaders and royalty. Indira, bonding with her daughter-in-law, often took her on trips—one was to the northern mountain kingdom of Sikkim, where they stayed in the palace as guests of the *chogyal,* or king, and where Sonia's former Cambridge housemate, Karma Topden, was also working as a deputy commissioner in the Sikkim Police.

Now in her fifties, Indira was a small-boned, petite woman, disciplined, calisthenics-practicing with boundless energy, stamina, and mental strength. Frank Christopher, the former director of the Parliamentary Library, remembers that "Indira Gandhi was a very brisk walker, and we witnessed that in the corridors of Parliament House. Her pace was such that the boys [junior staff members] and the officials used to literally run to keep up with her."[21] Arriving at a political rally, Indira would be met by officials and workers holding outstretched garlands to present to her; with a curt smile she would grab these in rapid succession and arrive at the end of the line within seconds. This prime minister had a Swiss sense of time.

As time ticked by and her family expanded, the prime minister needed more space, so the bungalow next door at 1 Akbar Road was provided to Indira for her offices and her staff. A small gate divided the two buildings. Every morning Indira, in the open-access manner typical of the Nehru family, received visitors on her front lawn. It was quite a sight for the public. Anybody could come along, and they did. Sometimes heads of state, journalists, and writers were invited home for meals—Indira preferred that to being away from the family in formal banquets. One editor, Inder Malhotra, who dined there a couple of times, described their talks as friendly and frank. Indira was always keen to elicit the views of her guests while putting her own thoughts across.[22] That dining table was the beating heart of India.

Contrary to a prevailing view that Sonia did not take an interest in politics at this time, she displayed a clear awareness of national and international events in the 1970s. Many years later, Sonia was invited by Ruud Lubbers, the former prime minister of the Netherlands and a friend of Rajiv Gandhi, to give a lecture at the Nexus Institute in the Netherlands. The annual Nexus Lecture is delivered by a prominent, internationally renowned personality and consists of his or her views on a theme of cultural philosophy. (The late Richard C. Holbrooke, US special envoy, was another of their speakers.) In her lecture Sonia described how, through the private, family world, the public, political spectrum "came alive for me: living in intimate proximity with people for whom larger questions of ideology and belief as well as issues relating to politics and governance were vivid daily realities."[23] Mushirul Hasan, author of *Nehrus: Personal Histories,* echoes this, noting that Sonia came to India at an impressionable age, so the greatest single factor that would have influenced her was the presence of "a towering figure like Indira Gandhi, who, with all her faults and failings, was . . . one of the greatest leaders of the twentieth century."[24] It was the best political kindergarten Sonia could have had, and she absorbed everything osmotically, even though she was never interested in *being* a politician. Why would she be? She was happy being Rajiv's wife, and for the next 14 years Rajiv was an archetypal urban, upper-middle-class family man earning 5,000 rupees a month from his job with Indian Airlines. He told a documentary interviewer, "I enjoyed the work . . . it was like a hobby and it gave you a lot of time to do what you liked; . . . we used to go to game parks, it was very nice."[25] At this time, Rajiv was a copilot, and over the coming decade he would progress to being a captain, a commander, then examiner—and would finally fly Boeing jets.

Meanwhile, Sonia and Rajiv also intended on having a family of their own. Sonia's first pregnancy was in 1969, but it sadly resulted in a miscarriage.[26] When Sonia became pregnant again toward the end of that year, she spent most of her term in bed. The family rallied around her; Rajiv was solicitous, and when he was away on a flying shift, Sanjay or Indira "would sit with [her] at mealtimes and do all they could to keep [her] spirits up."[27] A family bond between the four of them had formed. Sonia and Rajiv's son, Rahul, was born on June 19, 1970, followed by their daughter, Priyanka, on January 12, 1972. Rajiv and Sanjay both had inherited from their father a taste for mechanics, and Rajiv was delighted that Rahul, when presented with a choice of objects (designed to represent possible future interests), selected a toy car. One of his early gifts from his father was a tiny, scaled-down tool kit.

It was a life of domestic bliss, and Sonia was fine-tuning her new self. She was occasionally homesick for her family in Italy while she adjusted to her new family in India. She soon realized that she would not be able to truly settle in her adopted country if her heart was still divided. "I decided that my roots had to be properly embedded in India. . . . This would be possible only if I severed all contacts with Italy. And this is exactly what I did. To make a new start, you have to break away totally from your old links.

And when I realized that, yes, I had settled down completely, I picked up my old contacts."[28] Rajiv learned some basic Italian, and initial biannual visits to Italy turned into yearly holidays: A sister at the Istituto Magistrale Sant'Anna in Turin remembers a two-year-old Rahul, accompanied by his Indian maid, being taken to greet his young aunt Nadia who was studying to be an elementary school teacher there in 1972.[29] There are images taken by Rajiv near Venice, Capri, Rome, and Naples, and a 1979 photograph shows Rahul in Turin, wearing his grandfather Stefano's Italian army hat.[30]

Eventually, Signor Maino's resistance collapsed in the face of Nehruvian charm. Though he was not at the wedding, he did visit India later in his life; photos were taken of him in Kashmir with Paola in 1982 and in a national park in Rajasthan in 1985. Former external affairs minister Natwar Singh, who was known to the Nehrus for more than five decades, met Sonia's father on occasion in India.[31] Stefano passed away in the late 1980s, but the family is still very close: Sonia, Priyanka, and Rahul have plenty of contact with their Italian side. Paola Maino came to Delhi most winters, and she often appeared in society pages attending a concert or event with several members of the Indian branch of the family.

In late-1960s Delhi, the world of national politics was literally never far away from the house. On July 19, 1969, there was a great deal of commotion outside 1 Safdarjang Road: Fourteen of India's largest banks had just been nationalized under a directive from Indira Gandhi. The enormously popular move made these banks available to lower-income groups in towns and villages up and down the country, contributing to her being seen as a champion of the poor. Millions who had never even been inside a bank could now open a bank account. It marked a social shift in money management (though, of course, political control of the banks also enabled political control over the whole economy). Low-paid workers, drivers, and the educated unemployed danced in the streets. They assembled in happy, jubilant rallies outside the prime minister's house. Indira had an instinctive feel for what would please people and would move heaven and earth to deliver.

Since the time of India's independence, its numerous royal families, in return for handing over their princely states, received the rupee equivalent of hundreds of thousands of dollars a year tax-free in privy-purse payments, guaranteed forever by the constitution. In 1971 Indira decided to abolish the privy purses, another move popular with the middle and lower classes, which also added money to the national exchequer. She is also credited with India's green revolution by helping India, through mechanization, to learn to feed itself with high-yield food grain production. On her watch, India joined the exclusive five-member nuclear club in 1974 with an underground detonation in the Rajasthan desert by Atomic Energy Commission scientists.

These were significant achievements in a highly controversial premiership, but for many Indira analysts, the jury is still out. Some do grudgingly admit, however, that the bank nationalization and regulatory system carefully managed by the Reserve Bank of India helped safeguard India's economy during the twenty-first century's global economic downturn. Though she was determined, Indira faced political opposition from within her own party as well as from the other side of the House in parliament. As a result, she was developing an autocratic style of leadership supported by a motley handful of advisers, a type of "kitchen cabinet" that limited access to her. Dispensing with most forms of consensus, she trusted her own leadership qualities, which would serve her well in her finest hour in 1971 with the creation of Bangladesh.

Pakistan's mainly Bengali-speaking, more populous eastern portion was separated by about a thousand miles from its western segment, where military rule prevailed and Urdu was the official language. The only tie between the two portions was the Muslim religion. A movement for autonomy in the eastern section began under Sheikh Mujibur Rahman, who ran the Awami League party. As Rahman and his group gained in power and strength, winning nearly all the region's seats in a general election, west Pakistan decided to impose central control—whatever the cost—and ordered a crackdown in the eastern part of the country. Hundreds of civilians were slaughtered, and Rahman was whisked away to a secret military trial and jail in west Pakistan. Ten million terrified refugees poured across the border from east Pakistan into India while the fight for a free Bangladesh started. They needed to be accommodated, fed, and sheltered. India could not afford to absorb them permanently, so Indira personally visited the camps and made sure the refugees were contained close to the border while doing her best to see that they were looked after. Horrified at their plight, Indira appealed to the world to help promote a political settlement in Bangladesh and take pity on the helpless refugees. She also asked the international community to make sure that Rahman was not harmed in west Pakistan.

While tensions between Pakistan and India started to rise, the Indian army chief of staff[32] began secret preparations for his military to strike when necessary. In August 1971 Indira signed a special treaty with Russia that allowed mutual military assistance in case of war and was warmly received when she went there the following month. Determined to influence international opinion, she spent three weeks visiting European capitals to raise awareness of the unfolding crisis and flew to the United States where she met with President Richard Nixon and National Security Adviser Henry

Kissinger. Most leaders were scared of a war between Pakistan and India and advised Indira to show restraint. The United States considered, at the time, India to be too close politically to the Soviet Union.

Nixon was pro-Pakistan and expressed his antipathy toward Indira, telling Kissinger after Indira's visit, "We really slobbered over the old witch."[33] Despite Indira's international lobbying efforts, none of the countries would intervene, so Indira settled for using the Western media to get her message across instead. Meanwhile, battle was raging on India's eastern border.

A Bangladeshi Liberation Army was supported with training and equipment on Indian soil by Indira's paramilitary Border Security Force and a Sikh Indian army general,[34] with her overall supervision. Just as the Indian military was readying itself to attack, the Pakistanis struck first. On December 3, 1971, Pakistan air force bombers attacked Indian advance air bases. Indira worked through the night talking to military chiefs and overseeing battle plans they had been working on in preparation for such an event. Broadly, the idea was to defend in the west and attack and conquer in the east. The United States sent its 7th Fleet across to the Bay of Bengal, but Indira was not intimidated by the menacing gesture. She dispatched one of her staff to Moscow, and a Soviet fleet was also soon on its way. On December 6 she announced in parliament that India recognized an independent Bangladesh. In the west, the Indian navy bombarded and blockaded Pakistan's only port. In 14 days[35] the war was over, and on December 16, 93,000 Pakistani officers and men laid down their arms and surrendered—the largest capitulation since World War II. The Sikh army general who had trained and helped the guerrilla Bangladeshi Liberation Army to victory later was dismissed over corruption charges. Limping off into the sunset in disgrace, he vowed revenge.

Sheikh Mujibur Rahman was released and became president of Bangladesh.

Bangladesh's high commissioner to Delhi in 2009, Tariq Karim, acknowledges India's role. "Without India's assistance . . . Bangladesh perhaps would not . . . have been liberated within the nine months that it was. Our struggle probably would have continued much longer. The Pakistani army would have been able to reinforce itself. The bleeding . . . would have continued, so in a sense this was perhaps the fastest liberation war that has taken place anywhere in history in modern times."[36] Mushirul Hasan comments that Indira became Mother India, the maternal goddess of the people, a symbol of national unity. "Maybe even Churchill did not enjoy the kind of good luck after the war that Indira Gandhi did."[37]

Sonia said that dining-table talk during those days was about the atrocities of the Pakistani army on the people of Bangladesh and the refugee crisis, and throughout the 14-day war, she found Indira calm and composed. "We lived every moment of that crisis in our family. I remember when Mujibur Rahman came to Delhi from London, there was a big reception at the airport. Though I was about to deliver my other child the next day, I made it a point to be there at the airport."[38]

While Indira engaged in war with the nation's neighbor, she was also growing to love Sonia "like the daughter she never had," as Sonia said in her Nexus Lecture. Gradually, Sonia learned how to communicate in Hindi, "to feel comfortable in Indian clothes . . . and acquaint myself with the cultural heritage of my new homeland. The glorious and multihued palette of India came to be as dear and precious to me as it was to them."[39] With flexibility and tolerance, and driven by the love she shared with her husband, Sonia successfully integrated into India's most prominent family. Now, with children of her own to raise, it was time to consider which arena and which part of Delhi society she would step into.

3

NOT JUST BRINGING UP BABIES

She opened her heart, her family, and her culture to me.

—*Sonia Gandhi*

Behind imposing iron gates, roads bounding the sides of a large expanse of grass and trees lead to Teen Murti Bhavan, or Three Statues House, a rectangular building designed by Robert Tor-Russell, which was the official residence of the former commander in chief of the British Forces in India before the country gained its independence. After that, the building was home to India's founding father and prime minister, Jawaharlal Nehru. It is the setting for a memorable photograph of Indira, Rajiv, and Sanjay that features in the pictorial essay compiled by Sonia after the death of her husband.

Formerly called Flagstaff House, the residence was renamed after the three-statues memorial to Indian soldiers who died in World War I, which stands on a roundabout opposite the front gates. On the ground floor, the spacious rear gardens can be seen through glass doors at the front and the back; in between them is a large rectangular room used for informal and formal occasions, and for entertaining in the old days when Jawaharlal Nehru and Indira, as chatelaine for her father, lived there. Later, it was used for lying-in-state ceremonies. It was a room that would bear witness to highly emotional times for Sonia.

Rajiv and Sanjay spent a good part of their childhood in the spacious stone and stucco building with its manicured gardens and bougainvillea bushes. Though they had the run of the place as children, when it came to their emotions, their mother quite deliberately taught her sons to be reserved; displays of feelings were discouraged. Indira once said to a friend that "one does not wear one's heart on one's sleeve." Self-control in public was a trait of this aristocratic family. When Nehru's two nieces visited their father in prison, he told them that "we mustn't let these people see us cry." And Indira once told a three-year-old Rajiv to go to a fountain in the garden if he wanted to weep. On another occasion when Rajiv needed an operation and the surgeon told him it would not hurt, Indira interrupted to say that it most definitely *would*—he would feel considerable pain and he needed to be able to bear it.[1] So the boy learned to control his emotions at a young age.

Rajiv and Sanjay had quite different personalities, too. One of Nehru's junior press aides remembered that while Rajiv was quiet and compliant—likened to "a doll" by staff members—Sanjay engaged in tricks on retinue and family alike. He would play pranks when his grandfather returned from his office, on occasion blocking his car and demanding that he ride Sanjay's new bicycle. A lanky prime minister Nehru riding a tiny two-wheeler was quite a sight. Sanjay liked to play hide-and-seek and once hid behind a bush, daring Jawaharlal to find him. Despite the driver joining in the search, no Sanjay was to be found, eliciting a muttered observation from his grandfather, "You are a clever boy. You always win!"[2] The child was bold and mischievous—later on he would play truant and, still later, crash cars, often turning to his mother for an alibi to get him out of trouble.[3]

Sonia decided that it was now time to have her own children start their formal education. At age two and a half, Rahul was ready for nursery school, and Priyanka soon would be too. Sonia wanted the best education for her little ones and considered one of the most exclusive kindergartens around. "Everybody who's anybody went to The Study, and those who didn't go didn't matter," the son of a president once stated about Mrs. Hemant Pasrich's establishment. In the 1970s The Study was situated in the Golf Links Estate, a quite fancy New Delhi residential colony. (Indians often refer to large clusters of homes as colonies, each with a separate identity, with their own places of worship, gardens, parks, shops, and markets.) Pasrich proudly claims that the school took children from all types of families in the professional upper-strata of academics, politicians, and industrialists. Tiny members of Delhi's elite in white shirts and blue skirts or shorts attended for three and a half hours every weekday morning. Pasrich said mothers like Sonia Gandhi, who were "discerning and caring," would be the type to choose her kindergarten.

One day in 1973 Sonia arrived, unannounced, accompanied by one of Indira Gandhi's assistants. She found the director, duster in hand, dressed in casual slacks and explaining to some newly hired cleaning ladies how she expected hygiene to be maintained. Pasrich noticed a "very good-looking" visitor in trousers, but not knowing who she was, distractedly admonished, "I wish you'd made an appointment." Mrs. Pasrich was sure that Sonia, not Indira, made the decisions about her children's education: "I know *Sonia* chose the school because she came to see it. She came, she saw it, and she met me, and the next day the form came in."[4] A couple of days after the registration document was submitted, Rahul arrived. The toddler appeared well balanced, like his sister who joined him later on. "He didn't cry or give us any trouble," Pasrich smiles, recalling his parents waiting at the gate to collect their children and regularly attending school functions.

Rahul's teacher, Jyoti Aluwalia, notes, "Rahul was one of my favorites; he understood what he was told and did it. I don't remember ever having to check him. He wasn't rowdy, he was very disciplined." Sonia enthusiastically followed up at home, helping the children to learn to read *Kitty and Rover* books.[5] Rahul adored story time, and Priyanka enjoyed art and poetry. Mrs. Pasrich found Sonia involved and interested in her children's progress: "She would ask simple questions; 'How is Rahul doing, is he all right?' . . . Rahul was not a boisterous little fellow. Priyanka was more outgoing." Compared to Delhi parents today who, Pasrich said, write letters to the newspapers about every little complaint, Sonia was just a normal mom, and to demonstrate the point, tells this story.

Toddlers bring a little midmorning snack to school. The director (using the suffix *Ji* to show respect), said that once Rahul "had some juice and a little thermos and he put it in a glass and out plopped a cockroach, in the juice. I was called by the teacher because—*this was Rahul Gandhi!*—we took it out with a spoon and we put it in an envelope and I called the security guard . . . and I called Sonia-Ji and I said, 'There's a cockroach in the juice!' and she was so casual and nice about it. She said, 'Oh yes, you know, they come in from the garden, and sometimes the kitchen has them.' She didn't get upset. There were never any issues with the Gandhis."

Mrs. Pasrich became a trusted friend of the family, and Priyanka often went with her to special places. They went riding together at the Delhi Polo Club, for instance, and swimming at the Gymkhana club (an old colonial-style members-only establishment with recreational facilities and a 30-year waiting list). "She must have been about ten. Sometimes I would correct her stroke. She said, 'Mrs. Pasrich, no one tells me when I do something wrong. They always tell me I'm doing everything wonderfully.'"

Rahul and Priyanka left the school in 1976 as Sonia and Rajiv "wanted to keep both of the children together." Mrs. Pasrich would like to see one of the next generation of Gandhi infants one day: "Rahul said, 'I'll send mine to you.' I hope Rahul remembers saying this when he has children of his own and I hope I'm still around to see them." Today's atmosphere is of course very different from the easy days of the 1970s when Sonia and Rajiv would turn up unguarded, and Mrs. Pasrich worries about the safety of her former charges. "Rahul is out all the time and there are lots of mad people in the world. I do think Sonia's very brave."

The Gandhis were all busy in those days. Vinod Mehta, editor in chief of the *Outlook* Group (an Indian magazine publishing and news service corporation), explains: "Sonia was helping out with hospitality, when people came to dinner, etc.—she was a perfect hostess; Rajiv was flying planes but . . . there was a ritual that, whenever possible, they would meet for breakfast together. . . . The younger brother [Sanjay] was very interested in politics and helping his mother. And they [Sonia and Rajiv] were very happy—they had their own circle of friends . . . people from corporate life, business managers, not in politics."[6] Eating together was a family tradition going back to Teen Murti Bhavan. In her own residence, Indira led the discussions from the head of the rectangular wooden dining table with its ten blue-cushioned carved chairs. It was a chance to bond and to learn. Barring official engagements, everyone would sit together for meals of mainly Indian vegetarian fare[7] and join in lively discussions. Indira also liked Sonia's Italian cooking as it reminded her of her own days in Europe.

Sonia and others remember that Indira was fond of quoting from a 1968 Peter Sellers film, *The Party,* in which the actor plays an Indian. Later on, in a *Washington Post* interview, Indira talked about how Hindu philosophy gave her "an inner strength," and how she did not like making small talk with President Richard Nixon. The interviewer expressed surprise at the amount of energy Indira had, to which she replied it came from "being an Indian." The interviewer said he could see why Indira "got on Nixon's nerves," and she retorted with a description of the scene in the film in which Peter Sellers was asked, "Who do you think you are?" to which Sellers's character replied, "Indians don't *think.* We *know* who we are."[8] Years later, Sonia quoted the line at a 2006 *Hindustan Times* leadership summit.

While Indira was getting to know her daughter-in-law, Sonia was absorbing all that she could about being part of the family that helped build the nation. Indira was, as her father and grandfather had been, president of the left-of-center Indian National Congress (INC) political party, formed in 1885. Mahatma Gandhi was the pioneer who converted the INC into an all-India movement, using nonviolent protest to fight for the birthright of Indians, to be free from the might of the British Empire. He used the simple technique of noncooperation with the rulers of the country. The Mahatma became a spiritual mentor to Jawaharlal, who shed his somewhat dandified skin and adopted the simple lifestyle of a freedom fighter—in clothes, in food, in language, in the way he spent his money. Nehru's mansion became the epicenter of the national struggle for independence, and the two British-trained barristers, he and the Mahatma, worked side by side, eventually becoming two of the leading founding fathers of the nation. The whole of the Nehru family, especially Indira, was influenced by the Mahatma; as a youngster she was captivated by the freedom movement and hero-worshipped its pioneers. She was imbued with the spirit of the age and with India: It was in her DNA.

Once India gained its independence in 1947, the INC became the nation's dominant political party and Jawaharlal Nehru its first prime minister. The quintessentially modern Brahmin family, actively involved in the politics of the country for so long, was seen, Dileep Padgaonkar, consulting editor with the *Times of India* points out, "as genuinely above and beyond everything that divides India."[9] The Nehrus were projected as belonging to everyone because they were seen as being above the rifts—region, caste, community, and class—of Indian society. The pan-Indian appeal meant, says one of Indira's former ministers, Natwar Singh, that 20 percent of the electorate was always with them.[10] Indira, who had lived through so many of India's key moments, was a fascinating role model for her family, and mealtimes were mesmerizing lessons in living history.

Indira would quiz the children with simple historical and geographical questions about the country, about the states. "What are the names of the states, what is happening?" "What is the capital of Goa, what is the capital of Andhra Pradesh?" Since they were in an English-speaking school, she wanted them to learn Hindi and be fluent, so she would ask the questions in Hindi. Sonia learned a lot and took part in these discussions too.[11] For Priyanka, it made politics really exciting: She told an NDTV interviewer in 2009, "I've grown up in an atmosphere where at the dining table you discussed big political issues—right from when you were a kid."[12]

The family spoke a mix of Hindi and English at mealtimes, Vinod Mehta says, in the same way upper middle-class Indians do. "There was no rule that you could only speak in Hindi, there was no taboo against speaking English. But the speaking of Hindi was encouraged."

The prime minister doted on her grandchildren. Rahul, as a toddler, would often go with his grandmother to her office. When she came home for lunch with her family and grandchildren, Sonia would wait on the porch, Rahul and Priyanka to either side of her holding her hands, to receive Indira when she arrived in her car. The children would scamper on ahead, while Sonia would accompany her mother-in-law into the dining room and sit with her through the meal, making sure that she had what she wanted to eat.[13] If Indira needed to meet certain foreign dignitaries or eminent Indians, she would often invite them to the house rather than somewhere more formal,[14] and it was a routine experience for Sonia and her young family to have prominent international guests.

There was a genuine bond between Indira and her grandchildren, who grew as attached to her as she was to them. Film footage shows Indira sitting on a tiny chair at a low table with the pair, chatting to them in Hindi and playing with them. Just as her father had educated her in unconventional methods, through detailed correspondence when they were separated by continents or the iron bars of jail, so Indira made it her mission to develop passionately close bonds with all of her grandchildren and expand their education. Priyanka described growing up with Indira in a 2009 NDTV interview: "I did idealize my grandmother. I grew up in a household where she was the head. . . . Not only politically powerful, but she was a powerful human being to be around. So being a little girl and seeing this woman who was strong and stood for so much, it did have an effect on me." It seems that though Priyanka adored her grandmother, it was Rahul who was "absolutely . . . her favorite . . . she had this bond with him. And she taught him and she spent a lot of time with him, talking to him."[15]

Indira's fierce love for her family and her need to have her grandchildren close arose out of her own loneliness as a child. As time passed and she grew fonder of Sonia, she told her all about her personal life. In an uncertain environment, her father in and out of jail, her schooling disrupted by periodic visits to the hospital to accompany her mother, who died of tuberculosis in a Swiss sanitarium at the age of 37, Indira grew up without siblings and felt insecure. She studied abroad at Oxford and fell in love with Feroze Gandhi, whom she had known for a while in India and who was at the London School of Economics. He had spent time around the family, in particular with her mother, and Indira decided to marry him, but both her parents were against the union—they thought he was unstable and not of the right pedigree, and he was from a different community (though this was not a major block in Jawaharlal's eyes). At any rate, Indira understood Sonia's position and empathized; she told Sonia that Feroze had been her one true love.

Sonia was inspired by Indira in many ways. Her mother-in-law, she observed, interacted "with the common man and with heads of state, with allies and with opponents."[16] Sonia would adapt that interaction to her own style, but with less of a sycophantic coterie than her mother-in-law had, and she would be much less confrontational. She realized that a collegiate system, taking colleagues with her, would be far more effective in the long run.

Indira was developing a populist agenda for herself, as she felt it was important to be in touch with the rural masses. When her detractors launched a new slogan, "*Indira hatao!*" (Remove Indira!), she responded with "*Garibi hatao!*" (Remove poverty!). It was a slogan that would last many years.

But Indira was her own woman, and the Congress Party had people of all factions within it, hungry for power. The old, conservative, right-wing leaders, known as the Syndicate, had initially thought that Indira would simply be a puppet for them to manipulate when she first became prime minister and were frustrated when she proved them wrong. There was a constant power struggle, and they were determined to oust her. Her bank nationalization and antipoverty agenda were too left wing, too new for them, and, distrusting Moscow's intentions, they resented Indira's growing warm relations with the Soviet Union. When the Syndicate and Indira supported different candidates for the post of the Indian president, a parliamentary vote went to Indira's man. Further tussles led to a final split in the party: Indira's group, which was recognized by the election authorities, became known as Congress (R) (for Requisitionist) and the old-guard faction, Congress (O) (for Organization). Sonia took note: She recalled her mother-in-law coming out "strongly, aggressively." It was the first time that she felt that Indira behaved like the "Iron Woman" she was often called. "She was at her best when faced with challenges. If she was pushed to the wall, there was pressure on her, she would come out and really fight back."[17] Faced with all the hostility from the Syndicate, Indira realized—and it was a lesson Sonia herself would later observe—that there were those within the party who could not be trusted, and she started to shrink her coterie. In 1971 Indira called a midterm election and steered Congress (R) to a landslide victory with an unprecedented two-thirds majority. India's victory in the Bangladesh war had helped Indira's image, but there was insurgency and agitation at home. What was brewing quietly in a smoldering cauldron would have a dramatic and lasting impact on all the family. However, the Gandhis were now preoccupied with a happy event.

In September 1974, Sanjay married 17-year-old Maneka Anand, the daughter of a Sikh army colonel. Maneka has been described in many quarters as someone who did not fit easily with the Nehru-Gandhi family, and relations between her, Indira, and Sonia were the subject of much gossip. Maneka's life at 1 Safdarjang Road was very different from Sonia's experience: "We had a tiny room. Sanjay and I were working people. I was much younger than everyone else . . . [except] the children. I was in college then and working at a magazine called *Surya.*"[18] Jad Adams and Philip Whitehead describe Maneka in *The Dynasty* as "energetic and demanding," requiring "more attention than the busy and rather sober home . . . could provide."[19]

Most Indira Gandhi biographers and those who visited the house at the time agree that there were differences between Sonia and Maneka. Maneka explains it this way: "I was into animal welfare works and college and the magazine, different things. There's a difference of ten years [in our ages]. That's a lot of difference when you're younger. When you're older, it doesn't matter at all. When you're 17 and someone's 27, 28, there's a whole world of a difference. There's a big gap always." The model and journalist (later turned animal rights activist and politician) has no doubt that everyone in the household was politicized to a greater or lesser degree, and she rejects the notion that any member of the family was able to steer clear of the subject. "It's an intensely political family. In a political family every member is politically aware. Everybody was involved all throughout with everything."[20]

A former friend of the Gandhis, ex-deputy chair of the upper house and ex-Congress senior Najma Heptulla, recalls, "Sonia used to cook and take care of the household. [She and Maneka] had two different roles, two different personalities. It wasn't a big house. They weren't at each others' throats, but they were two different people, involved in two different things."[21]

Though Sonia was primarily a kindergarten mother at this stage, life was not at all simple for her on any front, and the complexities were about to increase tenfold.

4

THE EMERGENCY

India is like a baby and just as one should sometimes take a child and shake it, I feel we have to shake India.

—*Indira Gandhi*

Sonia and Rajiv were standing by Indira's side at the Boat Club in New Delhi on June 20, 1975, when the prime minister addressed a rally of roughly 100,000 people.[1] Indira spoke passionately, pledging she would serve the people of India "till her last breath."[2] Sanjay and Maneka were there too; the entire Gandhi clan lined up to demonstrate their unity to the nation. The show of family strength was deliberate because Indira and her Indian National Congress Party were in trouble. Rising prices, a drop in the supply of essential commodities, unemployment, and perceived government corruption had led to mass protests and the party's loss of a key territory, Gujarat, in a recent state election. Sanjay, now his mother's principal political support, had been defiantly arranging pro-Indira marches, rallies, and "spontaneous" demonstrations in front of the family home.

Indira, caught at the center of all this, was feeling increasingly isolated, trusting few outside the family. Many of her female friends had died; others had broken ties with her or moved to a different continent. Convinced that a dynastic project was compulsory as both an insurance policy and a shield, she was leaning more and more on Sanjay, and he liked that. Shorn of her friends and betrayed by those she once thought loyal, she was now determined that authority should remain with her and hers forever. While this was happening, Sanjay was acquiring an extraordinary power over his mother, and she was finding it difficult to say no to him. Her own father had been reluctant to fast-track her to the top position, often leaving it to others to encourage her in politics, but Indira made it very clear to everyone that Sanjay was her appointed heir.

All leaders need a key adviser, and who can you trust not to let you down if not your own son? Indira was very fond of Sonia, her favorite daughter-in-law, depended on her for personal support, gave her responsibility for running the home, and even took fashion advice from her, but she still needed to share with someone steeped in politics, someone hardheaded and ruthless who could play the game. That person was Sanjay. Rajiv was unassuming and liked to spend time with his young family; Sanjay provided the psychological and professional support his mother craved.

Sanjay was hardworking and did not drink or use drugs,[3] but he did seem to have an obsessive-compulsive nature, and, inspired by Henry Ford, still was keen to produce a small, cheap, Indian-made car to bring road mobility to the masses. In 1969, amid public charges of nepotism, which were denied by Indira, he was awarded a license to set up a factory to produce 50,000 Maruti cars a year, a challenge that proved beyond him. In the early 1980s, the brand was rescued by Indira Gandhi through an agreement with Japan's Suzuki Motor Corporation. The mass production of Maruti-Suzuki cars transformed the Indian automobile industry and Maruti-Suzuki into India's leading car company.

On June 12, 1975, Indira's stunning electoral victory of 1971 crumbled. The High Court in the state of Uttar Pradesh (where the constituency that had elected Indira to parliament was located) declared the vote invalid because of corruption charges leveled against her campaign. She was barred from holding the office of prime minister, but the order was stayed for 20 days, giving the party a chance to choose another leader as it had a parliamentary majority. Sanjay would not hear of his mother withdrawing from office, even temporarily; Congress chief ministers and cabinet colleagues, fearing for their own futures, also objected noisily to the notion of their leader stepping down. Indira, meanwhile, was convinced that forces both abroad and in India were trying to destabilize the country by manipulating the opposition parties.

Her fears had been aroused to the point of paranoia with the ousting and assassination of the Chilean president, Salvador Allende, two years earlier in 1973 in a coup supported by the Central Intelligence Agency.[4]

A groundswell of protest had started to develop around the country, leading to a period of high agitation. Indira was quite ruthless when she wanted to be. In 1974 she had used the army to break a national strike of millions of railway workers; though she espoused socialism, she was quite disdainful of trade unions. Nor was she one to relinquish power without a fight. She looked for stringent measures to stop the situation from getting out of hand and started to hatch a secret plan with the few aides whom she trusted.

Indira's enemies, meanwhile, were jubilant, prematurely foreseeing the mighty fall of the Iron Lady. They organized strikes and demonstrations to force her resignation and planned to urge the army and the police to mutiny and support them. At a large rally in Delhi, they announced that they would encircle her house for a whole week and called for a mass street protest in the capital. One opposition leader told a foreign journalist, "We intend to overthrow her . . . for good. The lady won't survive our movement. . . . Thousands of us will surround her house to prevent her from going out . . . we shall camp there night and day."[5]

Though Sonia and Rajiv were not directly involved in high-level decision making, they were uncomfortably caught up in unfolding events as their home was the center of action, such as the pro-Indira rallies orchestrated by Sanjay, while counterdemonstrations raged elsewhere. During these days Indira had Maneka Gandhi, a "curious, intelligent girl, who talked readily," sent to Kashmir, to avoid jeopardizing the covert operation she was designing with Sanjay.[6]

The morning of June 25, the threatened opposition protest packed the streets while Indira consulted a prominent lawyer and chief minister[7] who was an expert on the Indian Constitution, telling him that "drastic, emergent action is needed."[8] The lawyer left to read and reread the constitution and returned with his findings. Indira then asked him to escort her to see the president, whom she informed that, as the Indian Constitution provided grounds for action when "a grave emergency exists whereby the security of India is threatened by internal disturbances," Indira and her government had decided to declare a State of Internal Emergency. (An external emergency was still in place from the 1971 Bangladesh war.) The president signed the proclamation. Back home, Indira and her lawyer worked on the draft of a speech to be broadcast to the nation the next day, and Sanjay worked with a staff member on a list of those to be detained. More than six hundred opposition leaders were arrested through the early hours of the morning. The cabinet, having been telephoned at 5 AM, met an hour later at 6 and endorsed the declaration. Indira had decided on a retroactive endorsement meeting so that news of her decision would not be leaked in advance and those to be apprehended would not be forewarned. The long night of June 25 was the start of one of contemporary India's darkest times.

The power supply in the area where most offices of the major newspapers were located was cut off to prevent them printing news of the arrests. The *Hindustan Times* front page informed readers, "The city edition of Friday and desk editions of Friday and Saturday of the *Hindustan Times* could not be brought out as no power was available from 12:45 PM on Thursday till 7:15 PM on Friday. The inconvenience is deeply regretted."[9] Under State of Emergency rules, censorship was permitted, and the free press was immediately muzzled. Where material had been cut out by the government, some newspapers just left blank spaces. When they were reprimanded, they simply published quotations from Mahatma Gandhi and Jawaharlal Nehru in defense of freedom of expression. They were rapped over the knuckles for this too.[10] It was the first time since independence that free speech was suppressed.

The Maintenance of Internal Security Act (MISA) was put in place, a draconian measure that gave the government wide censorship powers. A *Hindustan Times* front-page story datelined June 30 said, "The Maintenance of Internal Security Act has been amended by an ordinance to the effect that no grounds need be given for detention to any [detainee] under the Act."[11] There were restrictions on the holding of meetings, demonstrations, processions, and the use of loudspeakers. Permission was needed for everything. In India, freed from the British nearly 30 years prior, with "liberty of thought and expression" enshrined in the country's newly minted constitution, there was now dread and loathing in the air. In parliament, seven Congress members accused the British Broadcasting Corporation (BBC) of "slandering India by false reporting. . . . It has often appeared to us the BBC picks up its news from Radio Pakistan." The authorities forced Mark Tully, for many years the BBC's bureau chief in Delhi, together with senior correspondents from the *Washington Post* and the *Baltimore Sun,* to leave India. Tully repudiates the charges. "The government was very angry about the BBC's coverage from the moment the Emergency was declared. They thought they had prevented all news . . . getting out . . . but we managed to get the names of all the opposition leaders who had been arrested out early on the morning of the declaration. . . . We had our network of stringers around the country. We never relied on Radio Pakistan. I was expelled because the BBC would not sign the censorship agreement."[12] Tully became the BBC foreign news editor in London during the Emergency period.

Human rights activist and author Kuldip Nayar, who was then the editor of the *Indian Express* newspaper, wrote articles critical of Indira Gandhi's governance, arranged a meeting of journalists at a local press club to lodge a protest against press censorship, and also wrote directly to Indira Gandhi in July. Arrested under MISA and sent to Tihar Jail for three months, he philosophically describes the experience as "quite educational. I was in a ward with about 30 other people; you had a *charpoy* [a four-legged frame strung with rope used as a bed] and a pot. The toilet was dry. The lunch, watery lentils and vegetables, had flies all over it. You conditioned yourself to put up with it."[13] Nayar, who has been the Indian high commissioner in London and a member of the upper house of India's parliament, says he feels no animosity at all toward the Nehru-Gandhi family for the Emergency action.

But the Emergency did bring about some temporary changes that astonished India. In contrast with the cacophony of disruptive strikes, sit-ins, protest marches, and clashes with the police in recent months, an uneasy orderliness descended on the county. It was behavior born of fear, for officials across the board, scared of whatever fate might be in store for them, fell into line like a row of ducks. Suddenly, trains ran on time, tea breaks were fewer and shorter, and pending files that had been gathering dust for months were miraculously processed overnight. Debts and bondage owed by the rural poor to moneylenders were voided. Slogans on roundabouts, buses, and billboards exclaimed: "She stood between chaos and order. She saved the Republic" and urged Indians to "let us get on with the business of nation building" and "work more, talk less" as "courtesy keeps everyone happy." In December 1975 Sanjay was made a member of the executive committee of the Congress Party's youth wing, the training ground for the party and government positions. The same day, to the wild, abandoned joy of much of the party, Sanjay was publicly proclaimed his mother's successor. This gave him the perfect platform from which to construct a power base, but the political heir-apparent got carried away. Indira biographer Inder Malhotra observed that he was "attracting dropouts, drifters and roughnecks to him . . . in large numbers in the hour of his power and glory."[14] Sanjay had become the second most powerful person in India.

Any reforms that took place during the Emergency were neutralized by Sanjay and his coterie, who exercised their authority without restraint, riling much of the country. Sanjay had a five-point plan to increase adult literacy (adopting the Frank Laubach program slogan "each one teach one"), to abolish bride dowry, to end the caste system, to beautify the environment by clearing slums and planting trees, and to introduce a radical program of family planning. As Malhotra describes in his biography of Indira, "the five-point plan, like the Emergency itself, became more a vehicle for Sanjay Gandhi's personal aggrandizement than for social improvement in India."[15] Sanjay's thugs extorted money from Delhi shopkeepers "for non-existent adult literacy or family planning centers."[16]

The birth rate per 1,000 in 1922 had been 48.1 and the death rate, 47.2. But with medical advances and improvements in nutrition, by the early

1970s the death rate had fallen to a record 17.4, and India's population was rising by 12 million a year.[17] There were more people living more reproductive years, and male sterilization seemed to be the most practical method of birth control. Slogans like "You have two, that will do" appeared in a drive overzealously directed by Sanjay, promoted on state television with willing or unwilling "volunteers" gazing into cameras as examples to their fellow men. Tents for vasectomy surgeries sprang up in cities, and vans drove around rural areas so that surgical operations could be carried out there. A quota system was imposed on government employees: They were paid to produce a certain number of people to be sterilized, and those who underwent the procedure were rewarded.

Many agree with Inder Malhotra's description of Sanjay as "brash and extremely tactless." He was often rude to his elders and those who worked with his mother.[18] Back then, even his family was starting to express doubts about him. Malhotra observes, "Rajiv was unhappy and always anxious to distance himself from what his brother was doing. . . . Sonia . . . shared her husband's thoughts."[19] Indira too was feeling somewhat helpless. Later, in 2004, Sonia told Shekhar Gupta in a television interview that during the Emergency, Indira had expressed doubts about the Emergency "through what she said, her comments . . . I can recall that at times she was uneasy about it."[20]

On the other hand, Bharatiya Janata Party vice president Najma Heptulla, who knew the family since she was then in the Congress circle, feels that Sanjay's reform plans could have worked if they had been handled differently. "Good programs were spoilt . . . because people wanted to show their eagerness to please some leaders." She says that while family planning is an important issue for India, "there was a misuse of power at the small level . . . to please the leadership. It so badly backfired that today no leader wants to talk about family planning or having a small family; they're scared of it." She also feels that it was wrong for important opposition leaders to be imprisoned: "In a democracy it shouldn't happen. A democracy is both the opposition and the ruling."[21]

Sanjay's beautification of cities plan misfired badly in Delhi. Tenements housing tens of thousands of people were cleared by bulldozers and demolition teams. At one location, Turkman Gate, it led to riots, when some 70,000 residents "were bundled off . . . at gunpoint and driven to their new homes—barbed-wire fenced plots of farmland."[22]

Mark Tully asserts that Sanjay was a major player at this time. "He was very much responsible for the image of the Emergency . . . the image of brutality. He was the one who forced through certain policies, supervised and was the driving force of the policy of compulsory sterilization, which was particularly disastrous from Indira Gandhi's point of view. Sanjay quite clearly played a very influential role indeed."[23] Indira, however, seemed to have had a complete blind spot where Sanjay was concerned, so strong was her belief in the dynastic construct. Her legacy project could not *allow* him to be faulty. The scenario was acutely awkward, and she soon had another reason for paranoia.

In August 1975, almost the entire family of Bangladesh's leader, Sheikh Mujibur Rahman, whom Sonia had met and whom Indira had supported so vociferously, was killed in a coup. For the first time, the repercussions of being part of the prime minister's family hit home. What had happened across the border could just as easily occur in Delhi. Indira was afraid that her grandchildren, daughters-in-law, and sons were all potential targets now. Alarmed, she took preventive action by increasing both detention without trial and intelligence activity. Sheikh Mujibur Rahman's daughters, Sheikh Hasina and Sheikh Rehana, were abroad at the time of the coup. They later sought refuge in India, where they became close to the Gandhi women, Indira playing a motherly, protective role to them and Sonia becoming a friend.[24]

Meanwhile, the Emergency was prompting international and domestic criticism of Indira. She wanted to regain her credentials as a democratic leader, so in the cause of egalitarianism was prepared to go to the polls. Businessman Swraj Paul notes, "Nobody in India and the western world thought she would call elections, but she proved them wrong. She was aware that she would lose. . . . It was an acceptance that the Emergency was a mistake."[25] Indeed, in January 1977, 19 months after the Emergency had been declared, Indira called for a March poll and had political prisoners released. Sonia explained in a 2004 interview on *Walk the Talk*, "Don't forget that at least the Indira Gandhi I knew was a democrat at heart, to the core. I think circumstances compelled her to take that action. But she was never quite at ease with it."[26]

For this 1977 election, Sanjay campaigned in Amethi, in the state of Uttar Pradesh, next to Indira's constituency, Rae Bareli. But the election had turned into a referendum on the Emergency. The opposition could smell blood; it was angry, as was the electorate. The most furious voters were where the Emergency had been most stringently enforced. A combination of political groups came together as the Janata (People's) Party to overthrow Indira. On top of opposition outside the home, tragedy hit the family that year: Maneka Gandhi's father was found dead in an apparent suicide.

Indira's friend Pupul Jayakar was at Safdarjang Road on March 20, 1977, the night the results came in: Both Indira and Sanjay were dramatically defeated. Sanjay and Maneka were due back that night from Amethi. Jayakar wrote, "I asked after Rajiv Gandhi and Sonia; they were in their room. . . . At 10:30, Indira rang the bell, asked for dinner and sent for Rajiv and Sonia. They came after a long time. Sonia was crying quietly, Rajiv was grim, tight-lipped. Dinner was served, Sonia and Rajiv ate some fruit, Indira her cutlets, salad and vegetables. . . ."[27]

The Emergency ended with a cabinet meeting and Indira's resignation: Jubilation on the streets mixed with hostility toward the fallen prime minister. One of her intelligence advisers had warned as the end of the campaign neared that, if she lost, such was the antipathy toward her and Sanjay, crowds might force their way into her house with violence in mind. He offered her paramilitary support for her safety. She refused his proposal while at the same time asking him to protect her children.[28] The night of the defeat, "the warnings . . . were in her mind. Her children and grandchildren had to be protected. She asked Rajiv and Sonia to take Rahul and Priyanka and spend the night with friends. She wanted them away from the house until the atmosphere in the city had settled down."[29]

On *Walk the Talk*, Sonia spoke about the adverse public feeling toward Indira: "There was a great deal of propaganda against Mrs. Gandhi. . . . Yes there were problems, but not in the scale that the opposition had built up." The interviewer, Shekhar Gupta, pressed the issue, asking, "Do you remember this coming up between Mrs. Gandhi and Rajiv or between Sanjay and Rajiv at that point?" to which Sonia replied calmly: "I do remember, but I wouldn't like to disclose it."

"Twenty-five years have gone past, maybe you should."

"Maybe another 25 years, maybe I'll write it someday."

Gupta was impressed by the outcome of his interview with Sonia, which took him several months of informal encounters to set up. There had been no preparatory meetings, no support team or entourage for this 2004 interview. Years later he commented, "I was very pleasantly surprised by how candid and how articulate she was . . . nobody had tutored her because I had given her no questions [in advance] . . . the conversation suddenly veered off onto the Emergency and she was quite game handling questions [about it]. I think that's when she for the first time made a statement that mistakes were made during the Emergency, excesses were committed, and in fact she even mentioned that Mrs. Gandhi was regretful. They had discussed it at their own dining table—and that, to an extent, helped the Congress Party to get over the trauma of the Emergency." Sonia chose Anand Bhavan in Allahabad, the ancestral home of the Nehru family, now donated to the nation by Indira Gandhi, for the interview setting. Gupta observed: "Nehru's father . . . had lived there; for [Sonia], it was the best way of showing the political legacy."[30]

5

WILLINGDON CRESCENT

Every insult hurled against me will rebound. Every punishment inflicted on me will be a source of strength to me.

—*Indira Gandhi*

Indira had lost the election. Thrown out of power, she and her family were homeless. Indira, Sonia, Rajiv, Maneka, Sanjay, 2 children, 5 dogs, and 13 years' worth of possessions, boxes, and papers needed somewhere to live—and fast. An old friend, Mohammad Yunus, decided to vacate his nearby bungalow at 12 Willingdon Crescent for Indira and her family. The house was smaller than the one on Safdarjang Road, though similarly designed: a whitewashed, one-story bungalow, with a pillared front veranda and a curved driveway behind a double-gated entrance.

Circumstances were far from the best for moving. The acidic atmosphere outside exacerbated the tension between the two brothers and the two daughters-in-law. Members of the new government had had their sights on Indira ever since she had imperiously ordered many of its senior leaders thrown into jail during the Emergency. Sanjay, excited at the chance to agitate and create an independent power base, was now entangled either in meetings with Youth Congress cronies or in designing grand strategy plans for his mother's comeback. Maneka was on fire too, politicking or working on her magazine. Rajiv was still flying with Indian Airlines, and Sonia still was responsible for maintaining hearth and home.

With Indira's loss of power came a loss of staff and some domestic help. Indira was still involved in political meetings and in any case had not set up or run a house for more than a decade. The home had to be furnished from scratch: air conditioners, a refrigerator, kitchenware, heaters—all were urgently needed. Sonia, the most domesticated lady in the home, "used to do all of the housework and the cooking,"[1] says interior designer Sunita Kohli.

The house was cramped, and Indira's room overcrowded with trunks. Files and newspapers were stacked up on the cases, and there were piles of books on the floor. As well as battling her opponents in public, Indira was constantly fighting a rearguard action. When her old cook died in a car accident, any replacement now could be a spy or someone assigned to poison her. Indira's friend Pupul Jayakar observed that much of the time Sonia and Rajiv were away from the premises, visiting their friends[2] as the atmosphere was tense and there was no space for guests. Maneka Gandhi confirms, "They were there on and off but without any interaction with any of us."[3]

A journalist commented, Sonia and Rajiv "withdrew into their one-family subshell."[4]

Despite the pressure-cooker atmosphere, the Sonia–Indira bond deepened. The reliable, discreet, and reserved Sonia was just the kind of trustworthy tonic Indira needed to maintain her home front. Maneka, who was not very interested in food stalls and the kitchen, found her own niche from which to support her mother-in-law: "I handled [Indira's] mail and generally became a secretary in spite of handling *Surya,* which was the only Congress-supporting magazine and which became very well known."[5]

With no formal administrative staff around to act as a barrier, Sonia was more directly exposed to the political colleagues, supporters, sycophants, hangers-on, and associates who routinely surround those in the political arena and were part of Indira's entourage. There was a constant flow of these people in, around, and through the house, which lacked designated office space.

Accusations, alleged scandals, and alleged corruption are endemic to any political landscape, and these beasts were now in Sonia's daily life. The Janata Party government, determined to wreak revenge on the entire Nehru-Gandhi clan, lit the fuse on a mammoth series of unsubstantiated accusations through the media, suggesting that the family had accumulated riches through illegal methods, even stating that they were preparing to leave India to avoid the authorities. Sonia called these accusations "lies and rumors."[6] The government dragnet fell on Rajiv, who was harassed by the Income Tax Department. Once he had spent his free time relaxing with the family, now the pilot with a passion for the simple things in life had to deal with countless vicious allegations. Their phones were bugged, and Sonia wrote, "Like everyone else in the family, Rajiv and I were followed by the CBI [Central Bureau of Investigation] wherever we went."[7]

Dr. Sanjay Sinh, parliament member and family friend, a former royal from Amethi, was sensitive to the pain caused to Rajiv and Sonia, whom he describes as "Simple and transparent . . . mud-slinging could never make them feel good . . . they were definitely unhappy."[8] After Indira's defeat, the foreign minister of the new government congratulated the electorate in "consigning Indira to the dustbin of history." Often, Indira's car was stoned—while she was in it. Congress Party men and women who had professed slavish loyalty to Indira now disappeared from her orbit. But she was too wily to stay down for any length of time. A true political boxer, Indira got on the comeback trail, thinking of ways to seize an advantage.

In July 1977, in a remote village called Belchi in the state of Bihar, there was a massacre of untouchables by upper-caste landowners. The Janata Party did nothing about this, so Indira, seeing a chance to turn her unpopularity around, immediately got into a jeep to ride to the village. It was raining hard and the roads were muddy and difficult, so a tractor was deployed. For the last part of the journey to Belchi, she climbed on an elephant in order to cross a flooded river. The terrorized villagers whose families had been murdered welcomed her with wild acclaim. Indira riding in on an elephant symbolized an urban politician coming to the rescue of the beleaguered helpless, and a photograph of her seated atop the animal looking quite thrilled has become a classic image in the Nehru gallery. Indira's visits to the countryside started to turn public opinion back toward her. The Janata Party decided that the only way to stop the petite dynamo was to put her behind bars.

The Nehrus embraced jail as part of their political struggle for freedom. Jawaharlal spent around ten years incarcerated. Departures for prison were occasions for excitement; Nehru and his family went "with a glad heart" and often with full pre-event ceremony. His wife, his son-in-law, and his daughter enthusiastically spent time behind bars. Indira in particular considered it an important rite of passage, and she was often completely involved with the process. It was such a ritual of the freedom movement that she viewed the experience with happiness, not dread. On one anticipated occasion, when the police came for her father at 5:45 AM, Indira woke him up and packed his suitcase. When informed that the arresting inspector was in a hurry, Nehru commented nonchalantly, "Tell him to go to hell!" as he proceeded to eat a full English breakfast of cornflakes, eggs, bacon, toast, and coffee. When the inspector complained that there was no time for a meal, Nehru retorted, "Shut up! I intend on having breakfast before I go."[9] Indira had learned how to handle going to jail with style. So on October 3, 1977, when the Janata government attempted to have the Iron Lady indicted and charged, she decided to use the situation to garner sympathy.

An officer from the Central Bureau of Investigation arrived late in the afternoon with some policemen but without an arrest warrant. Indira kept them waiting several hours while she made herself ready and telephone calls were placed. Supporters, lawyers, and the press arrived instantly. When she did come out of her house, immaculately groomed, she demanded that the police handcuff her (it would look so good for the cameras). Embarrassed, they refused. Amid noisy protests from her supporters, she spoke to the press from the roof of the black police van, explaining that the arrest was politically motivated and apologizing for not being able to carry out her scheduled village visit the next day. Rahul and Priyanka, bewildered and crying, were left in the care of servants[10] while Indira was driven off, with Sanjay, Maneka, Rajiv, and Sonia following protectively, ahead of a cavalcade of vehicles. At one point, it looked as though the police were actually heading out of Delhi's administrative jurisdiction into the next state, something Indira's lawyers advised her could not be done without an arrest warrant.

At a railway crossing where they were held up for half an hour, her followers surrounded the van and started arguing vehemently with the police. Amidst the squabble, Indira quietly slipped out and sat down on a culvert while the press took photographs. When the trains had passed, the police had no choice but to turn around and return to the capital, where they brought Indira to an officers' mess. She said goodnight to Sonia, Rajiv, Maneka, and Sanjay, and as she proceeded to her quarters, took a police salute. The next day, while hostile crowds, friendly crowds, and tear-gassing policemen clashed, the case against Indira was dismissed due to a lack of documentary evidence. Indira was getting energized. The government blocked her from appearing on television or radio, and the print media was hostile, so she figured the only way to reach people was to appear in front of them and talk to them directly. Her enemies, however, were determined.

On returning from a trip to London in 1978, Indira was expelled from parliament. Soon afterward, she was arrested and confined in barracks for six nights by herself—in the very same cell complex that one of the senior opposition leaders had occupied during the Emergency. Being relatively open, her cage-like quarters were very cold in December, but the jail authorities did their best to provide some warmth.[11] Rajiv described the vilification years from 1977 to 1980: "The whole family went through a very difficult period. Sonia stood up even when my mother was in jail. Sonia used to cook the food and take the food to jail, and even when Sanjay was in jail Sonia had to cook the food and then it was sent to the jail; she's very tough. . . ."[12] The experience of visiting her family in prison may have been new for Sonia, but for the Nehru-Gandhis, this was just some of the currency of political life. For Sonia, times were now very different from the idyllic days at Safdarjang Road; the long evening drives, soft music, ice cream trips, and craft activities in the workshop seemed a lifetime away. For the days that Indira was in jail, Sonia would take her something to eat in the morning, then a meal in the evening, and some milk that her mother-in-law would drink the following morning after waking up at 5 AM to practice yoga.[13] Sonia was received courteously by the guards and sometimes was allowed to exchange a few words with Indira.[14] On one occasion, Sonia brought Priyanka to visit her grandmother in the Tihar prison.[15]

The prison terms were a period of high anxiety for the family. Sanjay Gandhi, Sanjay Sinh, and others threw themselves into loud protests. Sinh remembers, "I was with Sanjay . . . going to jails for agitations and everything many times. We were fighting against the Janata regime. When Mrs. Indira Gandhi was jailed, we definitely used this against the opposition and we were doing agitations all over the state."[16] Indira, who visited Sanjay the day he too was sent to Tihar in 1978, told him that his jail term was his political rebirth. Maneka took his meals to him every day and reveled in the great adventure of supporting her husband.[17] During 1979 Sanjay went to prison six times, spending five weeks in different jails. Working hard to attack the family's enemies, Maneka used her magazine to expose the alleged improper conduct of the son of a prominent member of the Janata Party government. She published compromising photographs of the son, a middle-aged married man, in graphically intimate poses with a teenage girl. The news made national headlines. Between all the jail visits, court hearings, and rallies, Indira tried to preserve some semblance of normalcy.

However hard Indira tried for the sake of appearances, the physical constraints of the Willingdon Crescent house, virtually open to all and sundry, and the plotting and machinations orchestrated by Sanjay contributed to frosty relations between Sonia and Maneka. In her biography of Indira, Katherine Frank described the two young women as "not on speaking terms" and avoiding "being in the same room together except when absolutely necessary." On one occasion, Indira's cousin and his wife were having breakfast with the family. "Sanjay went into a rage and threw his plate across the room when Sonia failed to cook his eggs in the precise way he had ordered. Indira did not utter a word of criticism but she was clearly embarrassed."[18] Pupul Jayakar qualified the reported atmosphere in her book: "The combatants rarely confronted each other, rarely met, but addressed curt notes to each other to express their hurt and anger." Indira occasionally explained Maneka's behavior with compassion; she wrote to a friend that Maneka was only 21, Sanjay was under constant threat, and her father had died—all placing the younger daughter-in-law "under great strain. People should understand and forgive her hysteria."[19]

Sonia and Rajiv had minimized their presence in the house. The lack of privacy was becoming unbearable for Sonia and Rajiv, and the continuing threats were making their nerves ragged. Sonia, who was not used to an atmosphere of strife, fretted about its effect on Rahul and Priyanka.[20] She also worried about their safety. Pupul Jayakar painted a picture of tension and angst in her biography: "The dogs were everywhere. Sanjay had two Irish wolf-hounds and Bruno, a bull mastiff, a ferocious dog. . . . Rajiv and Sonia had a daschund, Reshma, and an Afghan hound, Zabul. The dogs fought, to the horror of Sonia."[21] It was as if the animals at Willingdon Road were embodying the unspoken tension between the adults in the house.

If the turmoil at home wasn't enough, a power struggle within the Congress Party caused Indira to split off from it for a second time. In 1978 she formed Congress-Indira (I), with the symbol of a hand raised in blessing and herself as the party president. The largest Congress coalition party to have survived in the Indian polity is this one; the various other parties with "Congress" as part of their name are generally factions.

Splits within the Janata Party were forming now; the group that had banded together with the common aim of dethroning Indira was falling apart. A struggle for the leadership of the party opened up divisions that Indira quickly exploited. On his birthday, Indira sent a bouquet of flowers to the man who, as home minister, had ordered her arrest—one of her most vehement detractors, Charan Singh. He responded by inviting her to his house to celebrate the birth of his grandson. Indira, completely fearless, went and made nice with the couple—to the horror and acute discomfort of the prime minister, who was also present. The seam of discord among her enemies that she mined, along with the infighting and backstabbing among the Janata groups, resulted in the fall of the government, and elections were ordered for January 1980.

Tension in the family home seemed to abate. Maneka comments that she and Indira grew closer during this time as Rajiv and Sonia stood aside from the political entanglements. "Willingdon Crescent is a whole new ball game. There were just the three of us and it was, in spite of the tension of losing [the 1977 election], the adjustments we made, the legal and political battles, a happy time for me because we became a family. . . . My mother-in-law and I went on holidays together . . . my son was conceived there—actually on a holiday to Darjeeling which the three of us took together."[22] By autumn 1979 Maneka was pregnant, the atmosphere at home softened, and Indira fussed over her second daughter-in-law.

For the election campaign, Indira and Sanjay marked out areas of potential support, and Sanjay arranged for Youth Congress workers to make sure that rural people could get to polling booths. The Nehrus covered vast amounts of territory and rallies at election time. With 22 meetings a day, a combined audience of 100 million, and 40,000 miles traveled,[23]

Indira outpaced her opponents, focused on the high price of essential commodities, and romped to victory. In fact, as Indian electoral rules allow candidates to stand for more than one constituency, Indira competed for and won two: Rae Bareli in the state of Uttar Pradesh in the north and Medak in the south. Sanjay won back his constituency, Amethi, which he had lost after the Emergency three years earlier. In a strategic move, Indira ensured that Rae Bareli passed to the son of a cousin, Arun Nehru, to keep the Uttar Pradesh constituency in the family. Maintaining a grip over the two constituencies ensured a smooth passage for members of the Nehru-Gandhi family to step into later on. Indira's Congress Party, which had ruled India nonstop from Independence in 1947 until 1977, was back in power. The atmosphere at Willingdon Crescent was now more upbeat; Indira's biographer and friend Pupul Jayakar noticed that flowers, servants, and familiar faces reappeared, and when she went over for a meal, Sonia Gandhi had "taken special care over the menu; there was soup, delicious pasta, fresh crisp golden lettuce, cheese, fruit and chocolate."[24] Najma Heptulla, a former family friend and Congress politician, now the Bharatiya Janata Party's vice president, notes that both Indira Gandhi and Sanjay had been chastened by their years out of power.

"Indira Gandhi learned a lesson by losing . . . she realized she could not throttle the voice of dissent. She was a changed woman when she came back to power in 1980."[25]

Significant changes were taking place across the subcontinent too. With the 1979 Soviet invasion of Afghanistan, India and her northern borders became a strategically important part of the world. The United Sates sought to enforce its strength in the Indian Ocean. Foreign leaders and dignitaries, including an emissary of President Jimmy Carter, began to visit New Delhi to consult with the Indian prime minister, for India's special relationship with the Soviet Union gave it a key negotiating position between the two superpowers.

The third and youngest of the next generation of Gandhis, Feroze Varun, was born in March 1980. Sonia wrote that he "immediately became the darling of our household."[26] Indira became even more attached to Feroze Varun than she was to the older grandchildren because Sanjay was her favorite.[27] Varun was reading at 11 months, and Indira later sent him off to The Study to be its youngest pupil ever at just under two years old.[28] The family moved back to Safdarjang Road, and things appeared to be back to normal, with Sonia and Rajiv picking up their old lives as best as they could.

PART II

BETWEEN TWO DEATHS

6

ANYONE BUT SANJAY

Sorrow . . . can be neither forgotten nor overcome. One has to learn to live with it, to absorb it with one's being as a part of life.

—*Indira Gandhi*

Sanjay and Rajiv had a privileged, unusual childhood. Indira was keen to be a hands-on parent, as she wanted her sons to have a completely different experience from her own lonely adolescence. She had an unconventional approach to education; high grades were not the be-all-and-end-all for this mother—which was just as well—as they were not for the boys. The disparity in the way Indira treated them in later years stemmed from when they were very little. She described her elder boy as "quiet and sensitive" and the younger as "talkative and lively and full of fun. He is generally more popular than his brother, especially with strangers."[1]

From her husband, Feroze, who died when his sons were still in their teens, the boys inherited a fascination with machines, gadgets, aircraft, and automobiles. The brothers were competitive, and though they disagreed over the way the Emergency was conducted, they still loved each other. Sanjay had grown up; he had learned from the excesses of earlier years and was less arrogant. He now wanted to be seen as a pragmatist, someone who could get things done.

With Indira Gandhi back as prime minister for her fourth term and living at 1 Safdarjang Road, Sanjay was now firmly lodged in the nation's consciousness as her heir, her partner in power, and possible future prime minister. Indira vetoed suggestions from Congress acolytes that he should now be made the chief minister of Uttar Pradesh, as he still had a lot of learning to do. Instead, she inducted him into the All India Congress Committee, the 1,000-member-strong, central decision-making assembly of the Indian National Congress Party, as a general secretary. While Maneka was busy working on her magazine, animal rights, and supporting her husband, Sonia often looked after her nephew, Varun[2]; regular visitor Najma Heptulla observed Sonia often carrying the baby out into the garden and generally caring for him.[3] Home life was now somewhat more stable than when they were living at Willingdon Crescent. In the summer of 1980, Sonia, Rajiv, Rahul, and Priyanka left for one of their customary visits to see the Mainos in Italy.

Sonia had become fond of Sanjay from her time in England and then her early days in Delhi. They were the same age, and Sonia and the brothers spent time together as a trio during her first years in India when the two men had interests and friends in common. If one was going out for a drive or a movie, he would most often check if the other wanted to come along too. Rajiv later told an interviewer, "There were a lot of things where Sanjay and I had very similar views. In some areas we had differences. Sometimes we fought like mad, at other times we were very good friends."[4]

Both he and Sanjay adored the speed and power of machines. While Rajiv respected the rules of aviation and nature, learning to fly and choosing a tightly controlled profession to progress in what began as a hobby, Sanjay, who won his license in 1976, found danger highly seductive. For the younger brother, the skies were a firewall he needed to break. He played as hard as he worked and often flew himself to engagements outside Delhi in a Piper aircraft.[5] Alert and always in control, a trained instructor with an excellent pilot rating, he kept his reflexes razor-sharp with regular sessions in the air every day when he was in the capital. While Rajiv had started off flying a sedate glider and progressed to becoming a good commercial pilot, Sanjay needed the adrenaline of power flying. He won several acrobatics prizes, excelled at exploding balloons with his propellers in the sky, and could achieve pinpoint landings.[6] Maneka, who had a student pilot license, says that Sanjay was regarded as an extremely good pilot. "Everybody flew with him."[7] While his mother was out of power, the government vindictively took away his pilot's license, so he started making radio-controlled model aircraft. With Indira back as prime minister and his license restored, Sanjay was hungry for his next flying fix.

In 1977 Indira's personal yoga teacher (who also had business interests) brokered the importation of a red-and-white two-seater Pitts S–2A airplane.[8] The only one of its type to be brought into the country, it was specially designed for aerobatics and had won four world championships. It was not cleared by Indian customs until May 1980; but then, within a month, it was assembled and housed at the Delhi Flying Club at Safdarjang Airport, roughly a half hour's drive from the house. It was subject to Indian Aircraft Rules and international flying regulations, which stipulated that this type of aircraft was not allowed to fly above residential areas or below 5,000 feet.

Sanjay was as excited as a child on Christmas Eve. He could not wait to play with the new toy—he wanted to take it for its inaugural flight but was told he couldn't; a Delhi Flying Club instructor took it for the trial instead. Sanjay got his first chance the day the Pitts S–2A received its certificate of airworthiness, Saturday, June 21. He took it for another couple of sorties the next day, accompanied variously by Maneka, Indira's special assistant, and her personal yoga teacher, spending just over 40 minutes in the air.[9]

By June 23, the two-seater had logged only 10 hours. That same day an animated Sanjay decided he wanted to go flying again and left home early in his Matador car after checking in with his mother, something he did most mornings. The aviation minister was due to be his flying companion, but Sanjay was in a hurry to get going and drove directly to the home of a former Delhi Flying Club chief instructor who lived just by Safdarjang Airport, Captain Subhash Saxena. He found him relaxing in his garden. Saxena had not planned to be airborne that day, but Sanjay was impatient and wanted to go up with him *right away.*

The captain told Sanjay that he was in no mood for flying. Sanjay insisted, brushing off his refusal with a casual "don't worry" before going off to park his car.[10] Captain Saxena, accompanied by his orderly, dutifully went to the flying club, where he, in no hurry, ordered a cup of tea. He had taken only a sip when an airport worker came to tell him that Sanjay Gandhi was demanding his presence; the captain had to oblige. He sent his orderly home, saying that he would be back in 10 or 15 minutes. The attendant did as he was told, watching the skies for his boss. Captain Saxena got into the front of the biplane and Sanjay sat in the rear, holding the controls. Sanjay decided they would spend about an hour in the air. They proceeded to establish weather clearance from the control tower and then took off at 7:58 AM from Safdarjang Airport, completely ignoring the safety precaution rules of not flying below 5,000 feet or over residential areas. Sanjay performed three spectacular loops in the air and was getting ready to go into a fourth. Sanjay descended perilously low over the houses below, while Saxena's orderly watched from the ground. As the plane swooped down, its engine stopped. The two-seater spun and took a nosedive; Sanjay tried to crash land, narrowly missing occupied barracks, but was soon hurtling toward the ground behind Willingdon Crescent. Those in the control tower looked on in horror as the plane disappeared behind a luxury hotel, the Ashoka. Captain Saxena's orderly reached frantically for his bicycle and pedaled like mad. The brand-new Pitts crashed into a small bunch of trees, forcing its way through the branches, spiraling into a mass of twisted metal. When Saxena's man arrived at the crash site, the wreckage was belching huge billows of thick dark smoke but was not on fire. The orderly said, "I saw the body of Sanjay Gandhi lying three or four feet away from the plane which was a total ruin. . . . Capt. Sahib's lower limbs were inside the plane and the head was outside . . . (they) were not dead and were gasping."

Indira received the news over the phone at 8:20 AM. Within minutes, she was on her way to the scene of the crash. When she arrived, medical personnel were desperately trying to extricate the bodies. The sides of the aircraft had to be broken open and the safety belts cut for the corpses to be taken out. The *Hindustan Times* wrote, "Dismembered bodies without any sign of life were gently being lifted into the ambulance." Indira stood frozen, rooted to the spot. Then suddenly, sharp spasms jolted her tiny frame. Sobbing, Indira accompanied the bodies of her son and Captain Saxena to the hospital. Sanjay was so badly injured that doctors were reluctant to show his body to his mother, but she insisted on seeing him. Telephones and cable lines were red-hot with the news, and senior politicians immediately rushed to her side at the hospital. She kept such a tight grip on herself—she was determined not to show any loss of control—that she quickly engaged one of them in a discussion about a particular political situation in one of the states. Maneka arrived as well, in shock, but she was not allowed to look at what remained of her husband until he had been stitched up. The doctors took around three hours to complete the medical formalities, after which Indira spent a few minutes alone with her favorite son. Around noon, Indira returned to her home, asked about the funeral arrangements, and went into her bedroom. There in front of her was a photograph of Sanjay. She fell apart then; but within 20 minutes, she was back at the hospital. At 1:45 PM, the body, wrapped in reams of shrouds and covered with flowers, was put into an official police van. Indira escorted Sanjay's body back home, where it was placed in a room at 1 Akbar Road, her office, in preparation for the cremation the next day once Rajiv, Sonia, and the children were back from Italy. Sanjay's face was exposed: "One eye and the head were badly damaged, the nose smashed."[11] His body was put on a raised platform. Indira, wearing sunglasses to hide her eyes swollen with crying, stood by it, her head covered. According to a friend, she did not seem to be registering what was going on, and Maneka, who sat down on a sheet next to her husband, oblivious to those around her, said to herself sadly, "Not Sanjay, not Sanjay, anyone but Sanjay."[12]

Sonia, Rajiv, and the children flew back on the first flight available, arriving at three in the morning. At their home, they spent some time alone with Indira and then went to the room where Sanjay's body had been placed. Rajiv had lost his only sibling with whom he had shared most of his life. Indira had lost the person she trusted most: her political aide and most beloved family member. For Sonia, this was the first major tragedy to hit her adopted family, and she took it badly. Today, Maneka still can't put her loss into words: "The pain of losing him is indescribable. It's still there . . . ," but she is able to eulogize: "My husband taught me to lead by example. He was an extraordinary man. He was passionate about India. He changed India with the Maruti and got reviled in the process. He was single-minded, intensely involved with the country, asked people to plant trees, stop dowry, have one or two children. He asked people to teach other people."[13] She acknowledges that she learned from him much that has influenced her work.

Eight miles from Akbar Road, along the river Yamuna, sit the cremation sites of Mahatma Gandhi, Jawaharlal Nehru, and other Indian leaders. Each location is large, separate but interconnected by pathways, and surrounded by grass, trees, lakes, and knolls to allow for thousands of tourists to visit each day and for dignitaries to pay formal homage on anniversaries. It is peaceful and spacious, a place for reflection. On June 23 Indira Gandhi visited the location chosen for Sanjay's cremation, approximately 300 feet from Jawaharlal Nehru's cremation site, Shanti Van (the Forest of Peace). She wanted him cremated there even though he had held no government position. The following morning, Rajiv arrived at the area to supervise the final arrangements. Though it was not going to be a state funeral—no reversed arms, buglers, or pageantry—hundreds of thousands of people still turned up from all over the country.

At Akbar Road a large contingent of the paramilitary Border Security Force was deployed to control the gathering crowds. For an hour, the immediate family was alone with the body behind doors closed to security guards and the public. Then the Gandhi women hurried into a waiting army jeep, Indira still wearing dark glasses, her head covered by part of her white sari; Maneka, her eyes red, looking at the ground; and Sonia.

A large group of Youth Congress (I) workers on scooters, wearing black armbands on their spotless white outfits, and two military trucks bearing newsmen and photographers led the procession. Behind them, Rajiv could be seen wearing the traditional outfit of a long white overshirt, trousers, and cap, with a symbolic striped cloth over his left shoulder. Amid frenzied cries from the crowd, he helped lift the stretcher carrying his younger brother onto the flower-bedecked Shaktiman, an open military flatbed truck, where it rested on a raised platform. Rajiv sat alongside the body of his brother with some of Sanjay's close friends. Once at the cremation site, the body was placed on a bier at the pyre. In keeping with the Nehru tradition of secularism, Hindu, Muslim, Christian, Jain, and Zoroastrian priests chanted hymns.[14] In the long shadows of their grandfather's cremation site, silhouetted against the setting sun, Rajiv walked around his brother's funeral pyre and lit it at 6:50 PM.

Sonia broke down and sobbed while Maneka looked shocked and numb, as if she could not comprehend what was happening. Rajiv held his mother around her shoulder, and she put her arm around his waist.

He was all she had now.

On June 25 the ashes were brought back in copper urns; the next morning, the three adult Gandhi women sat in the room where Sanjay's body had lain, mourning with visitors. Later Sonia, Rajiv, Maneka, Youth Congress workers, and many of Sanjay's cohorts traveled to Allahabad to immerse Sanjay's ashes in the holy river confluence at Sangam. Despite her pain, Indira was back in her office within four days of her son's death.

But there was now a void, and the spotlight suddenly turned on Rajiv. As people came in hordes to offer condolences according to custom, delegations began to demand that Rajiv step into his brother's large shoes. Mark Tully, for many years the BBC bureau chief in Delhi (who at breakfast had heard about Sanjay's death and had headed straight into the BBC office to report on it), explained the forces that were pushing Rajiv toward his fate: "There were some people like Vijayalaxmi Pandit,[15] for instance . . . his aunt told him that he must come in and help his mother. A lot of the politicians—not all the politicians, the Congress ones—of course put pressure on him because they were terrified; they wanted the Gandhi succession to be continued because they felt . . . the Gandhi family was the cornerstone of the Congress Party. Without the Gandhi family, the Congress Party falls apart was their view. So a lot of them wanted him to follow."[16]

Pressure was building in the Congress Party, but Rajiv was just not willing to enter politics. Indira enlisted party workers in the "draft Rajiv" campaign, asking them to speak to her son, so many youth leaders came to talk to him wherever and whenever they could. Despite the tangible squeeze, there was no diktat from Indira; she was too smart to force her opinions on her children, knowing that somehow, Nehrus tended to do what was expected of them anyway. Party workers, anxious about their own futures, had their own motivations for wanting Rajiv in the game, and they delivered impassioned speeches all about the hard work they had done for the party, organizing support, agitations, and demonstrations. He would listen quietly—it was all resonating—but would not give them a decision.

Sonia, however, was set against Rajiv entering the family business full time. A relative and former friend of his, Arun Nehru, said, "I spent hours with her. It was not easy convincing her, but we had to take the same line with all the wives who were reluctant for their husbands to go into politics. After all, the family is political, there is a responsibility, and you can't run away from it."[17] Natwar Singh, who was the Indian ambassador to Pakistan, was asked to use his influence with the reluctant man. "Indira was very keen. She asked me to have a word with him. . . ." Natwar wrote a letter to Rajiv, saying that the responsibility now rested with the elder son, and that it would mean a great sacrifice of his private life and impose some strain on his family, but that he was the senior member of one of the most well-known political dynasties in the world, and that involved a certain duty. Natwar met with Rajiv when he was in Delhi and pushed the point again, even though Rajiv pleaded that he was "not Sanjay" and had no other money apart from his salary as a pilot. Indira herself was a little unsure of how Rajiv would manage, as she knew he lacked Sanjay's "dynamism and concerns" while appreciating the help he could give her. "If he gives up the job how will he help me? Sanjay was very frugal, but Rajiv and his wife need certain comforts."[18]

But the sustained campaign to draft Rajiv was having an effect, and he soon realized he had no option other than to support his mother by joining the Congress Party.[19] Sonia, meanwhile, still tried to resist the inevitable. Her husband managed to keep the persuasive delegations at bay for nearly a year. He continued his flying, but the destiny that would change Sonia's life was inching closer.

There was no good reason for Sonia to agree to what she perceived as the destruction of all that she had carefully built; the tension and the torment went on for months. The prime minister was skilled in the art of suggestion: When anyone advised her to bring Rajiv into politics, she would urge the person to speak to him instead. Indira too had to undergo a change of mindset, for until Sanjay's death she had been content to wrap herself around her younger son for comfort. She had always regarded Rajiv as less capable than his brother, on one occasion telling reporters that Sanjay was irreplaceable. Yet she had no choice now but to lean on him to carry the dynastic project forward.

7

THEIR TOUGHEST DECISION

We both knew exactly what life for Rajiv as a politician would be.

—*Sonia Gandhi*

The death of her brother-in-law Sanjay caused a huge problem for Sonia. Indira, suspicious of nonfamily members and confident in her second son's abilities, had envisaged no other successor. In this, she was different from her own father, who was not as dynastically driven and who thought that his home minister, Lal Bahadur Shastri, might one day inherit his job. The Indian Constitution decrees that when a prime minister dies, another one should be sworn in by the president at once to avoid a vacuum. When Nehru died in 1964, the ruling Congress Party did select Lal Bahadur Shastri to succeed him. Shastri died of a heart attack in 1966, and only then was Indira elected to the post.

By 1980 Sonia had seen enough of politics up close to believe it to be a "weapon to obtain personal or group dominance."[1] She knew that authority can be used for good, but the overriding feature for her at that time seemed to be the ugliness of the game. The endless attacks on her husband's family during the late 1970s and the ability of those in public life to distort the truth also taught her another valuable lesson: the value of silence. Though the tone has moderated to a degree, even today opposition parties can be crude and base in their often highly personal comments toward her and Rahul. While members of the public may flinch, Sonia seems completely impervious, laughing off jibes about her Italian-ness, observing in interviews sometimes that opponents do it when they have no other arguments to run.

Since Rajiv had no political experience, Indira was criticized abroad for being a slave to dynastic manipulation. Dynasty, however, is a big part of South Asian politics, at both regional and national levels. In fact it is a big part of all professions in India—the progeny of doctors often become doctors, the offspring of lawyers become lawyers—it continues until a member of one generation decides to do something different.

South Asians believe knowledge and experience increases from one generation to the next and, if possible, should not be squandered. Critics of dynastic succession like the Bharatiya Janata Party (BJP)—the second largest political group in India, established in 1980 and supporting a nationalist cause—trumpet the fact that the BJP does not have one family name ascending to its highest posts, unlike the Indian National Congress, which has had a Nehru at its helm for the better part of its life.

Maneka Gandhi did not fully agree with Indira's view of dynasty and saw herself as the one to carry forward her husband's political legacy. Many who had supported Sanjay now supported her. Indira, busy working and traveling, tried to keep an eye on her second daughter-in-law but could not give the matter her whole-hearted attention.

The world that Sonia had carefully built with Rajiv was threatened. The choice that Rajiv had to make vis-à-vis his ascension to power was causing stress within their marriage. For the first time in 15 years, Sonia noted that "there was tension between Rajiv and me. I fought like a tigress—for him, for us and our children, for the life we had made together, his flying which he loved, our uncomplicated, easy friendships, and, above all, for our freedom: that simple human right that we had so carefully and consistently preserved."[2]

Both Rajiv and Sonia faced harrowing choices. Sonia had come to love Indira; she understood her needs and that it would be selfish to turn the other way when Rajiv's mother needed him most. It was the political system that Sonia railed against. The Nehrus, their sacrifices, prison sentences, their part in building the Indian National Congress Party, the glory days of Jawaharlal, universally accepted as visionary—all this makes misty-eyed party men and women want to have someone with the family name at the helm; to them, the name symbolizes leadership and success. Sonia described her husband's relationship with the party as one that "demanded him as a sacrificial lamb. It would crush him and destroy him—of that I was absolutely certain. . . . I remember that long year as being one of complete helplessness, with every minute drawing us closer to the abyss. I kept hoping for a miracle, a solution which would be acceptable and fair to all of us."[3] Eventually, the woman with the strength of will to bear a year apart from the man she loved, and to take on a whole new country for the same cause, had to capitulate against her better instincts. Rajiv told a television interviewer, "We had very long talks, my wife and I, before I left flying and joined politics. She was not too happy about it mainly because she felt in a sense she would be losing me . . . that was the crux of the issue. But when we talked about it and discussed it was a joint decision."[4] Former minister Natwar Singh says that Sonia had made her case for not disturbing the status quo.[5] She realized that the biggest deposit she could make in her relationship with Rajiv was to support him wholeheartedly.

In her memoir Sonia wrote she did not want him to suffer indefinitely. "I could no longer bear to watch Rajiv being torn apart. . . . I would bow to those forces which were now beyond me to fight, and I would go with him wherever they took him."[6] The anguish took a physical toll on Sonia; it was reported that she withdrew to her room, cried for four days, lost weight, and looked drawn.[7]

Rajiv agreed to join the family business only on condition that he did not have to join the government and was reminded that Indira did not have to either when she supported her father. He resigned from Indian Airlines on May 5, 1981, 11 months after his brother's accident. Later that month he formally entered politics by becoming a primary member of the Congress Party. He became a contact point between the prime minister and the outside world, meeting people whom she might not have time to see.[8]

Indira, behind the scenes, wanted Rajiv and Sonia to build their rural experience, to get to know the real India. She told her political adviser M. L. Fotedar, "Ensure that when he goes on tours, she accompanies him," which Sonia did, Fotedar adds.[9] With little formal political training, Rajiv would need to become a member of parliament with his own constituency. Rural Amethi, which his grandfather Jawaharlal and then Sanjay had held, was perceived as the most suitable as it had been in the family. He decided to take Sonia with him on his visits. It was an adjustment for the couple. In 1982 Rajiv wrote to Rahul about his upcoming visit to the constituency: "Mama is also going. . . . It will be difficult for her as everyone will be staring at her in the beginning and she will feel very embarrassed till she gets a bit used to it. She is being very brave."[10]

Amethi lies about 280 miles east of Delhi in the state of Uttar Pradesh, one of the poorest and most populous states in India.[11] To get there from the state's capital city, Lucknow, the bumpy main road passes low, often fallow fields, then winds through villages with stalls selling everything from toys to fresh melons and oranges to car and bicycle spare parts. More than 70 percent of Uttar Pradesh works in agriculture, raising mainly food grains (wheat, barley, rye, rice) and potatoes; it is the largest sugarcane-producing state in the country. Amethi has a sleepy atmosphere, a far cry from the sleek boulevards and giant shopping malls of New Delhi.

Congress Party stalwarts from Uttar Pradesh go back a long way. One of them, nonagenarian Ram Sewak, a member of the Legislative Assembly, witnessed the filing of nomination papers by successive members of the Gandhi family and helped Rajiv when the latter toured the constituency. When they visited Amethi, Rajiv would drive an Indian military jeep, known as a *Jonga*, with Ram Sewak jaunty in the back seat, and he would occasionally translate Sewak's words for Sonia who was seated beside her husband.[12]

Sonia's work over the years in the constituency was completely hands-on, focusing on education and women; she was very concerned about the running of the schools, visiting them one by one, assessing the adequacy and attendance records of teachers and the amount of time they devoted to the syllabus. She wanted every primary school in Amethi equipped with crayons, slates, blackboards, and chalk. As Rajiv got busier, she began to visit without him. Even in this dozy, dusty, cow-belt location, she would insist on punctuality, leaving her guest house promptly at 8 AM—very often not returning before 8 PM, eating breakfast in the car if someone turned up unexpectedly to meet her—she would not be late.[13]

Locals noticed that Sonia didn't have any problem making herself understood by constituents, many of whom spoke a dialect. "Even when she couldn't speak to them fluently in their language, whenever there was a problem, she would touch the person—woman, man or child, she didn't discriminate—and would help the person to feel, 'I am with you, don't worry, everything will be solved.' People responded to her very well."[14] Rakesh Singh, another party worker, said that from the moment she arrived, Sonia was "part of the system at ground level. She was moving around with people, working with them, trying to build them up, guiding them, she was there physically. She would sit with people, and by her actions, her gestures, she would motivate them."[15] Little by little, as she got to know the locals, Sonia learned Avdi, the local dialect of the eastern state.[16]

Sonia's life and to some extent their public image changed dramatically. Previously, a few days of work for Rajiv were followed by periods of relaxation; now, the endless wall of demanding constituents and supplicants surrounded her. Natwar Singh remarks candidly, "She didn't just marry a man—she married a public meeting!"[17]

Rajiv was away on duty much more. He shed his pilot's uniform and day-off jeans and shirts for the traditional politician's outfit of white handwoven cotton overshirts, trousers, and pointed caps, a hallmark of the Nehru-Gandhi men. During the years of protest against British rule, Mahatma

Gandhi, Jawaharlal Nehru, and Congress Party workers had refused to wear British imported or synthetic materials. They preferred indigenous hand-woven or hand-spun fabric, known as *khadi,* to fabric processed in mills; it symbolized strength and self-sufficiency that could provide employment to millions and was a hallmark of the independence movement. The raw material, usually cotton, though silk and wool are also used, is woven into yarns on a manually propelled spinning wheel. Khadi is not only the uniform fabric of many Indian politicians today, but it is also a very strong part of the fashion and home furnishing industries. Indira followed the example set by her father and by Mahatma Gandhi by wearing hand-woven cloth saris, and gradually Sonia adopted the same look, mixing it sometimes with the female version of the overshirt and long trousers worn with a scarf. In Rajiv's constituency, Sonia started several centers where illiterate women were helped to become independent by hand-weaving cotton. She assiduously wears handwoven cottons and silks, and designer Sunita Kohli calls her "the most elegant woman in India, with a deep knowledge of Indian textiles."[18]

Although Maneka was keen to take on a role as political secretary, Sonia's compliant nature and shared passions kept her firmly in position as Indira's favorite. In an effort to be even-handed, however, Indira tried to involve both daughters-in-law in international tours and public life. So Sonia undertook these in addition to accompanying Rajiv to his constituency. She still ran the household, and now she also attended a course in restoring oil paintings, "an old interest of mine which I could not pursue earlier. I was careful to adjust my timings and engagements as far as possible to coincide with Rajiv's and my mother-in-law's free moments."[19]

Dalip Mehta, a former Doon School pupil who had been a few years ahead of Rajiv at Cambridge, later joined the Indian Foreign Service and was posted to Paris during a relaxing visit by Indira and Sonia. He recalls the trip with nostalgia: President François Mitterrand and his wife, Danielle, held Indira in high esteem, so the Gandhi ladies stayed in the guest wing of the Elysée Palace, the French presidential residence, "which was a special honor because it was a private visit. My ambassador . . . said to my wife, 'They're very interested in art. Take them to some museum which you think they may not have seen.'" Mrs. Nandini Mehta, an editor for Penguin Books, took them to the Marmottan, which contains Monet's famous painting *Impression, Sunrise.* Indira and Sonia were absolutely delighted. Dalip Mehta recalls that the women saw pieces by "Monet, Manet, Gauguin, all the great painters of that period. They moved around very casually within the museum . . . they didn't want to be surrounded by security or to disrupt the flow of tourists. So we went there with just one police car accompanying us. . . . They both spoke very good French." Sonia loved the museum: "She noticed everything carefully and reacted to everything quickly. She would appreciate beauty in all its forms."[20]

Frank Christopher, former director of the Parliament Library, attended a four-month, roughly three-sessions-per-week "Appreciation of Art" course in the early 1980s with Sonia at the National Gallery of Modern Art in New Delhi, though she was involved there over a longer period of time than he was. "[Sonia] was doing another course before coming to this class . . . Conservation and Preservation. . . . I remember her listening to talks and watching the slide presentations on art work, after which we all used to walk out together." Most of the time she was chauffeured, but sometimes Rajiv would come and pick her up after class. At the end of the course, a National Gallery of Modern Art certificate[21] was awarded by the faculty of History of Art and Conservation, which fell under the aegis of the Government of India's Department of Culture. Christopher remembers Sonia's "graceful beauty . . . her confidence." She was at ease in this milieu, in a class of 25 or 30 students: "Of course, hailing from Italy, she must have known quite a bit about the art of her land, but her deep interest was to know more about the artworks of India. And she always used to ask questions." Art was just one way for Sonia to learn and grow in the company of Indira. Frank Christopher recalls an exhibition he attended in New Delhi by the eminent artist Krishan Khanna. "Despite her busy schedule Mrs. Indira Gandhi took time out to see this work, and Sonia was a companion and a friend."[22]

Sonia enjoyed spending time with her mother-in-law, but she missed Rajiv, and he missed her too. On one of his tours he wrote, "Hindu tradition says, a man is only half a person and his wife makes up the other half. . . . I know that without you I would find it very difficult . . . even more so now that I am in politics."[23]

The year 1981 marked Rajiv's full entry onto the political stage. During the time that Rajiv campaigned for his seat in Amethi, he was joined on different occasions by Rahul, Sonia, and Indira. Indians took to Rajiv; he had a fresh face, a clean image, and a friendly disposition. He was confident enough to ask for information if he needed to learn about a topic—unlike many Indians who are often reluctant to admit to ignorance. On June 15 he won Amethi with a huge majority, and at age 36, he joined the House in August. His mother gave him the task of organizing the Asian Games in Delhi, and in 1983 he was appointed a general secretary of the Congress Party. All the while, Sonia saw herself as homemaker-in-chief, needing to provide a secure domestic environment. Though politics had entered their lives in a big way, she was still determined to fence off, away from the public, some sort of space for her family.

8

ENEMIES WITHOUT AND TENSIONS WITHIN

> The situation here is a disturbing one . . . the terrible period we are going through . . . I am truly depressed.
>
> —*Indira Gandhi*

Rajiv was caught in a political flytrap; Sonia knew this and was trying to keep the atmosphere calm at home. Indira, consumed with grief over Sanjay's death, poured her affection into his toddler son, Feroze Varun, and drew on her love for all three of her grandchildren to comfort her. Meanwhile, there was trouble brewing all around them in the house. Sanjay's widow, Maneka, aided by allies of her late husband, was trying to assert herself as the rightful heir to Sanjay's position. But Indira wanted some of Sanjay's friends to be denuded of their power and influence. Maneka, however, was focused and ambitious. She was not old enough at age 23 to become a member of parliament, otherwise she might have stood against Rajiv when he was elected to the lower house in June 1981 from his brother's constituency, Amethi. But, as she later told the press, Sanjay had taught her to "plan strategies four steps ahead," so she was methodically preparing for her future.[1]

Relations between Sonia and Maneka had again soured.[2] It is easy to paint the picture as saint versus sinner, calm, angelic homemaker versus noisy, attention-seeking young activist, but things were not so black and white. Though Sonia *was* the homemaker-in-chief, she also was protective of her territory. As Sonia liked art, restoration, and looking after her family, so Maneka had causes that she wanted to pursue on the political front, including animal rights and the environment, causes Sanjay believed in. Although Indira found her younger daughter-in-law to be a little impetuous, she decided to be compassionate toward Maneka and offered her the job of personal secretary, in which capacity she would travel with the prime minister. Sonia, who was now probably the closest she had ever been to Indira, emotionally as well as in every other sense, was not happy about this and objected emphatically.[3] Indira and Sonia exchanged letters on the subject: "Very upset, she was, so Mrs. Gandhi told Maneka, 'I'm sorry, Sonia does not want it,'" remarked a friend of Indira.[4] Jad Adams and Phillip Whitehead suggested in their book *The Dynasty* that Rajiv and Sonia may have been unwilling to hand the position of "dominant representative" of the younger Gandhi generation to Maneka.

But the younger Gandhi daughter-in-law did not sit idle. She compiled a photographic book on Sanjay and asked Indira to write the foreword to it. Perhaps with the growing tension in the house and Indira's increasingly busy schedule, the prime minister decided not to, saying that she could have done it when she had more time immediately after her son had passed away. Though the book, according to Indira, was "very well conceived," she would not now write the foreword, she told a friend, as "she had erased Maneka from her cherished ones; she saw her now as an outsider, but Feroze Varun was of her blood."[5]

Rival camps were forming within the household, and there was a clear intent to isolate Maneka. She was on a visit to Mumbai (then called Bombay) when Indira and the family were at the cremation ground of Indira's father on his birthday; next to it lies Sanjay's site. Indira, Rajiv, Sonia, Varun, Rahul, and Priyanka all proceeded to plant trees at Sanjay's ground, while no mention was made of Maneka.[6] At formal dinners, she was seated with staff members rather than the family.[7] Little Varun, however, was kept close to his grandmother all the time and slept in her bedroom at night.[8]

Tension was growing between Indira and Maneka over some captions and text in the photographic book on Sanjay. Indira felt that they were damaging and distorted, so the release of the book was postponed until the captions were altered. She claimed that she had not been shown the final proof of the book and simultaneously delivered a veiled ultimatum: Maneka could decide how the relationship would proceed from there on in; she could leave the house if she wished. Maneka apparently took the hint. The captions were altered, and the book was published.[9]

Relations between Maneka and Indira may have deteriorated further if not for Maneka's tender tie to the household: Feroze Varun. Sonia was still helping raise the child, taking care of him during the day. Given the domestic tensions, Maneka might well have been ejected from the premises earlier if not for Indira's affection for the little boy. During this time, Sonia was supportive of Indira but did not get directly involved in the daily bickering, according to one of her mother-in-law's biographers.[10]

Sanjay's friends were coalescing around Maneka while Rajiv brought his Doon schoolmates in to join his team. "Goons versus Doons" soon became a popular phrase in media circles. Now fully aware that Indira was transferring the political mantle to Rajiv and not Maneka, she sold her magazine, *Surya,* which she had used to attack Indira's opponents, to a group of Indira's political enemies. Realizing that her behavior was bound to result in expulsion, Maneka timed her exit meticulously. In March 1982, while Indira was in the United Kingdom for a Festival of India, Maneka had most of her own belongings from the household removed.[11] She declared that she wanted to give a speech in Lucknow, the capital of Uttar Pradesh, to a conference of Sanjay loyalists who would set up a new organization promoting his ideals. She had been invited to do so. From London, Indira sent word that Maneka was not to attend. Upon her return from London on March 27, Indira sent another message forbidding Maneka from attending the assembly, condemning the convention. She said that disobedience would result in expulsion from the Gandhi household. Maneka was already on her way to Lucknow and disregarded the messages. Her speech there was conciliatory though, encouraging supporters to be loyal to the prime minister, stating, "I shall always honor the discipline and reputation of the great Nehru-Gandhi family I belong to."[12]

Despite the contents of the speech, Indira was incensed that her instructions had been disobeyed. The rebellious daughter-in-law was served with a notice to quit.[13] Maneka returned to Delhi, ready for a verbal shoot-out with Indira. As it all kicked off, Varun was taken to Indira's room and, in front of staff, Maneka was told to pack her bags and to leave the house. After a yelling match, she was given a letter from Indira listing her misdemeanors and explaining why she was being sent away. Referring to Maneka's "different background," Indira accused her of being in collusion with her enemies. Eventually, with a tired and bewildered Feroze Varun, Maneka left that night in the prime minister's car. Photographers and reporters hovering around the house—they had been alerted by Maneka's people in good time—caught the moment. The next day, Maneka released a letter to the press, accusing Indira of having insulted her and her family, of confiscating her son, and of ordering her luggage searched.[14] It was a very public and acrimonious split.

Indira was hugely upset that Maneka had taken Varun with her, and from that time on had less and less contact with him, which compounded her sorrow at the loss of her own son, Sanjay. Both sides were left scarred by the schism in the family. Talking about her life, Maneka says that since Sanjay died, she does not get attached to anything now, and it gives her a kind of freedom. "The freedom to walk away and not be hurt. I don't want to be frightened into doing something I don't want to do. Nothing scares me. I have a mother with liver cancer. I have a brother who died, much younger. My husband died when I was 23 . . . my father committed suicide when I was 18. So what do you think would scare me?"[15] At the end of February 2011, Amteshwar Anand, Maneka's ailing mother, passed away.

In her book *Rajiv,* Sonia did not detail the reason for Maneka's departure. In this instance, she did not even refer to Maneka by name. She reduced the months leading up to the exit to one short paragraph, with a pointed reference to Maneka's going and the fact that Sonia and Rajiv now provided the love and nourishment that Indira required: "[Indira's] anguish following the loss of her son had recently been compounded by Sanjay's widow's decision to leave our home. . . . My mother-in-law . . . drew strength and comfort from Rajiv's supportive presence in her work, and from us at home."[16] Sonia marks important dates to do with Sanjay, visiting his cremation site, but has said little on Maneka over the years. Sonia learned from Indira that a cold shoulder is sometimes more devastating than a direct confrontation. Silence is often used by the Nehrus as a negative response, buying time and keeping opponents guessing.

On the other side, Maneka is also discreet. She says simply, "Sanjay died, and some years later I went into politics." She became an "independent" member of parliament and converted a pressure group of those who supported Sanjay's way of thinking (those who had been with her when she gave the speech that infuriated Indira) into a political entity. In 1984 the party won a victory over a Congress candidate in the state of Uttar Pradesh. Maneka was gathering strength and supporters and declared that she would fight Rajiv in any election he stood for. She forged her own political career: "In 2004 the BJP asked me to join so I did." Her work was always based around the causes she and Sanjay were passionate about. Maneka now lives not far from 1 Safdarjang Road, in the Lutyens zone, dealing with injured or abused animals from all over the country while also being a member of parliament. She has turned her garden into a conservation area for rare plants and trees. But she does not display the ruthless ambition ascribed to her. "By choosing the environment and animals, I shut off the door to becoming prime minister [in a BJP-led government]," she says, as working for her causes takes up so much of her time.[17]

The feud between Indira and Maneka played out against a backdrop of sectarian violence in various quarters of the country. With trouble in the eastern states of Assam, the northern states of Punjab, and later on Jammu and Kashmir, the 1980s became known as "the age of terrorism" in India. In Punjab, Sikh separatists were calling for an independent state, described as "the land of the pure, Khalistan." Sikhs (the word means disciples) are a religious minority that represents roughly 2 percent of India's population. They felt that their language, their script, and their religious norms were being undermined. There was also the issue of control over rivers that run through Punjab. The Akali party was formed to represent their interests; Sikh militancy was on the rise.

While multiple insurgencies and an atmosphere of unrest and instability afflicted parts of India, back in Delhi, Sonia had a family to raise and nurture. After attending private day schools[18] in the city, her children were now starting the secondary phase of their education. Sonia and Rajiv chose Rajiv's alma mater, Doon School, for Rahul, who entered in 1982. Priyanka was sent to Welham Girls' School, where many Doon siblings went, in Dehradun, in the foothills of the Himalayas. Rahul and Priyanka were now firmly established on a conventional route, the old boys' and girls' network of establishments favored by upper-class families. According to Indira supporter Swraj Paul, the choice of school was firmly left up to Sonia and Rajiv; Indira did not interfere other than to discuss pros and cons with the family.[19] For Sonia's children, it meant a different atmosphere from the one they had experienced at home.

Vikram Lal, who had been at Doon School three years ahead of Rajiv Gandhi and is now on its board, explained that at Doon, everything is run by the clock. Bedtime was at 9:15 PM, the boys would rise at 6 or 6:15 AM, and by about 6:45 they were on the field for physical training. Sports were still compulsory. Children can find it hard to settle in for the first few months. Homesickness often sets in, and mothers can find the separation difficult too. Sonia sometimes sent "tuck" for Rahul if another parent, like Hemant Pasrich, director of The Study, was going up to school.[20] Vikram Lal said that Doon did have its clever pupils, but academic brilliance was not mandatory: "Every class had its top order . . . but academics in those years . . . was not a very important matter because kids from Doon school somehow got into colleges anyway. . . ."[21] But Sonia and Rajiv were aware that their now public lives might have an adverse impact on their children.

They both worried, because apart from the normal, sometimes tough, teasing that can go on in Indian educational institutions, the family's high profile left them open to all sorts of vicious personal onslaught. As Rahul had always appeared the more sensitive and vulnerable of the two children during his formative years, Rajiv wrote his son explaining that he would read stories about Sonia, Indira, and himself, and would likely be teased, but that he would need to learn to face such behavior.

The children did not end up spending much time as boarders. By 1984 Rahul and Priyanka were prime terrorist targets, their parents were told, and managing their security in a boarding school was a problem not just for the Gandhis but for other parents who worried an attack might affect their own children. Mark Tully and Satish Jacob, coauthors of a book on this period, stated, "Mrs. Gandhi knew the risks to her own family. . . . Rajiv Gandhi had already been told by the prime minister's security advisers to withdraw his son and daughter from their boarding schools. . . . The advisers said that the children's security could only be guaranteed if they lived in the prime minister's house in Delhi."[22] The children were moved to day schools in the capital in the spring of 1984. Their extraordinary lineage and the current events of the time would soon further disrupt all their lives.

Terrorist offensives were starting to hit some Indian cities in the 1980s. In Delhi, there was a wave of transistor bombs and improvised explosive devices, for which Khalistan militant groups were blamed. In Punjab, almost daily, moderates were targeted with drive-by shootings or bomb attacks. One armed militant, Sant Jarnail Singh Bhindranwale (who had initially been supported by Indira's regime to work *against* the Sikh separatists) became the centrifugal force of the movement. He was arrested for murder but abruptly released, and the insurgency gathered momentum around him. Deciding that violent assertion was the only way forward, he moved into a guest house in the complex of the holiest shrine of the Sikhs, the Golden Temple in the northern town of Amritsar. From there, Bhindranwale directed gangs of motorcycle-riding killers who caused mayhem around the countryside. A senior police officer visiting the Golden Temple was shot dead by Bhindranwale's men; the police felt powerless to arrest their leader as he had taken sanctuary on holy ground and no action against him was ordered by Delhi. He continued to send his terror squads into the Punjab countryside.

The Golden Temple of Amritsar, a place of pilgrimage for Sikhs from all over the world, houses the Sikh holy book, treated with great veneration by believers. Built on and around a square lake of religious significance, the large temple complex includes buildings where devotees work and serve the community. As the militant movement intensified and Bhindranwale gained confidence, he and his followers moved into the second most-sacred part of the temple itself and began turning it into a fortress. He was helped by the vengeful disgraced army officer, Major General Shahbeg Singh, who had trained the Bangladeshi Liberation Army so successfully for India in the

1971 war. Bricks and sandbags were used as barricades, and Bhindranwale accumulated a huge arsenal of AK-47s, 12-bore and .303 rifles, improvised grenades, and light machine guns, all smuggled into the premises hidden in sacks of flour and rice. There was also a rocket launcher. By now, violence in the state had reached fever pitch. Buses were hijacked and Hindus shot dead. The separatists had to be quashed. Indira needed to act quickly; she had only one option now.

On June 2, 1984, Indira Gandhi ordered the army into the Golden Temple in an action known as Operation Blue Star. She told her friends that she was signing her death sentence when she ordered the storming. Former BBC Delhi bureau chief Mark Tully viewed the decision as constricted. "Operation Blue Star came at the end of a longish period of trouble in the Punjab during which the government had really wavered a lot and failed to take decisive action, in my view, until they had it forced on them—by the fact that Bhindranwale was occupying the Golden Temple and flouting their authority, challenging them to come and get him."[23]

For Operation Blue Star, in addition to the army, a special forces group, the SG, led by Lieutenant Colonel Mahendra Pratap Choudhary, was deployed. Still moving with some stiffness today due to injury, Choudhary described the battle. "On the evening of June 3, we were flown from our base 320 kilometers from Delhi to Amritsar. . . . For this operation, we were part of the Indian army . . . we and they suffered a high rate of casualties . . . so then it was decided by the general to bring in tanks." The general in charge of Operation Blue Star had to seek permission from Indira Gandhi to send in those vehicles. This decision—to send tanks into what was universally acknowledged as the Vatican of the Sikhs—caused uproar and outrage all over the world. "Armored cars were brought in. The first armored car that came in was shot down by a rocket launcher. Then a tank was brought in; the terrorists were still fighting; they were hardened; they didn't give in."[24]

The army used all the hardware it could, yet hundreds of soldiers perished in bloody battles. On June 7 the violence subsided but Sikh militants were still hiding out in the basement of the complex. When the president and supreme commander of the Indian armed forces visited the site on June 8, accompanied by the Lt. Colonel, one of the militants opened fire on him but hit Choudhary's shoulder and spinal cord.

According to Sonia, Indira knew that this marked the beginning of the end for her: "After Operation Blue Star . . . my mother-in-law spoke separately to Rajiv and me about arrangements for her funeral. She wrote down her instructions. She talked to Rahul separately. She told him to be brave when the time came: she had lived her life and done all she had to do and could do; he was not to cry for her."[25]

Following the military operation, one of Indira's own bodyguards, sub-inspector Beant Singh from the Delhi police, went to view the damage for himself. He saw a sacred place of worship decimated, disrespected, and torn apart by an armed conflict. Devastated, he decided to take revenge on the politician whom he saw as the culprit and villain: Indira.

9

EVERY DROP OF MY BLOOD

People come and go but the nation continues to live.

—*Indira Gandhi*

Indira was fully aware that the June 1984 events in Amritsar had sealed her fate, and she indicated this to her loved ones. The family was living on a knife-edge, as it was impossible to know when and where an assassination attempt would happen. The call for an independent homeland for the Sikhs now posed the biggest internal security threat any Indian prime minister had faced since independence. One-tenth of the then million-strong army came from this religion, and a few thousand mutinied in protest at Operation Blue Star. Not surprisingly, questions were continually raised over the fealty of some Sikhs on duty close to Prime Minister Gandhi. Indira was advised to remove the Sikh bodyguards from the home she shared with Sonia, Rajiv, and the children, but she rejected the idea, saying that she was not going to differentiate between one community and another, that she was the prime minister of the whole country. Besides, as Sandeep Unnithan, *India Today*'s defense editor, points out, no twentieth-century head of state had ever been killed by his or her own bodyguards.[1] No Indian prime minister had ever been assassinated. The Sikh protection, which had been with her for a number of years, was retained.

Indira was busy: State elections meant that she and Rajiv had work to do. Away from politics on the domestic front, Indira appeared to be shutting down her life and bidding farewell to all that was dear to her. In 1984 Indira had told Sonia that she wanted to go back to Kashmir, nostalgically describing the tall, indigenous plane trees that show their best colors in the fall. Their whole lives, Jawaharlal and Indira had remained attached to Kashmir, often returning for spiritual nourishment to the valley an emperor from ancient times once referred to as "paradise on earth."

In her memoir, Sonia questioned whether her mother-in-law's urge to go back to Kashmir signified a need to say good-bye to her roots, the memories and the meanings the place held for Indira. Indira planned a fall trip: "She was hesitant to stay overnight because she was worried about my being unwell and alone. In the end she decided to go with the children."[2] Sonia believed that Indira knew her life was in danger. A document handwritten by her mother-in-law "in the nature of a will" during the fall of 1984 stated that if she were to die a violent death, "as some fear and a few are plotting, I know the violence will be in the thought and action of the assassin, not in my dying—for no hate is dark enough to overshadow the extent of my love for my people and my country."[3] It was found after the end of October among her papers; she had mentioned it to no one.

Security was still light in 1984. Delhi police handled the bulk of the protection for prominent personnel.[4] Though they were supplemented by paramilitary organizations, such as the Indo-Tibetan Border Police, they had no special training for important personnel security. For about an hour every morning, Indira Gandhi hosted janta durbars, people's courts, in her garden, where hundreds of people would come to submit a petition, air a grievance, or just to gaze upon her. Indira adored going into crowds, holding the hands of ordinary Indians—she thrived on contact with the people and often rode in open cars. With the assassination of President John F. Kennedy in 1963, however, protection officers had begun to realize that an open vehicle might not be such a good idea. The Nehrus, like the Kennedys, were famous for their accessibility: The more transparent they appeared, the more their mystique grew.

On October 28, the day Indira returned from Kashmir, she spent a quiet evening in Sonia's room, carrying in her cane stool and files herself, talking to Sonia and the children, and taking the odd glance at the television.[5] She was to be back on the campaign trail the following morning, in the state of Orissa on the east coast of India. In a speech to a mass rally of thousands at Bhubaneshwar, on October 30, 1984, she sent a defiant message to her critics and to those who wished her dead. "It does not matter to me whether I live or die.

As long as I draw breath I will carry on serving. And when I die, every drop of my blood will nourish and strengthen my free and undivided country."[6] Her words demonstrated that she had no concern for her own life, but Indira did appear to be quite afraid for those closest to her. She had good reason. Disgruntled Sikhs, furious at the army attack on the Golden Temple, had been sending threatening letters to each member of the family.[7] Indira was always concerned for the children. "On more than one occasion she gave them strict instructions not to play beyond the gate" that connected the house to the building used for official business.[8] That pathway crossed a stretch of grass and was lined, as it is now, with tall straight trees. Looking straight down it toward the office, there was a large green sentry box to the right at the far end. Every morning the prime minister took the short walk along the pathway from her home on Safdarjang Road to her office on Akbar Road. The garden at Safdarjang Road was often filled with the sound of children laughing and playing or adults indulging in a game of badminton, watched by others placidly sipping tea and chatting on the veranda.

On October 30 in the morning, while the children were on their way to school, a car turning in from a side road hit their escort jeep. There were no injuries, but the grandchildren were immediately taken back to the house. When Indira found out about the incident that night, she told her principal secretary that she was sure that it was part of a plot to kidnap or injure Rahul and Priyanka. That night she was restless in the dark hours. In the bedroom next door Sonia awoke around 4 AM, needing her asthma medication. She quietly switched on the lamp at her bedside and started creeping toward the cabinet where medicines were kept. Sonia thought that Indira was asleep. "I was surprised when the door opened. With her torch on, she helped me find my tablet and gave me a glass of water. She told me to be sure to call out for her if I felt ill again."[9]

On protective guard duty the next morning was a young uniformed Sikh constable named Satwant Singh. He had just spent two months in an area of Punjab by the Pakistani border, known to be a hotbed of Sikh extremism. He had been cleared by security chiefs even though Rajiv's suspicions about him had been aroused some time ago.[10] Satwant had feigned an upset stomach so that he could be on duty at the same shift time on October 31, 1984, as Sikh subinspector Beant Singh. Beant Singh had been part of Indira's guard unit for more than nine years. This morning he was waiting in civilian clothes by Indira's gate with his revolver fully prepared. The sun was glinting through the trees and the manicured green gardens looked crisp.

When Priyanka came to give her a customary kiss before setting off for school that morning, Indira hugged her extra tight. She then called Rahul to her and reminded him about the conversation she had had with him about being brave when the time came.

Indira sat in front of her dressing table with its glass top and tall mirror on a low, blue-cushioned stool. On the table top was a pair of her large-framed glasses. To her left was a trunk with a miniature portable cotton spinning wheel and some knitting needles with a couple of balls of wool. Behind her was a set of shelves with fewer than ten pairs of low-heeled, functional shoes. A full program of events lay ahead for Indira, ending with a formal dinner at home with Princess Anne of Great Britain. Sonia entered the room, and they spoke for a short while about the dinner menu before Indira had to prepare for her first appointment. They decided to complete the conversation at lunchtime, and Sonia went back to her room to get dressed.

After a filmed interview with British actor Peter Ustinov, Indira was scheduled to meet a former British prime minister, James Callaghan. Makeup artists came to prepare her for the recording. Her personal physician, who stopped by most mornings,[11] talked with her briefly. As she was expecting to go on camera, Indira did not put on the thick bulletproof vest that she had been wearing since Operation Blue Star.[12] The filming was taking longer to set up than anticipated and was set back 50 minutes. At 9:10 AM, Indira stepped outside the back door and hurried toward the path connecting her home with the office. Sonia was inside the house getting ready for the day, Rahul and Priyanka were starting their lessons at school, and Rajiv was campaigning in West Bengal.

Indira should have been surrounded by a ring of security men while she walked. Instead, she was escorted by a constable who held an umbrella, her assistant, R. K. Dhawan, her personal servant, and a subinspector. As she approached the green sentry box, subinspector Beant Singh came forward to open the white wooden gate. She smiled and as she saw him raise his hand as if to salute her, she folded her hands in greeting. Just three feet away from her, he was holding a revolver. As Indira asked, "What are you doing?" Beant Singh fired a bullet into her abdomen. She moved her right arm and hand up to protect her face. Beant Singh fired another four shots point-blank. The bullets entered Indira's waist, chest, and armpit.[13] Holding an automatic Sten gun and standing just over four feet away was Satwant Singh, paralyzed with fear until Beant Singh yelled at him to open fire. Those around Indira froze, unable to move to protect her. She was probably not mortally wounded yet.[14] Constable Satwant Singh stepped out and shot a volley of 25 tungsten carbide bullets, designed to pierce through armor, at the fallen prime minister.

Sonia was still getting ready inside the house. At first she had assumed the gunshots were fireworks for Hindu festivities taking place: "I had started my bath when I heard what sounded like an unusually close burst of Diwali firecrackers—but with a peculiar difference. I called out to the children's nanny to see what it was. I heard her screams. I knew at once something terrible had happened."[15] After 25 seconds, the subinspector ran forward but was shot down before he could get to Indira.[16] The assassins dropped their guns. "Beant Singh hung his walkie-talkie on the fence, lifted his hands above his head and said, 'I have done what I had to do. Now you do what you have to do.'"[17]

Indira's constable escort felled Beant Singh to the ground. Her personal servant ran into the house and got Dr. Opeh, the duty physician, as Indo-Tibetan Police Force paramilitaries seized Satwant Singh. Dr. Opeh tried mouth-to-mouth resuscitation on Indira. There was an ambulance on standby at 1 Safdarjang Road, but the driver had gone for a tea break. No blood supplies or specialist medical team were kept at the ready. Indira's political adviser M. L. Fotedar shouted for a vehicle to take her to the hospital, the All India Institute for Medical Sciences (AIIMS), nearly three miles away. As the domestic staff and security men went into a panic, a car arrived. Fotedar and Dhawan sat in the front, next to the driver. Before they could start off, Sonia ran down the path in her dressing gown, barefoot, burst into tears,[18] and shouted "Mummy! Oh my God, Mummy!"[19] She pulled open the rear car door and leaped in where her mother-in-law was stretched out lifeless in the back. "My first thought was that I hoped very much that she would survive."[20] Sonia cradled Indira's head in her lap; no one in the car could utter a word. The drive to the hospital was slow because of heavy traffic. Sonia's dressing gown was drenched with blood and her mind was racing. She was desperately wondering if Indira could be saved, while also immediately terrified about the safety of the children and Rajiv, none of whom was there.

No one had alerted the AIIMS that the car was on its way. Once at the hospital, one of the men, described as a "'short foreigner [probably M. L. Fotedar, who is light-eyed and fair-skinned] in a blue suit' who was screaming hysterically"[21] at the hospital porter, jumped out of the car followed by Sonia, who was crying. She went straight to casualty and announced that "Madam has been injured."[22] For some moments, nobody knew who she was talking about. Then a stretcher boy recognized the prime minister of India lying bleeding in the car outside the hospital.[23] Three aghast junior doctors tended to the blood-soaked leader. Around 10:30 AM, as doctors were trying to revive Indira with a cardiac massage, Sonia fainted.[24] Within a few minutes an urgently summoned senior cardiologist and a team of 12 top hospital doctors put Indira on heart and lung bypass apparatus. Blood was pumped into Indira's body, but she had arrived at the hospital clinically dead. The doctors did not declare her deceased until 2:20 PM. Arteries and veins on the right side of her body had been punctured by the bullets, along with her liver, one kidney, and her arm.[25]

Maneka Gandhi visited the intensive care unit with her son Varun and stood for hours outside the operating theater. Pupul Jayakar, a close friend of Indira, rushed to 1 Safdarjang Road, where a friend of Sonia's, Nina Singh, was attempting to calm two hysterical and frightened children—Priyanka and Rahul had been brought home from school. They cried out to Jayakar, asking her what had happened to their grandmother and where she had been taken.[26] She remained with them for a few minutes before being driven to the hospital, where she found Sonia in the anteroom next to the operating theater. Sonia was in a state of severe shock.[27] Rajiv's aide and distant cousin Arun Nehru had arrived at the hospital within minutes of Sonia. Instantly reminded of the massacre of the prime minister of Bangladesh and his family, including a ten-year-old boy—close to Rahul's age—Sonia was "hysterical about the safety of her children, fearing the same fate for them," according to Nehru.[28] He was sent to the house on Safdarjang Road where he discovered that there was no security guard, so anybody could have just walked in off the road. He quickly organized protection for Rahul and Priyanka.

At the hospital, Pupul Jayakar gave Sonia news of her offspring. Sonia "started to tremble, could hardly speak and I didn't want to ask any questions. . . . Sonia was anxious to see her children. She asked me whether I would accompany her back home to bring back fresh clothes to dress the prime minister."[29]

Things move very fast after an Indian leader dies. The body needs to be dressed appropriately for ceremonious removal with certain rituals before the lying-in-state. Sonia was the only one who could deal with the necessary formalities at this stage. At the time when she most needed the support of those she loved, there was no one for her to lean on. Arriving home, when Sonia saw her children, she broke down.[30] Clinging to her, they asked about their grandmother. Jayakar and Sonia spent an hour there, during which Jayakar "helped Sonia choose Indira's favorite . . . saree and . . . *Mala* [necklace] . . . Priyanka and Rahul refused to be left behind and accompanied us back to the hospital."[31]

BBC Delhi correspondent Satish Jacob had broken the news of the assassination; Rajiv had been informed and had heard the radio news and was flying back.

Rajiv arrived at the hospital at 3:15 PM. There were people everywhere. Sonia wanted to be alone with her husband if only for a minute. She was crying, the children were scared, and Rajiv looked devastated. Jayakar left them alone in the anteroom. Party leaders were already pushing Rajiv to step into the premier position. Indira's principal secretary, P. C. Alexander, went into the waiting room and saw Sonia in a terrible state, begging Rajiv not to take over: "They were hugging each other, he was kissing her forehead." Sonia was in tears and saying, "'You should step back and allow someone else to hold this job.'"[32] She knew she was fighting a losing battle. Rajiv kissed his wife's forehead and said, "'It's my duty. I have to do it. I have to do it.'"[33]

The affairs of state were calling—and they had to be handled in whatever space was available to them in the hospital. P. C. Alexander stood "very close" to Rajiv and Sonia, tapped Rajiv on the shoulder, and told him that he wanted to talk to him urgently. "He suddenly broke loose of her and then said, 'Come on, let us discuss what you want to.' He took me to the bathroom and straightaway said, 'I agree with you. Let the CPP [Congress Parliamentary Party] board take a decision nominating me, and let the president be informed, and let's fix a time.' He said, 'You go ahead with this.'"[34]

In an instant, Sonia's and Rajiv's destinies had changed, and a new dawn was breaking in their lives. Rajiv knew that there was a need for decisive action, and he took it. With Sonia beside herself, the children distraught, and Rajiv trying to deal with it all, those around him were making important plans. All hell could break loose once Indira's death was announced, but there was a technical hitch preventing them from proceeding to the next stage. Natwar Singh, former minister of state, said that the official announcement of Indira's death, though reported by the BBC just after 12:30 PM, was not cleared to be broadcast on a government-controlled radio station until 6 PM. The president was in Yemen and the principal secretary to the prime minister was in Bombay (now Mumbai). It would have been perilous for the government to make a declaration until all key players were back in place. "You don't announce it. Everybody was out of Delhi at that time . . . so you had to keep her publicly alive until the president came back. Otherwise there would have been no government."[35]

Back at Safdarjang Road, a family friend found Rajiv calm and strong in front of his associates, allowing himself just a brief moment of grief when he greeted his uncle. For many, the ghosts of the slain leader of Bangladesh and his family were suddenly present.

Who knew how far the conspiracy went? Who else might be in the firing line? Sonia and Rajiv were steeling themselves for an impending destiny that neither of them wanted. To Rajiv, it was now clear that he had to fulfill his duty; he knew what was coming as he moved center stage. As soon as news got out that the prime minister had been killed by Sikhs, mobs went on the rampage, looting, burning, and killing in Delhi.

Later that evening, in an atmosphere of high emotion, at 6:30 PM[36] in Rashtrapati Bhavan (the president's palace), a brief swearing-in ceremony was held, and Rajiv Gandhi signed the oath of office and secrecy at 6:45 PM.[37] At age 40, Rajiv was India's youngest-ever prime minister. Outside, different groups of all ages continued to wreak havoc, seeking revenge. Dr. Sanjay Sinh, a friend of the family, had been at the hospital with Rajiv and a few others when news of the anti-Sikh violence broke. Rajiv wanted to see for himself what was going on. Singh remembers during the next day or so, "He took me in his car and took a drive round Delhi. He spoke to officers that this should be controlled. He saw burning houses. For some time things were absolutely . . . out of control."[38]

The mobs dragged Sikhs out of their cars and hacked them to death, poured petrol over them and set them alight, and wrecked and burned Sikh homes (often with whole families inside) and businesses. Columns of smoke rose over the city as over 2,000 Sikhs were butchered. More than 50,000 fled and another 50,000 sought refuge in camps.[39] Shekhar Gupta, then a reporter for a news magazine, described the scene: "We were covering the story by day and . . . guarding Sikh households in our neighborhoods at night. Many of our neighbors used to put motorcycle helmets on and carry cricket bats . . . to patrol round the houses of our Sikh neighbors . . . it was a very traumatic three or four days. There was a great deal of uncertainty in the city because of the way Mrs. Gandhi had gone, and because it had followed so soon after Operation Blue Star and the troubles in Punjab."[40] The army was called out three days after the attacks started. The carnage halted, but not before its intensity had been carved into India's contemporary history and memory.

The upheavals that Sonia had feared arrived in one great blow, but there was a state funeral to prepare for. Twelve official days of mourning were announced. Indira's body, draped in the national flag, was brought to Teen Murti Bhavan for the three-day lying-in-state. The *Hindustan Times* reported that "Mrs. Sonia Gandhi, carrying a *diva* [candle] was the first to enter the room,"[41] and while the body was raised onto the dais, Rajiv stood strong as his family wept around him, seeking comfort from their patriarch. Many hundreds of thousands came to grieve for the woman who had come to be known as the mother of the nation. On the political front in India, at times of death or illness, rancor disappears, and men and women come together not as opponents but as a community.

When the lying-in-state was over, it was time for the slain prime minister to leave the home she had shared with her father, Jawaharlal, for the last time. Clad in a white silk sari with a black border, Sonia sobbed as Indira's body was carried out from Teen Murti Bhavan to be cremated. Among close friends and family present was Varun, Indira's third and youngest grandchild. Young Priyanka, holding her face close to her mother's, tried valiantly to comfort Sonia.[42]

Fate was moving Sonia inexorably along an arc she had neither imagined nor desired.

PART III

TEMPERED BY TRAGEDY

10

RACE COURSE ROAD

On his young shoulders now lay the responsibility of a whole nation.

—*Sonia Gandhi*

Sonia stood at the pyre for Indira's cremation, holding on to Priyanka's shoulders, Rajiv and Rahul at her side. The loose end of her sari covered her head; dark glasses hid her swollen eyes. She and the children wept as they threw sandalwood sticks into the fire. Indira had been the pivot of the family, the rock, the backbone. She had always been there to solve problems, settle squabbles, and celebrate special events. There had been a place in her heart for each member of her family; she had guided, reprimanded, supported, and loved them. She was as mighty in death as she had been in life.

After the three-day lying-in-state at Teen Murti Bhavan, on November 3, Indira's last journey began at 2:30 PM. She was robed in a rose red sari with a gold-yellow border, and the national flag was draped over her, powdered with marigolds and white lilies. Rajiv and the three military service chiefs placed her body on a gun carriage bedecked with white flowered railings, her face clearly visible.

Four thousand men drawn from the three services had lined the route, while tens of thousands of civilians massed behind them. The crowd was small by Nehru-Gandhi standards, minimized by the violence of the previous few days. The president was part of the cortege. Rajiv was one of the pallbearers, his right shoulder at his mother's bier, his left hand reassuringly steadying the uplifted right arm of Rahul, the youngest of the pallbearers, who walked in front of his father, biting his lip. Next to them Sonia, still numb with shock behind her dark glasses, looked in their direction and held Priyanka's hand.[1] At the cremation site, the gun carriage stopped, Indira's body was taken off and placed on the pyre, and the national flag was removed.

More than a hundred political leaders and dignitaries, among them British prime minister Margaret Thatcher, had flown into New Delhi for Indira Gandhi's state funeral, but the fallen prime minister was the center of attention. Thatcher, struck by the sight of Sonia, remarked that she appeared "absolutely grief-stricken. Had anyone painted that scene, her grief alone would have communicated itself to other people."[2] Devender Khanna, a friend of Rajiv's, recalls grimly, "We were all in shock and just focusing on the body and the pyre. We didn't even bother to talk to the visiting VIPs."[3] Maneka Gandhi and her son, Varun, were among those paying their respects, Maneka circling the pyre, bowing and offering flowers to her estranged mother-in-law.

Hindu ritual calls for the elder son to walk around the pyre seven times before lighting it. At 3:50 PM, amid chanting, Rajiv lit the sandalwood. As the flames rose, one onlooker was struck by the sight of Rajiv's face against the mirage of the heat of the fire and thought Rajiv was like an ocean of pensive strength. The Nehru restraint his mother helped him to learn at an early age was evident. Rajiv later told a television interviewer, "The shock went through me but I kept it in myself as something private and personal, mine rather than something that the world must share with me."[4]

When the ashes had cooled, they were collected in brass urns and placed ceremoniously under a tree in the garden at Teen Murti Bhavan. The official photographer,[5] in a haunting black-and-white image, captured 14-year-old Rahul facing his father, their arms around each other, naked pain etched on both their faces. Sonia stood with the children and Rajiv before bowing and paying respect to the vestiges of her mother-in-law. Rajiv took the ashes in an airplane and scattered them, as his mother had wished, over her beloved Kashmir mountains. Indira's cremation ground, situated near her father's and Sanjay's, is known as Shakti Sthal ("the place of strength and courage"), a grassy complex with pathways and dotted with trees. The centerpiece of Shakti Sthal is carved from ferrous rock, symbolic of the strength of the fallen leader. Boulders from every state in the country are interspersed along paths and mounds, to which seven days a week tens of thousands of Indians from all over the country come to honor their fallen leader.

For births, deaths, and important anniversaries, Sonia and her family visit significant cremation grounds along here. Often, there are hymns from major religions sung while Sonia, her family, the prime minister, and noteworthy guests sit cross-legged on white sheets, with the Special Protection

Group in their safari suits (for summer; jackets and ties in winter), identity labels hanging from their pockets visible at all times. These events are picturesque, with flowers placed in patterns over the central piece of the cremation site. Sonia approaches the cremation centerpiece, completely focused, serious, and somber, and is often photographed sitting or standing barefoot, her hands folded in respect. Each site has a designated area for guests to sit when formal functions take place.

The Indian need for ritual, icons, custom, and celebration is in harmony with the Nehru family values. Dileep Padgaonkar, consulting editor of the *Times of India,* notes that going to the cremation grounds of Mahatma Gandhi or Indira Gandhi, for instance, is an important rite, one that gratifies the cultural side of politics, which is as important as the economic and social side. The cultural aspect of politics reflects a strong sense of community—a community that creates icons, whether it is in cinema, cricket, or politics. In India hysterical displays of emotion on the streets, whether happy or tragic, are common. It is why, in the West there are celebrities and in India there are icons. For Sonia, Rajiv, and their children, Indira was iconic despite her faults. One politician who knows her says that Sonia still sees Indira as a role model, eulogizing her and thinking about the way she would handle any given situation as a guide for her own decisions.[6]

The ease with which Indira was assassinated resulted in an immediate security clampdown on Sonia, Rajiv, and the children. After the murder of their grandmother, Rahul and Priyanka had to be home-schooled for five years. The security system had proved to be highly inadequate, and another shocking fatality had to be avoided. A highly trained team, the Special Group, was assigned to guard the family. At any one time, shifts of between 20 and 30 men guarded the residence. Electronic equipment and closed-circuit TV cameras were installed.

The Special Group carried a variety of weapons, including 9-mm pistols, MP–5 sub-machine guns, and AK–47 rifles. When the family was on the move, jeeps, each with a commander and four men, drove in front and behind, along with other police vehicles and an ambulance.[7] A circle of Special Group men surrounded Rajiv and Sonia when they were out in public. There were usually a second and third ring of men farther away, all able to communicate with each other and all on the lookout for potential threats. After six to eight months, the Special Group was removed and replaced by the Special Protection Group (SPG), formed under a government act and drawn from the police, the Border Security Force, the Indo-Tibetan Border Police, the Central Industrial Security Force, the Central Reserve Police Force, and a Border Guarding Force.[8]

In the 1980s Sonia and Rajiv were torn between the need to feel that their children were safe and the knowledge that they were being deprived of valuable experiences. Rajiv regretted the situation: "They can't go out and play . . . they can't be normal children . . . even their education has got all messed up because of the security problems. If anyone has had to sacrifice it's been the children."[9] The family were protected and guarded as never before.

Rajiv, keen to refute the notion of dynastic rule, wanted a mandate from the people, and in any case the maximum five-year term of any government was nearly over. He announced a general election for the end of December 1984. Maneka Gandhi was now of age to campaign and fought very hard against Rajiv in Amethi, often seen with her toddler son, Feroze Varun, in her arms. But she was up against a monolithic vote tide that swept the Congress Party to victory. Some think that Indians voted in a wave of sympathy; others postulate that Rajiv won because he had a clean image and represented change, hope, energy, and modernity. More likely, it was a combination of both—plus his Nehru heritage—that gave him the appeal that resulted in the biggest number of votes ever accorded to an Indian prime minister and the largest mandate in world history.[10] An untried, untested leader who had neither been in the cabinet nor held a ministerial post captured the imagination as well as the heart of the nation. Not since Jawaharlal's exhortations to his countrymen on the eve of Indian independence in 1947 had there been such excitement and anticipation. The election was two months after the day Indira was assassinated. It was the last time that the Indian National Congress (I) party would have enough seats to form a government on its own.

Rajiv was keen to "build an India of the twenty-first century" and chose a new team of his own: ex-corporate managers, a former flying colleague, men and women with a practical, logical point of view. He dispensed with some of the hangers-on and sycophants who had trailed his mother. Though able officials were retained, his colleagues tended to have a connection through school and university, and they shared his vision.

Not surprisingly, he was impatient with the long-winded flattery of politicians and railed at "the brokers of power" who stalled attempts at democratization. Appreciating the complaints of businessmen about government bureaucracy, he relaxed controls. The rising middle class had created material demands, so he liberalized import policies, making televisions and electronic goods much more widely available. He introduced computerization to India and gave birth to its IT industry. Before long, Rajiv came to be identified with upper-middle-class India.[11] But he was idealistic, and in an effort to empower the grassroots of India, Rajiv worked for the consolidation and strengthening of the elected village councils, or *panchayats,* through a special bill he introduced into parliament aimed at the decentralization of authority.

Sonia, now spouse to the prime minister of the world's largest democracy, had a bigger role on the public stage with more foreign travel, and in New Delhi, more formal meals at the president's palace, Rashtrapati Bhavan, and Hyderabad House. Former minister Natwar Singh comments, "She was the official hostess of the prime minister. I don't think she was overjoyed, but she had no choice."[12] It was not a new activity for her: She had already hosted many events with Indira and traveled extensively with Rajiv on official tours. Her husband remarked, "She's fighting very hard to see [that] her family remains a family and doesn't weaken in any way because of my being prime minister."[13] Within three weeks of Rajiv's new role, he and Sonia had met with the leaders and their wives of the two world superpowers: Mikhail Gorbachev and Ronald Reagan. They developed a good personal rapport with both the Russians and the Americans.

In footage and images from this period, though, Sonia appeared hesitant and stiff. The slightly frozen look she bore was because Rajiv's safety was always on her mind, as she explained in later years when asked about it by interviewer Vir Sanghvi: "There was perhaps this impression of me being aloof and distant. Part of the reason behind it could be, I was often tense because I was worried that something may happen to my husband."[14] Up to the point when Rajiv became prime minister, Sonia had only spoken twice in an official capacity.[15] Rajiv was keen to let the world know that Sonia was keeping a distance from politics. "She's not really interested; because then she gets involved. Well, we just decided we would keep these things apart. . . ."[16] Sonia was genuine in her dislike of the spotlight, but it was also important to quell any potential criticism of "foreign" influences. In any case, Sonia had already become an Indian citizen by registration in 1983.

While the family was adjusting to their new official life, they also were grieving. The psychological damage of the slaughter is not much discussed; the culture of mental trauma does not yet have as high a profile in India as it does in America or Europe. In her television interview with Vir Sanghvi, Sonia frankly admitted, "It was a very traumatic experience and it took me a long time to recover from it." Indira's harrowing murder hurt Sonia more than many realize, as evidenced by Rajiv's words in a television series called *India's Rajiv:* "It took her almost two years, perhaps more, to get over it. It really shattered her . . . she's not completely through with it. Also because she was the only one at home—there was nobody else—she took mummy to the hospital."[17]

Whatever she was going through inside, Sonia just got on with what she had to do. She had for some time been visiting Rajiv's constituency of Amethi in the state of Uttar Pradesh. Local party workers who accompanied her at that time said that she connected with constituents. During this period, she was particularly busy supervising eye and medical clinics, sometimes for several days at a time. She was with Rajiv on all of his rural tours, and he spoke of her "*dard* [pain] for the people of India. You can see it when she goes into houses and talks to people."[18]

Congress member of parliament and family friend Dr. Sanjay Sinh remembers, "While Rajiv was addressing a meeting, Sonia used to sit down with the women. She used to chat, listen to their grievances and problems. She used to talk in Hindi and dressed in saris."[19] Ram Sewak, who often accompanied Rajiv and Sonia when they came to his district, said, "As Rajiv was there in Delhi, she used to be here, taking care of the constituency, going to schools . . . seeing how education can be promoted here, and how people can be made literate."[20] Sonia was solicitous of those constituents who came to the capital, often taking doctors from Delhi to work in Amethi. Devender Khanna, who was involved with certain relief projects, noted that Sonia would support those who made the trip to the capital: "For heart surgery, to get married, major things that couldn't be handled there. The work was a kind of fixed long-term deposit."[21] She and her children continue to be concerned for those from the constituencies who travel to the capital for help.

Back in New Delhi, the Home Ministry designated a new official residence for the prime minister—around the corner from where Sonia had lived, with one interlude, for 15 years. The new home, along with a separate office, was on Race Course Road. Larger than the house on Safdarjang Road, it was set back from the street and easier to secure. The Gandhis were the first prime-minister family to move into the new premises in March 1985. Interior designer and architectural restorer Sunita Kohli helped Sonia and Rajiv organize numbers 5 and 7 Race Course Road into a home and an office, respectively. Many of the Lutyens zone buildings had been altered to suit changing Indian taste over the years, but Sonia wanted this place to reflect the original architectural design.

Sunita Kohli was invited to restore the new home for the Gandhis, who, she said, both possessed "a very fine design sensibility" and "were equally and fully involved in terms of design." Kohli found Sonia easy to work with. "There was a perfect collaboration as to which rooms would be used for what . . . we worked together at each step because Mrs. Gandhi has a very keen eye for what needs to be restored. She has a very highly developed sense of volume and proportion, and is very collaborative. She knows what restoration is all about."[22]

Kohli thought that Sonia's experience of having close relationships with two prime ministers helped develop her natural interests and instincts. "She's deeply interested in languages, etymology, very well read, very interested in cultures—she's an Indian woman with this wide sense of being, an awareness of things that are happening. . . ." That awareness was bolstered by a family affinity for books: Nehru and Indira were, and Sonia, Priyanka, and Rahul are, voracious readers with different tastes. Natwar Singh finds Sonia's appetite for books "exceptional for an Indian politician."[23] Jhumpa Lahiri's *Unaccustomed Earth,* Fadia Faqir's *My Name Is Salma,* Marjane Satrapi's *Persepolis,* and George Crile's *Charlie Wilson's War* were among her choice reads in 2008.[24] Among the many works presented to her, she was given a copy of Dan Brown's *The Da Vinci Code* by a politician.[25] Sonia's meeting room at her home is lined with books, just as Indira's study and bedroom were.

At Race Course Road there was much work to be done, as some of the changes to the buildings over the previous years had been quite radical. Structures needed strengthening, rooms needed restoration "to their original meaning . . . generally trying to remove the accretions which had piled up during the last 70 years," Kohli said. The gardens that had been truncated were restored so that the white bungalows were once again "set in the sweep of the verdant lawns." At Race Course Road, as in her other homes, Sonia managed to close off some part of her life to the outside world. Natwar Singh says that on Sundays, Sonia still tends to relax when possible, "putters around the garden," and spends time with her family. In 1984, such deliberate "fence-building" was a surprise for those in the media who were used to 24-hour access to politicians. Mark Tully, the BBC's Delhi bureau chief for much of Indira Gandhi's and Rajiv's ministries, states that "Rajiv always insisted that his family, including Sonia, should be kept out of interviews and such things. . . . I remember once we made a film about Rajiv and I specially said 'We must have some shots of your family,' and he said, 'I'm sorry; I'll let you make the film, but Sonia'—and he put the responsibility for this on Sonia—'will not allow the family to be filmed.' He just said it like that, which was understandable."[26] Rajiv told another interviewer that Sonia "feels that part of her family life has been taken away or stolen and that's why she's so protective about what she's got left."[27]

Apart from security problems, the restoration of the new ministerial residence respected the family's need for seclusion. As Sunita Kohli stated, "Five Race Course Road was the one place that was private; just for their family and a few close friends."

11

REMEMBERING INDIRA

> You've got to put away your personal sorrow, and you have to discharge your responsibility.
>
> —*Indira Gandhi*

Sonia and the family were slowly adjusting to their new life. The children had their lessons in the morning with tutors and found ways to keep themselves occupied in the afternoons because the tight security restricted their contact with the outside world.

Rajiv was too busy to devote as much time to being with them as he had before, but they enjoyed two of his own passions: photography and ham radio—Sonia and the children became amateur radio operators. There were pets around the house to play with—dogs and a parrot. Rahul enjoyed football and target shooting; Priyanka learned Bharatanatyam, a form of classical dance incorporating stories from Indian mythology. Both of them enjoyed reading newspapers and comics that often recounted episodes of Indian history and the stories and legends woven around it.[1] Rajiv would work long days, staying up until three or four in the morning, returning to his work at nine. Sonia, and sometimes the children, waited up for him most nights, altering their lifestyle to fit in with his.

Seeking a constructive way to spend her time while Rajiv was away seeing to state business, Sonia resumed her work at the National Museum and immersed herself in editing two volumes of letters between Indira and her father. Through most of Indira's youth, while her father was in British jails, "their loving and close relationship found expression in this flourishing correspondence, recording a rich and vivid interplay between two lively minds."[2] *Freedom's Daughter* and the second volume, *Two Alone, Two Together,* contained letters written between 1922 and 1964, when Nehru died. The letters gave Sonia insight into the minds of two of the most powerful leaders of the twentieth century, a perspective that would help her later in the creation of her own brand of socialism. The correspondence heavily features the battle for Indian independence that Jawaharlal spearheaded alongside Mahatma Gandhi, which Indira enthusiastically embraced. Sonia found that the correspondence "brought alive to me the freedom struggle as it was felt and acted by two people who went on to play important roles in shaping modern India . . . they provided a philosophical and historical underpinning to my direct experience of observing my husband as he carried forward their vision."[3] Giving life to inanimate objects was a way for Sonia to express her own love for the departed, and reaching out to her mother-in-law through the letters helped with the grieving process.[4]

Later on, after 2002, Sonia wanted the two volumes condensed into one. Nandini Mehta, an editor with Penguin Books at the time, worked on the new edition, periodically soliciting Sonia's review. Nandini observed that Sonia's concrete suggestions went toward making the volumes as accessible as possible by cutting out the "everyday kind of stuff" and keeping the best bits.[5] With the intention of making Indira's legacy more available, in 1985 Sonia turned 1 Safdarjang Road into the Indira Gandhi Memorial Museum with the help of architect Ranish Rai. Sonia pored over every detail that went into the design, selecting and handling each artifact herself, according to an assistant, in order to lay out the narrative of Indira's life.

The pale-pink cotton sari made of material spun by Jawaharlal when he was in prison hangs close to the entrance along with a shawl: It was the one that Indira, Sonia, and, later, Priyanka all wore at their weddings. The contents of Indira's bedroom, with a narrow single bed, jug, and angle lamp on the bedside table, the round cane stool that Sonia described her carrying into her room three nights before she was murdered, her many books, and modest photo frames (there are at least five, plus a small pocket travel album on one low bookshelf opposite her bed), are all carefully preserved there.

Indira's prayer room contains artifacts and books from different religions—prayer beads, little icons of Buddha, Hindu gods, Jesus Christ—the main table top is covered with Hindu-centric statuettes, books, and accessories. On the windowsill sits a Sanyo cassette player with a tape of Hindu devotional music still looking as though it is just about to be switched on. Indira's study—with its Eames and Breuer chairs, huge collection of books, Rubik's cube, a notepad on a low side table, simple couch covered in green hand-woven fabric, and more photographs of her family (there is a small plastic concertina album that she used to ask Rajiv to update periodically)—allows the visitor to gain some insight into what Indira held dear. Press photographs, clippings, and speech extracts compiled after her death adorn some walls. Indira wore a man's watch so that she could read the large dial easily, and it is in a showcase along with other everyday items like a Scrabble game and binoculars in a well-worn case. Chillingly, an orange sari with the faint outline of large blood stains, a red patterned tasseled shoulder bag with a white strap, and a small pair of black sandals—the outfit Indira wore the day she was assassinated—are laid out in a glass case. Outside, past the immaculately kept garden, is the pathway that led to her office, now preserved and marked out as a work of art. Made of crystal glass on a steel frame, it has the appearance of a moving water stream and shimmers eerily in the sunlight. The exact spot where the murder took place is marked by a sheet of clear glass. Sonia's affection for her mother-in-law and her desire to preserve these memories for the nation has led her to create a highly atmospheric place of remembrance, charged with emotion.

Sonia's visits to the heartlands of India with her husband after he took office in 1984 underscored what she had learned of the philosophies of the Nehru-Gandhis. Rajiv said that Sonia was with him on "almost all"[6] of his rural tours to distant areas of India to meet with the deprived, to listen and to show them that there were those who were concerned about them. By focusing on these people, the Gandhis were also able to ascertain the extent to which antipoverty programs were actually reaching those they were designed for. A discussion would often become a micro-investigation into what was happening locally: Was there a grain store? Were there vegetables in the house? Rajiv would never enter without asking for permission first; once inside, he would often taste the food that had been prepared and take a sip of water. The couple would stay on the move on these joint missions; in order to visit numerous villages, interactions could be as brief as two minutes or twenty minutes. They would often stay in *dak* bungalows or circuit houses, originally built by the British for their administrators.

These countryside trips were not glamorous; whether in the hills or the plains, smooth roads and paths were seldom encountered; more often they traveled rough mud tracks and tried to avoid ditches. If it had been raining, Sonia would pick up her sari hem and hold it inches above wet ground, walking at a brisk pace alongside or just behind Rajiv. She said, "He walked so fast that sometimes I had to ask him to slow down, seeing that the others with us were struggling to stay in step."[7] In marginalized areas of India,

Sonia was always by Rajiv's side, always part of the conversation. They were close and affectionate, iconic as far as their marriage was concerned, and people would often notice this in how they looked at or spoke to each other.

The marginalized rural people, those outside urban areas, those on the geographical periphery of India occupy the majority of the political, social, and economic space of the nation, which in the late 1980s had a population of around 850 million people. (It is now 1.21 billion and projected to reach 1.3 billion by 2021.[8]) Within India's 28 states, there is a rich variety of cultures and customs. In the countryside, where women tend to be more modestly dressed than in towns, Sonia often wore the loose end of her sari covering her head. The locals liked this, especially in the family constituencies of Uttar Pradesh. When the couple went to tribal areas in the northeast, the tribal leaders would often dress the pair in local garb. The groups greatly appreciated these outsiders identifying with them, observing their customs and rituals, and they both cooperated with great ease and composure. Sonia and her family took genuine delight in the variety of costumes of India; her Cambridge housemate Karma Topden was deputy secretary to the king of Sikkim and remembers Sonia, her sister Nadia, and Rajiv on holiday in the dominion once; the ladies wanted to have their own *bhakus*, traditional Sikkimese outfits of a wraparound long jacket worn over a full-sleeved silky blouse, so Topden got the palace tailor to make one for each of them.[9]

The trips included islands in the Bay of Bengal to the east of India; the Andaman and Nicobar islands; and, to India's southwest, the islands of Lakshadweep with their coral reefs. They also visited remote desert locations, made deep forays into forests and jungles, and journeyed into the mountains. While the Special Protection Group was generally in full force on visits, sometimes an aide would travel in a jeep with the prime minister and his wife. Although one of these aides recalls that Sonia didn't appear to have much interest in politics or policy, he did note that she was deeply interested in people and their living conditions. She was endlessly interested in the folk traditions of India and really enjoyed tribal music and dancing. When speaking to local women, she wanted to know about their everyday problems and worries. Rajiv and Sonia shared this zealous concern for the rural populace and for women's empowerment. During his term of office, Rajiv introduced a bill for a constitutional amendment that guaranteed women a 33 percent representation in elected local bodies. A sympathy for the underprivileged, the ordinary Indian, was never far from Sonia's mind. The aide remembered an early occasion on a tour of a central Indian state, Madhya Pradesh, where Sonia and Rajiv spent three or four days in dense jungle. At one point, a group of excited tribal children was running after them. He heard Sonia say softly "*dolce*" and "*bambini*" to Rajiv and deduced that she was asking her husband if they had any sweets to give to the children. Speaking in Hindi or in English would have been too obvious; she chose to ask him the question more discreetly. None of the party had any sweets with them, but it was a reflection of Sonia's sensitivity to her situation.

An affinity with the people is something she and Rajiv shared. She wrote of a "charge of excitement"[10] when Rajiv met with men and women, whether poor or rich. Dr. Rita Bahuguna Joshi, who now works with Sonia as one of her state Congress committee presidents, says that whether in a crowd of fifty or of hundreds of people, Sonia will make a beeline for the neediest and the weakest. "A person who is not properly dressed, who's humble, who's subdued, who's frightened—she'll hold her hand and say, '*Kya baath hey, kaisey ho, kahan sey ayey ho* (what's the matter, how are you feeling, where have you come from)?' That gives the person a lot of confidence. This is how the family has been trained; this is the message they send out—we need to work for the poor."[11] Sonia Gandhi seems to draw her strength from looking into the faces of the destitute; it is as though she gets her motivation from them. Rajiv's aide said that she never strutted across the stage as the wife of a prime minister; her feet were always firmly anchored on the ground.

12

GLIMPSES OF FREEDOM

As I was frequently touring with him, the children saw much less of us. This was the only time when Rahul and Priyanka could have their father to themselves.

—*Sonia Gandhi*

The Gandhis tried to spend a precious few days together wherever they could between official engagements. There were occasional magical vacations, for instance, on the Lakshadweep Islands, where the family could explore new territory and pursue water sports in a relaxing, safe environment. The white-beached islands lie on the southwestern tip of India, 36 of them on a spectacular coral reef in turquoise lagoons. According to Wajahat Habibullah, a mellifluous-toned former joint secretary in Rajiv Gandhi's office who was with Sonia and Rajiv on many tours, these magnificent coral islands in the Arabian Sea are the most beautiful part of India. With several portfolios, including environmental conservation and poverty alleviation, Wajahat found that though he might frequently be part of the prime minister's team, Sonia remained a mystery as she always kept herself apart, sitting alone, sometimes reading a book, not having much to do with Rajiv's staff except for politely making sure everyone was looked after if they were all eating together.[1] Evenings, if Rajiv was ensconced with his aides, she would go off to her room. There was, of course, the odd exchange or two. On a formal visit to the Lakshadweep islands, Habibullah found himself standing next to Sonia on a jetty, watching a flaming sunset. He was waxing lyrical about the spectacular scenery, the golden sinking sun, the magnificence of the deep aquamarine ocean, the calm evening air, and the wonder of the islands. After rambling on a while, he turned to Sonia, who simply responded, "Yes."

What he did not know then was that she has a near-photographic memory and a capacity for keeping track of individuals among the thousands she routinely meets. Sonia, Rajiv, and Wajahat were on an official visit to the east coast state of Orissa, when they came across two homeless, destitute little orphan girls in one of the villages. Rajiv told Wajahat that "something should be done for them," and while the latter dutifully took notes, Sonia listened silently. The joint secretary followed up and issued instructions via the prime minister's office that the girls should be given some financial support and a place to live. To his surprise, several times after that when he met Sonia with a "Good morning," she would reply, "Good morning," and add, "'What is the news of those two little girls?' She remembered it so clearly!"[2] She still hardly spoke to Wajahat—or to anyone else on Rajiv's team. However, the barriers came down when Wajahat received a different position, away from the prime minister's office.

He became the administrator of the Lakshadweep islands, moving there from New Delhi along with his Pakistan-born wife, Shahila, and their sons. In January 1988 the prime minister and his wife made another visit to the island. While Rajiv was on an official tour, Sonia chose to spend time with the Habibullahs, away from the formal part of the visit where, Shahila felt, "people would have been hovering around her and she would have had to be the center of attention."[3] She preferred to stay low-key and backstage.

Shahila remembers that Sonia just wanted to spend quiet moments with them. Not knowing what she was like, the Habibullahs trod cautiously around her. "It was an island development meeting. She was an important guest for us. So that there'd be no noise, I told my children, who were home from Doon School, to go to their rooms." Sonia, though, knew quite a bit about the family before she got there. When she arrived she asked, "'Where are your children?' and I rather sheepishly said that they were in their rooms. She said, 'Please send for them, I'd like to talk to them.' She put them at their ease immediately, asked them about their school, what their thoughts were about living on the islands, and if they were happy."[4] She was relaxed; so the Habibullahs relaxed too. She was curious about the logistics of island life and asked questions about maintaining a supply of food and other necessities. Compared with the distance Sonia maintained when he was working in Rajiv's office, Wajahat now found her "most open and free, extremely friendly! She bought a huge box full of shortbread and chocolates, which was given to the children. So she was not the same person I knew, actually, she was very open and affable; I felt that I only came to know her after I left her [husband's] office." Shahila Habibullah at the time was looking after the Indian Council for Child Welfare in Lakshadweep. "We had a lot of state projects; including a book-binding unit for women. She visited the book-binding unit with Rahul and Priyanka, and she visited the school which was on the main island, Kavaratti. The children in their island gear sang for her." While Rajiv's wife enjoyed the folk art of the island kids, Shahila noticed that Sonia was rather watchful with her own children. "When [the Gandhis] had gone to the islands; the helicopter was going to the mainland to collect something . . . everybody must have said [to Rahul and Priyanka], why don't you come along for a ride," but Sonia restrained them in Hindi, saying 'don't go off by yourselves in the helicopter . . . don't take undue advantage.' She wanted them to stay low-key and not be seen to be misusing government machinery." The discipline paid off. Rahul and Priyanka "were extremely well-brought-up children, polite, like their parents—they never had any airs and graces."

Sonia, having moved away from her native land and her family in northern Italy, was clearly intrigued by her hostess, who had done something similar. Shahila told the prime minister's wife that she had been educated in Pakistan and half her family was still there. Sonia asked if she felt like a foreigner, sensing, Shahila thought, that they might be kindred spirits. Mrs. Habibullah's reply seemed to resonate with Sonia: "I said wherever the children and my husband are, that is home. . . . I felt I could understand her a bit because where her husband and her family was, that was where *her* heart lay. She could relate to that."

After the official part of the tour was over, the Gandhis spent a week with family and friends on Bangaram Island, which had just developed as a tourist resort. It was a spectacular, tropical bolt-hole, the security only needed to be minimal, so they were left to themselves. Sonia would relax on the beach while Rajiv and Rahul swam back and forth to Tinnakara, a small island half a mile from where they were staying. Enchanted by the coral life, the family snorkeled and went scuba diving. With Rajiv and Rahul often dressed in blue-and-white nautical-style beach wear, the family appeared more photogenic than usual, with the white sand, beach houses, and transparent ocean as backdrops. There appeared to be a slightly heightened fragility to Rahul at this time (Sonia described him as "soft and sensitive"[5]), an impression of a greater vulnerability about him than the other three members of his family.

During these off-duty days, Wajahat kept in the background but has an abiding memory of watching Rahul from a distance on one occasion, "sitting at his father's feet and listening . . . on the beach. I remember very graphically the adoration and the admiration in the boy's eyes as he looked up to his father, and the way his father was talking to him. It looked as though he was teaching him something or telling him something which the boy was lapping up. He was a very quiet child, he hardly spoke at all in my presence . . . but he loved swimming. . . ." After leaving the islands, the Gandhi family did not forget the Habibullahs. Just under a year later, Shahila was surprised to receive a huge parcel. In it were "the loveliest cakes—Christmas cakes and dried fruit—and Sonia said, 'This is for your children.' I thought it was so touching that she felt these things might not be available on the island." "Such spectacular islands, such a wonderful time," Wajahat recalls. He says that members of Sonia's family from Italy spent time there, too, and that because of the sentimental attachment, Sonia developed a great affection for Lakshadweep, which she still visits occasionally with her children.

In 1986 Rajiv was in Jammu and Kashmir, the mountainous northern territory over which India and Pakistan had fought two wars.[6] He was there to sign an accord with the chief minister; Sonia and the children were on the trip too. India holds approximately 43 percent of the territory and considers the state an integral part of the country. Pakistan, which controls roughly 37 percent (China holds the remaining 20 percent), desires the implementation of a 1948 United Nations Security Council resolution for a referendum to determine the wishes of the Kashmiri people, most of whom are Muslim. Some Kashmiri groups want greater autonomy for themselves and the right to decide their own futures. Since the late 1980s, over 60,000 people have died in clashes between Indian security forces and separatist militants or in crossfire between the Indian and the Pakistani armies. The prisons are full to overflowing.

Despite roughly a quarter of India's 1.2 million-strong army[7] being deployed to the state, maintaining law and order continues to be a problem. In 2010 violence on the streets flared again, with young people throwing stones at Indian forces, some of them dying during the skirmishes. Sonia Gandhi described the events as "painful," saying that she grieved at the loss of young lives and urging "dissatisfied" Kashmiris to "give peace a chance."[8] As a confidence-building measure, a delegation of three interlocutors, led by *Times of India* consulting editor Dileep Padgaonkar, was appointed with a minimum year-long mandate to go to the Kashmir Valley, engage with different groups and compile recommendations for the prime minister. The valley, though, remains restless, a harmonious endgame a distant prospect.

Back in the 1980s, whether it was to a troubled region or to a peaceful one, if the prime minister took his family along, the media pack was able to scrutinize their every move close up. Sonia was known for her public silence, which led to her being dubbed "the Italian sphinx" in the media. Although by Rajiv's side, his wife appeared very quiet. But Sadia Dehlvi, one of the journalists who covered the Kashmir event and traveled back to Delhi with the prime minister's group in a small civil aircraft, "could sense that he was drawing his strength from her a lot. You could see that she was a strong influence and a big support in his life."[9]

Despite the fact that Sonia and her family were part of a press caravan, Dehlvi found that the Gandhis were rigorous about keeping their public and private lives separate while staying very involved with each other. "The kids, they were just so close-knit. You could see there was an effort being made to draw that line between family and politics." Sonia apparently kept herself and the children in the background for two reasons: maintaining that line allowed the family some privacy, and it also kept the focus on Rajiv. As in her relationship with Indira, Sonia excelled at being the quiet supporter.

The state of Jammu and Kashmir is spectacular any time of the year but even more so in the winter months; crisp snow covers the alpine slopes, and on occasion the Gandhis could be seen in relief against the mountains, playing with snowballs. But the impression of the youngsters' politeness noted by the Habibullahs was also picked up by Sadia Dehlvi. In a family already under scrutiny, Sonia tried to make sure that her own behavior and that of her children gave no cause for complaint. Dehlvi feels that sometimes the children were *too* correct; they were very guarded and conscious of everything around them. She remarks that Rahul and Priyanka "would duck the camera, they didn't appreciate it if you took pictures of them. They were not willing to smile and be happy. . . . Sonia was very reticent and very guarded. . . ." If she or others in the media corps met the family, few words beyond pleasantries would be exchanged. Gandhi family members are invariably civil and cordial to everyone. They have friends at home and all over the world. Yet, one of the most noticeable things about them, Dileep Padgaonkar opines, is that they maintain an air of detachment: "They do not encourage intimacy, or even any kind of friendly approach."[10] It is a paradox, because all of them are highly physical in their interactions with the needy, with the electorate, with villagers. They freely embrace the old, hold children and babies close, and grasp the hundreds of hands that stretch out toward them wherever they go. They try to narrow the distance between themselves and ordinary Indians more than many other politicians. They have an ability to maintain psychological space around themselves while at the same time providing more corporeal proximity than most other Indian legislators.

At the time of the Kashmir tour, Priyanka was seen as the Gandhi who had inherited Indira's public ease and confidence, while Rahul was described as shy and quiet. For many years, Congress watchers excitedly predicted that Priyanka would be the next generation's leader. Rahul was more like Sonia, people thought. "Rahul takes a lot from his mother. He is guarded, humble. He shows an ability to control and self-reflect; we all assumed Priyanka was the one. She was very sure of herself—she just needs to smile and you're Priyanka's forever. Rahul has worked hard to prove himself. In those days he didn't give the impression of having the promise of leadership," comments Dehlvi, who was then a columnist and editor with the Shama Group of publications. No one, not even Rahul perhaps, thought at that time that he would come to be hailed as a future prime minister.

In the late 1980s, Rahul, Priyanka, and Sonia accompanied Rajiv to the kingdom of Bhutan, a country on the northern border of India, as guests of the fourth king, Jigme Singye Wangchuk. The friendship between the Nehru-Gandhis and the Bhutanese royal family went back to the relationship between Jawaharlal Nehru and the third monarch, Jigme Dorji Wangchuk, which was followed by warm exchanges between Indira Gandhi and the third and the fourth rulers. Doon School and Cambridge alumnus Dalip Mehta was with the Gandhis in his official capacity as a joint secretary in the Ministry of Foreign Affairs. After the official part of the visit, there was to be a two-night break in the kingdom, but on the third and fourth nights the helicopter couldn't take off because of bad weather. "We were all delighted that we were forced to stay on," the gentle-mannered former Indian foreign service officer says, smiling.[11] The Bhutan trip provided an opportunity for more of those unofficial, off-duty times when Sonia let her guard down slightly, when she relaxed with her family and was at her most comfortable—in short, when the real woman was revealed. The same is true of her children, who have now spent nearly half their lives with just one parent, their mother.

The Buddhist kingdom of Bhutan sits in the eastern Himalayas, and the Gandhi family spent "a happy few days" in Bumthang, central Bhutan. The broad valleys are largely unspoiled, and for Sonia, Rajiv, and the children, it was liberating to be away from New Delhi and the claustrophobic presence of the security team, enlarged since Indira's assassination in 1984. Mehta remarks, "I never could imagine them so relaxed, so happy, and somehow so unburdened by the affairs of state and responsibility." There was security, but it was unobtrusive. The family stayed in an enclosure around the royal guest house, where the monarch had beautiful, special little huts made for them. Sonia and Rajiv stayed in one, the children stayed in another, and the king in yet another. The thatched huts were completely Bhutanese in design but had all the necessary modern conveniences inside. There was no bifurcation of activities in this liberal family, no question of the men going off to be macho together. Sonia was always present, and they did everything as a unit. Mehta remembers fishing and visiting monasteries and *gompas* (places of religion). In the evenings there would be a bonfire, and they would sit around it talking and laughing. The king appointed one of his cousins to make all the arrangements and look after them.

In *Rajiv,* Sonia described how her husband's personal relationship with the king echoed Rajiv's message advocating regional peace and stability; India's relations with Bhutan exemplified the Indian premier's approach to the country's neighbors. "South Asia's biggest nation and its smallest evolved bonds based on trust and common interests."[12] One of the few official photos of this visit shows Sonia sitting between Rajiv and the king, watching an archery display. Behind the archer, next to Priyanka, a rapt Rahul stands with his hands behind his back, a classic Jawaharlal Nehru pose he can often be spotted in today. There was an easy, casual tone to the holiday. "They would go for long walks. They were free to wander; you didn't have all these soldiers everywhere, so they had a sense of privacy."[13] Officials made themselves as scarce as possible unless invited to formal discussions or bonfire evenings. The stringent preservation measures that kept pollution at bay bestowed on Bhutan a pristine environment that greatly appealed to Sonia and the children. Rahul and Priyanka observed and absorbed everything they could about the kingdom, wanting to know about the murals, images, religious artifacts, and *thangkas* (intricate silk paintings with embroidery, usually depicting a Buddhist deity or scene).

Dalip Mehta saw the relationship between the two dynasties, the Nehru-Gandhis and the house of the Bhutanese royal family blossom during the time the fourth king was in power. The friendship continues; in November 2008, Sonia and Rahul, along with Priyanka and her husband, Robert Vadra, attended the coronation of the fifth king of Bhutan, Jigme Khesar Namgyel Wangchuk.

Sonia and Rajiv would sometimes go to extraordinary lengths to find time for the family. In 1985 Satish Jacob, former deputy chief of the BBC's Delhi bureau, was asked by his far east colleague, the late Jim Biddulph, to organize some filming with Rajiv. Jacob was told that Rajiv, whom he knew, was in his constituency, Amethi, so Satish arranged for himself and Biddulph to fly to Lucknow from Delhi. The two journalists spent hours driving all around the constituency searching for the prime minister. Disappointed, they returned to Lucknow in the evening only to find a relaxed Gandhi family emerging from a restaurant in the same hotel where the BBC pair had checked in. Recognizing Jacob, Rajiv told him that he had given instructions to his aides "not to reveal my whereabouts as I wanted to be alone with Sonia and the family."[14] He made it up to the pair by allowing the journalists to accompany him later and gave them hours of interview time.

For the Gandhis, the chance to have quality time together was rare now that Rajiv was in politics, but when it did come, it provided some special recollections to lock away. The islands of Lakshadweep and the Himalayan kingdom of Bhutan were refuges, calm places of happy memories in turbulent lives.

13

THE PREMIER'S WIFE

I dream of an India—strong, independent, self-reliant, and in the front rank of the nations of the world in the service of mankind.

—*Rajiv Gandhi*

As the prime minister's wife, Sonia usually traveled with Rajiv when he went abroad—according to an aide, he made more than 54 foreign trips. Sonia had been with Indira on a number of such visits, and now her role was that of an enhanced companion in chief. Having learned realpolitik, costume, and protocol at the side of an accomplished player, Sonia started off on the international circuit at a higher level. The prime minister and his wife liked aesthetically pleasing surroundings when possible, and given India's rising profile in the global economy, Rajiv asked interior designer Sunita Kohli to work on a couple of Ministry of Defense Boeing aircraft that were for the use of the prime minister, the president, and two top officials. In the personal seating cabin, where the chairs converted to narrow beds, Kohli created a small conference space, two seats for Rajiv's personal assistants, and chairs for the accompanying cabinet and secretariat delegation. As was often the case with Sonia and Rajiv's personal and professional environments, there was a high design element—unusual in Indian aircraft in those days. The two aircraft were given different themes: monuments of India for one, and birds of India for the other, with specifically appointed watercolors. Kohli said that "everything was specially commissioned—including the linen napkins." The woolen aircraft fabrics with inflammable coating, previously imported from Switzerland, were woven by an Indian firm.[1]

Sonia didn't have makeup artists, stylists, or dressers traveling with her,[2] but her choice of apparel and jewelry on showpiece state occasions was usually, as it was with Indira, appropriately glamorous. Sonia travels abroad for official visits much less now than she did then. But on the rare occasion when she does leave India to give a speech or, more frequently, when she meets with high-profile international statesmen at home, fashion journalists comment on what she wears. (The Indian press tripped over itself with delirium at Sonia's dark blue silk sari when she attended a formal dinner for US president Barack Obama in November 2010 in New Delhi.)

Back in the 1980s, on foreign trips Sonia's slim figure always drew admiring glances, draped to great effect in a show-stopping sari, her fair skin contrasting with her long, dark brown hair. Rajiv too was a grand figure, always neat, often sporting an Indian formal jacket with a high Nehru collar. The combination was potent enough to make them the poster pair of their generation. It is a fashionable conceit to compare them with that other star couple, Jacqueline and John F. Kennedy, and the Nehru-Gandhi and Kennedy dynasties are often mentioned in the same breath. Apart from their stunning good looks, the Kennedys and the Nehru-Gandhis are regarded in their respective countries as having charisma and mystique by the bucketful, though some Indians like to point out that the Nehru-Gandhis surpass the Kennedys in the number of generations in political power, as well as the actual top positions held.

Rajiv had many informal exchanges on the world stage, with both sides keen to learn about the other. Kenneth Clarke, British lord chancellor and secretary of state for justice, remembers meeting him at a specially arranged political lunch in London along with six or seven ministers in Margaret Thatcher's government: "He gave the impression of a man who was surprised to find he was no longer an airline pilot and was eagerly getting into politics. I remember being impressed by Rajiv—he was very modest, very restrained and very intelligent." Rajiv came across as "a nice guy with great prospects."[3] Clarke found that political diplomacy was clearly something he had adapted to quite well.

Cultural diplomacy was another of the hallmarks of Rajiv's premiership, a concept he advanced through the Festivals of India, which his mother had supported. Designed to promote artistic exchanges and strengthen international appreciation for the country, several of them took place across the globe. Sonia was always closely involved in the promotion of India's culture, having developed an early bond with craftsmen and artists in their villages, on occasion even traveling with them. It gave her an understanding of the need to preserve the cultural heritage of her adopted country, which natives might take for granted. India has at least eight million artisans, the largest skills base of craftsmen left in the world. Many of them are women and from the poorer sections of society. Those who have worked in the field with her say that Sonia's early days visiting rural India instilled a passion in her that influenced Rajiv's ideas, such as the concept of national cultural center zones that cross state boundaries. Rajiv was also keen on cultural dissemination: taking art into village fairs or large grounds where people would congregate, rather than keeping it in air-conditioned urban halls. He wanted to promote the connection between all art forms, combining the visual with food and clothes, for instance. In 1986 seven cultural zone centers were set up by Rajiv's government. The North Central Zone center, for example, covers six states and concentrates on the preservation of dying art forms as well as tribal and folk craft skills. Alongside festivals and workshops, there are artist camps that encourage contemporary painters, handicraft fairs that coexist with seminars and story recitations, and theater workshops for disabled children that are organized to raise awareness and take the arts to the rural masses. The centers also search for new talent and award training courses in various art forms. Accessible, away from city centers to maintain close links with rural communities, many performances take place in public spaces and open areas, such as the large courtyards in front of the centers themselves (sometimes housed in large converted historic buildings), and in local villages.

In November 2010, opening an exhibition at the National Gallery of Modern Art in Delhi, Sonia recalled Indira Gandhi's words that the development of an individual was about attending to aesthetic and spiritual as well as material needs. She added, "Art, and particularly, public art, plays a vital role in this process. It improves taste and sensibility. It helps open new windows in our mind, freeing it from prejudice and narrowness."[4]

Though Sonia most often preferred to be in the background, even in the arts environment in which she felt comfortable, she would at times happily leapfrog into the front seat. Sonia and Rajiv were very involved in the Festival of India in the United States in 1985. At the Smithsonian Museum of Natural History in Washington, the American president's wife, Nancy Reagan, was to open the exhibition. She was escorted up through a secret entrance, via the back door and the kitchen. In the hall where the Festival of India was set up, Sonia told Mrs. Reagan all about the displays. Mirroring the way their two countries were now coming to see each other, the Gandhis and the Reagans had a friendly relationship: Photographs taken at a formal White House dinner show the two couples clearly at ease with each other. Setting off her silk sari, Sonia wore heavy drop earrings and a choker and carried a tasseled bag. While Indira had been distinctly unimpressed by Ronald Reagan's intellect,[5] the new generation of Gandhis had little time for such snobbery and was bridging gaps the older one could or would not. Upper-middle-class Indians were thrilled at seeing their leader and his gorgeous wife with statesmen and women on the world stage. They felt that Rajiv and Sonia represented them much better than some odd-looking, male figures from the past with strangely antiquated habits.

In 1985 Sonia and Rajiv flew to France for a state visit with several official functions on the agenda, including the joint inauguration of a yearlong Festival of India with President Mitterrand and his wife, Danielle. According to Dalip Mehta, then deputy head of mission for India in Paris, Sonia, Rajiv, and the children received a "truly grand reception that was accorded where the Mitterrands went out of their way to make it historic, often sweeping aside considerations of protocol." Sonia and Rajiv's gift to the French first couple was a baby elephant called Tara, which was presented, after the animal was taken up in a lift specially modified for her, on the first floor of the Eiffel Tower. Danielle Mitterrand became very fond of the elephant and visited her at the Zoo de Vincennes for many years.[6]

Rajiv, with Sonia at his side, was effective in the international arena. In 1985 at a Commonwealth Heads of Government meeting in Nassau, he was asked to take the lead in proposing economic sanctions against South Africa (he later famously battled British prime minister Margaret Thatcher on this topic). He also addressed the US Council on Foreign Relations and the United States Congress in Washington, saying, "India is an old country but a young nation, and like the young everywhere, we are impatient. I am young, and I too have a dream." He spoke to the United Nations Special Committee on Apartheid, and the UN General Assembly on its fortieth anniversary. In 1987 he returned to speak on two more occasions at the UN, and the same year he gave a talk at Harvard University. Rajiv traveled east, too, with Sonia, praising the "new scientific knowledge" of Japan (she had also accompanied Rajiv's mother there in 1982).

The family of a former Indian ambassador to Burma, Dr. I. P. Singh, recalls Sonia arriving for a reception on a visit with Rajiv in the late 1980s. Presented with a tray of freshly made juices, Sonia studied the options carefully: papaya, lime, orange, fresh mango, and coconut water, before choosing the last one; her husband selected lime juice. She complimented the ambassador's wife on her high-quality silk brocade sari[7] and something else she noticed as soon as she entered the diplomatic residence: Tanjore paintings, representing an ancient South Indian school of art, usually executed on wood panels and often inlaid with semiprecious and precious stones or even gold.

An aide recalls a time when the couple was passing through Prague, and Sonia suggested that she would like to see the city: She had always wanted to do so but did not want to have to do so with all the usual protocol. The Czechs did their best, and she succeeded in touring all the places that she wanted to see, just like a normal visitor. The chauffeur-cum-tourist guide who accompanied her seemed to be receiving some deference from the police wherever they went, but Sonia apparently dismissed it from her mind. When she got back to India, she discovered that the head of the security forces in Czechoslovakia was actually her driver. The Czechs had very subtly ensured that she got what she wanted while ensuring that there was no danger to her person or her property.

The new leading-power couple was able to establish enjoyable and excellent relationships with leaders across the globe. According to one aide, there was a fair amount of electricity in the air when Rajiv was with Margaret Thatcher. Closer to home, they established a very good rapport with the Gorbachevs. Rajiv made his first state visit to the USSR in 1985; Sonia described the relationship between Gorbachev and Rajiv Gandhi as "enduring and fruitful. . . ."[8] Rajiv also visited two countries with which India had issues—Pakistan, where he developed a positive connection with Benazir Bhutto, and China, which received its first Indian prime minister in 34 years when Sonia and her husband met with Deng Xiaoping in December 1988. Sonia was always with Rajiv while he was building relationships with power-states—communist and capitalist alike—though India remained resolutely nonaligned with any one power bloc.

Yasser Arafat was a particularly close friend of Rajiv. The relationship had crossed generations as Arafat and Indira had shared a warm friendship. When Arafat and his men were being shelled by the Syrian army in Tripoli, Lebanon, in 1983, she telephoned Damascus, urging President Hafez Al-Assad to cease fire and allow the Palestinians to leave through Syria. Her request was denied, so she sent a message through Arafat's envoy that he must make contact with Europe. "Tell him that India loves him," she had said.[9] She also sent a warning for Arafat to be wary of those around him, to protect himself as many sought to kill him. He would later try to return the favor to her son. The following year in New Delhi, Arafat stood in sorrow, saluting the slain Indian leader after her state funeral.

The fact that the Gandhis could shake hands with leaders of different persuasions right across the globe, and that their own circle was completely eclectic, threw into relief one dark aspect of their own country. Communalism, the exploitation of religious feeling for electoral advantage, is as abhorrent to Sonia as it was to Rajiv. His stand against communalism can be linked directly to later views of hers on the subject, notably in the case of the demolition of a mosque in north India by Hindu fundamentalists. Another link to the time of Rajiv is Sonia's passion for nongovernmental organizations: "Rajiv greatly valued the initiative and commitment" of these groups, . . . he was particularly appreciative of those who worked for the disabled and the deprived," she wrote in her photo-memoir.[10]

The symbiosis that developed during these years, when the line between the ideas of Sonia and Rajiv became blurred, gave rise to the mission that drives her now. Nongovernmental think tanks she set up are the children of Rajiv's legacy and are responsible for taking forward the ideas and policies of social inclusion that the fathers of India's independence dreamed of. In this period, Sonia felt that she and her husband were building so much together, personally and politically, but always, lurking at the back of her mind, was the fear of an assassination attempt on her husband. Deep down, she knew that they were living on borrowed time.

14

SHADOW OF DEATH

> Carrying cyanide on one's person is a symbolic expression of our commitment, our determination. . . . In reality this gives our fighters an extra measure of belief in the cause, a special edge.
>
> —*Tamil Tiger leader V. Prabhakaran*

It was October 2, 1986, the anniversary of the birth of Mahatma Gandhi. Sonia and Rajiv were on their way to a prayer meeting at his cremation site by the Yamuna river in Delhi, the landscaped ground in the area known as Raj Ghat, or the court of the king, where memorials to Indira and other significant Indian nationals were built. The president and other important officials who always appear on these occasions were following.[1] Among them was one uninvited guest: Hiding in a thicket was an athletic-looking gunman with a 12-bore revolver. Dressed in army fatigues, he was lying on his stomach on top of the 8-foot-high canopy of a concrete shelter. He had been waiting there for several nights.

Sonia was still in constant fear of an attack on her husband, and she had good grounds for her instincts—she knew that he was never fully protected. At Raj Ghat, security sweeps had taken place on the ground and on top of adjacent buildings, but there was no helicopter surveillance prior to or during the arrival of Rajiv and Sonia. Anyone hiding in a thicket would go undetected by sniffer dogs, which were trained to sniff out explosives only. On this day, commandos, armed policemen, plainclothes officers, and security guards lined the wall of the open ground. No one saw Karamjit Singh, the man who was planning to murder Sonia's husband, or the camouflaged shelter he had built using sticks and polyethylene. He had a jerry-can with water in it, a green blanket, toothpaste, mosquito repellant, medicines, castor oil, and a religious novel.[2] The gunman looked out over the cremation site, his revolver aimed and ready, just under 30 feet from Rajiv and Sonia.

It was a solemn, ceremonial occasion commemorating the revered leader, Mahatma Gandhi, whose life had been terminated by another gunman who had bowed respectfully before shooting the Mahatma point-blank in this same city. That assassin had belonged to a right-wing Hindu group.

The prime minister's car arrived, and the couple got out. Singh got ready to pull the trigger. "As we walked into the Raj Ghat memorial . . . a shot was fired in our direction," Sonia wrote in her photo-memoir of her husband. Rajiv put his hands together in the air as if to give thanks for not being hit.[3] Sonia, the media, and the commandos, who were supposed to form the inner security ring, were all startled. Rajiv asked one of the personal security officers to find out what had happened. "We were told that the noise was that of a scooter backfiring."[4] The couple carried on with the ceremony.

Standing by Rajiv's side with her hands folded in respect and homage to the father of the nation, Sonia bent her head forward in contemplation at the memorial before sitting down for the prayer meeting. Around 8:10 AM, Rajiv and Sonia left the enclosure by the memorial and headed back toward the gates. "It was yet another opportuntity for me to take aim and fire one more shot at him," Karamjit Singh said later. On hearing fresh gunfire, there was chaos; everyone ran helter-skelter. "While Rajivji was running, I fired a third shot aiming at his head."[5] Around six people walking with Rajiv and Sonia were hit by bullet shrapnel; the personal security officer to Sonia's right was grazed on the forehead.[6] Commandos immediately encircled Rajiv.

The gunman had missed his target, and surprised security personnel started shooting randomly into the bush, risking the destruction of any evidence connected with the assassination attempt. Singh, who had been within the second ring of security surrounding the prime minister and his wife, put his arms up, surrendered, and was given a good thrashing by the police before being taken away for interrogation. Panic and fear set in among those gathered at Raj Ghat, and a WTN cameraman who caught the whole incident on film was asked to erase his footage by an overzealous senior police official. The shock set in among the crowd, but Rajiv stayed calm. Despite the fact that Sonia's nightmares were very nearly realized, she and Rajiv continued the day's program. Whisked off in a car, they went on to the memorial of former prime minister Lal Bahadur Shastri, which was nearby.[7] One of Rajiv's aides said that Rajiv then asked Sonia to go home while he continued with the rest of the day's program and advised the president of India to send his family to safety as well. Later, speaking quietly to the aide en route to Mahatma Gandhi's headquarters in the southern state of Maharashtra, Rajiv told him that he had wanted to make sure Sonia was protected and that the family was not exposed to further risk. He and the president continued with their itinerary to avoid any sense of panic in the country and to show that the assassination attempt had not succeeded. That day, armed policemen took up positions at all the sensitive locations in the city. It emerged that the gunman was a 26-year-old Sikh from the portion of the community that still harbored resentment against the Gandhi family for the storming of the Golden Temple in 1984. Notwithstanding the assassination of Rajiv's mother barely two years earlier, glaring holes in security procedures had again been exposed and were criticized in the media. Rajiv's own relative who was responsible for security was immediately suspended. Although this time an assassination was averted, somewhere along Rajiv's path there would be the watchful eyes of those who wished to kill him. As a safety precaution, since the time when violence and unrest in various parts of the country had started to escalate, the prime minister had been given bulletproof vests to wear for protection. With temperatures on his trips varying from subtropical to freezing, Rajiv found them uncomfortable and constraining. His aide observed him often struggling to get into one prior to descending the steps of his plane or helicopter or to going out and about, but said that after a while he wore one only where the threat assessment was particularly high, such as in the Punjab and in Sri Lanka.

In Sri Lanka, the small island near to the southern tip of India, there was an ongoing conflict that had major repercussions for India. The 2.5 million ethnic Tamil minority, mainly concentrated at the north and the east of the island, sought independence from the Sinhala majority. The Tamils had more linguistic and racial affinity with the 55 million Tamils of the southernmost Indian state of Tamil Nadu than with the island's Sinhalese, from whom their militant leaders wanted to establish separation in identity, language, and culture.

An armed faction of the Tamils, the Liberation Tigers of Tamil Eelam (LTTE), was led by Vellupilai Prabhakaran. Following the Maoist theory of power emanating from the barrel of a gun, he formed units of committed, highly trained guerilla fighters capable of deadly warfare on land and at sea. At its height, the LTTE was the most potent terrorist organization in the world. An LTTE fighter would routinely carry an AK-47, strap grenades to his waist, and wear a necklace with a glass cyanide capsule. The cyanide was meant to be swallowed if the Tamil Tiger was threatened with imminent capture; a Tiger caught alive by the enemy was condemned by his fellow fighters. They were willing not just to fight and to kill, but also to sacrifice their own lives for the cause of an independent state. A cadre of Black Tigers or Panthers (who would don black armbands on the eve of their assigned operation) volunteered for the task of suicide missions. One of the thousand or so Black Tigers was a man with a glass eye; one of his aliases was Sivarajan, but Indian detectives would refer to him as One-Eyed Jack.

The Tigers received logistical support, arms, money, and refuge from some in Tamil Nadu, and with the Sri Lankan government engaged in fierce armed conflict with the rebels, Tiger and non-Tiger Tamil refugees flooded onto the mainland. In the Indian state, a hotbed of sympathizers was soon incubating. Consolidated into a powerful network of intelligence, munitions stores, and safe houses, by the mid-1980s it was a solid rear base for Tamil Tigers fighting in Sri Lanka. The deluge of refugees into India was looking as though it could escalate to the level of the 1971 exodus of Bangladeshis, who fled to safety in India during that war. It was a big problem.

Rajiv wanted to promote stability in Sri Lanka and head off a possible crisis by providing potential refugees with "no urgent reason to move,"[8] so he sent fishing vessels with relief items to Tamil areas blockaded by the Sri Lankan army. The ships were turned back by the Sri Lankan navy. In early June 1987 he ordered a series of transport planes, escorted by fighter aircraft, to drop a healthy amount of supplies into Tamil areas. A humanitarian gesture, it was an effort to provide support to the Tamils in a nonviolent way and also demonstrated some Indian muscle in the region.

Such measures contributed to the formulation of the Indo-Sri Lanka Agreement signed on July 29, 1987, by Rajiv Gandhi and the president of Sri Lanka, Junius Richard Jayawardene.[9] It was a pact designed to provide the Tamils with what they wanted within the framework of a unified Sri Lanka, and it was hoped that the agreement would end the conflict on the island. But whatever was done by India in Sri Lanka, one side or the other was always going to be annoyed. In this case some of the majority Sinhalese, fearing the erosion of their privileges, became disgruntled. Sonia was with Rajiv in Sri Lanka for the signing of the pact, and, as with all official visits, there were ceremonial duties for the couple to perform on the last day of the trip, July 30, 1987, in Colombo, capital of the island republic. Sonia, in a beige patterned sari, stood under a red awning with the president of Sri Lanka, his wife, and other officials while Rajiv, against the advice of some of his own civil servants, went to review the first row of a farewell guard of honor in the bright sun in front of the presidential palace. Rajiv was near the end of the line of the white-uniformed, rifle-bearing Sri Lankan naval ratings, when one of them reversed his rifle, striking him with the butt. "As

I walked past one person at one point of time, I saw through the corner of my left eye, some movement and I saw a reverse gun coming up. . . . He missed my head and the brunt of the blow came on my shoulder below the left ear,"[10] he told reporters later on the flight home with Sonia.

Rajiv did not allow himself to be deflected. He continued with the inspection and the final formalities, including a group photograph, just a few minutes later. An anxious Sonia stood awkwardly between her husband and the president's wife, her face tense, the upper part of her body straining forward and her neck at an angle. Her hands were clenched together while nearly everyone else had theirs at their sides.[11] The president, his wife, and even Rajiv were smiling. A security officer stood right next to Rajiv, who continued with the ceremonial function and received medical attention only when they were in the air. On the plane, he told his high commissioner for Sri Lanka that "the character tried to kill me!"[12] as he took off his bulletproof jacket and showed his deep-blue bruises. Rajiv could not sleep on his left side or move his shoulder too freely for a while after the incident.[13]

Since July 30, 1987, 3,000 (the number would later rise to more than 70,000) Indian peacekeeping troops deployed across Sri Lanka's northern Jaffna peninsula, responding to a formal and specific request from the Sri Lankan government invoking Indian commitments and obligations according to the July 29 agreement.[14] Though the Indian forces were initially sent to help maintain peace, they soon lost their shield of neutrality and found themselves fighting against the Tamil Tigers in what would turn into a two-year confrontation between the Indian Peace Keeping Force (IPKF) and the LTTE. Deep in the forests of northern Sri Lanka, surrounded by his guerrillas, the Tamil leader Prabhakaran began plotting revenge against Rajiv Gandhi. By October 1990, his carefully laid plans to have the former Indian prime minister murdered were falling neatly into place.

All prime ministers have their share of enemies—colleagues disgruntled at not having been given what they thought was their due or political opponents on the lookout for the exploitable moment. Corruption is part of the Indian political landscape, and Rajiv, always seen as India's Mr. Clean, suffered from an accusation that refused to go away. Rajiv wanted to equip India's armed services so that they could defend the country's borders with vigor and was particularly keen that the long coastline should be well protected. While India was one of the globe's most prolific producers of intermediate-range missiles and mostly used home-manufactured weapons (the country was the largest arms maker in the developing world), some items, like the long-range field gun, needed to be bought abroad. A Swedish company, Bofors, won the contract, but in 1987 Swedish radio broadcast an allegation that commercial bribes had helped the company win the deal. Though Rajiv's government immediately refuted the story, his opponents made huge capital out of it. Rajiv continued to deny any wrongdoing, but the media accused him of not moving fast enough to kill the rumors.

Later, he reflected that he and his team could have handled the matter better, especially since the contract had been a good one, obtained at a low rate: "And so we opened up and said, we'll have an inquiry and we were quite frank. But the more frank we were, the more of a mess we got into."[15] Though parliament was stalled for a while amid cantankerous shouting from the opposition benches on the subject, no legal culpability was ever attached to Rajiv and his family. This was confirmed in 2004, when a Delhi high court judge ruled, after 16 years of investigation by the Central Bureau of Investigation, that there was no evidence of involvement in the deal by the former prime minister. Sonia commented that after the years of "abuse and vilification," it was a "special moment" and that she hoped that "the people who caused [Rajiv] so much pain" would now "rethink the falsehoods they spread about him."[16]

The problem with corruption allegations—a problem exploited by opponents to the hilt in India—is that long after the detail is forgotten, the headlines—or even just the subject—remain in the collective memory, and the *perception* of possible corruption can do harm electorally. It certainly dented the image of Rajiv's government at the time. Rajiv was under pressure as there were also vested interests who were supposed to be on his side of the political divide, power brokers who wanted to kill his vision of reducing the bloated bureaucracy and opening up the economy. He became distanced from some former friends and colleagues, like Arun Nehru, and even, many observed, from the ordinary Indian, as the strains of office began to tell on him.[17]

In 1987 a series of legalistic religious disputes gave way to outbreaks of Hindu-Muslim violence. Rajiv called an election toward the end of 1989, and during the campaign the interreligious strife reached a horrific level—particularly in the state of Bihar, where more than 1,000 Muslims were killed and more than 20,000 were left homeless. Sonia, with Priyanka at her side, concentrated on Rajiv's constituency of Amethi during the election. It meant many days of work, but in politics as in all matters, the family was united and pulled up its collective sleeves. While Priyanka accompanied Sonia, Rahul was with Rajiv, gaining valuable on-the-road campaign experience at 19 years of age.

The years and effort Sonia had put into working with constituents paid off. Although he lost the general election, Rajiv was elected by his constituency in Amethi again. Maneka Gandhi campaigned hard and won a constituency called Pilibhit near Rajiv's in Uttar Pradesh. Congress gained enough seats to make it the largest single party but needed others to form a government; the selection of groups open to a coalition would still not be enough. So the winner of the second largest number of seats, the Janata Dal party, formed the government. It was led by Vishwanath Pratap Singh, who had once been a minister in Rajiv's cabinet and who had resigned over implacable disagreements between the two. Maneka Gandhi gained a ministerial berth in V. P. Singh's government, one of four posts she held at that rank. She won Pilibhit five times over, handing it to her son, Varun, also now with the BJP, to fight for and win in 2009.

Her sister-in-law, Sonia, now wife to the leader of the opposition, found that life became less pressured. Yet the stream of visitors remained constant enough for Rajiv to tell a magazine reporter that he sometimes felt like taking a break from the political world. On February 5, 1990, Sonia and her family moved to 10 Janpath, which is where she lives now. Smaller than the Race Course Road house, it has a similar colonial design to other buildings in the area. She spent 16 happy months there with Rajiv. In June, Rahul left for the United States to study economics at Harvard, after spending a year reading history at St. Stephen's College, which was—like Jesus and Mary, the college where Priyanka studied psychology—part of Delhi University. During 1990 Christian von Stieglitz, the person who had introduced Rajiv and Sonia to one another in Cambridge, visited India and took a photograph of the couple that reveals how close and relaxed they were: nestled warmly against each other, at rest in the garden. At the end of that year, Sonia and the family spent a few days at their farmhouse in Mehrauli. It was the only time they were all there together.

Caste violence increased around this time with disputes over social-status-based job quotas; at least one man tried to set himself on fire as feelings heightened. Clashes and attacks were centered around Delhi and eastern states like Uttar Pradesh, known as the Hindi-speaking belt. This, in a homogenous country where major religions were born (Hinduism, Buddhism, Jainism, and Sikhism) and other enormously important faiths were brought by settlers (Islam, Christianity, Judaism, and Zoroastrianism). Meanwhile, Sonia mingled freely with the ordinary Indian, gaining insight into how politics and policies can adversely affect people at the grassroots level. In October 1990 she and Rajiv ventured on a pilgrimage of goodwill, an old tradition, through the streets of Delhi to promote peace between religious communities. It was Mahatma Gandhi's birthday again, and the crowds were so thick that it took nearly seven hours to cover six miles.

While Sonia had reluctantly settled for the fact that her time alone with Rajiv was almost nonexistent, their aching need to escape the spotlight was at times unbearable. Sonia was working in Amethi in February 1991, and their wedding anniversary, February 25, which they had always spent together, was approaching. Rajiv sent a message to Sonia that he would be going on official business to Tehran and wanted her to join him. "I feel like [being] with you, only you and I, the two of us alone, without two hundred people about us." They traveled on February 24, and at midnight Rajiv gave Sonia the anniversary present that he had brought with him from Delhi. Rajiv had official duties all day on February 25, but they were able go out to a restaurant that evening, an event that had not happened for a very long time. When they came back to their hotel room, Rajiv took out his camera and took a self-timed photograph of the two of them, something that he had never done before.[18]

A period of two unstable governments led to a general election being called in April 1991. For Sonia, this was again a time when she was needed to provide support as well as hard-core constituency campaign work. She was so familiar and loved in this part of rural Uttar Pradesh by now that when Rajiv filed his nomination papers, local Congress workers loudly called for Sonia to stand for Indira's former seat, Rae Bareli[19] next door—something everyone knew Sonia could now handle if she wished to. Her husband, too, "was very keen" that Sonia fight an election in her own right, but she flatly refused.[20] Rajiv threw himself with gusto into his campaign, wanting to reverse public perceptions of him and freely admitting to journalists that he had learned from his past mistakes—a humility not normally found in more dyed-in-the-wool politicians. He gave the media plenty of access, and he worked hard at the campaign, covering 600 national and state constituencies by plane, helicopter, and car, promising a program of government stability and law and order to counteract the growing violence around him. The approaching Gulf War had sent the price of oil rocketing, and the economy was in poor health. Rajiv, with renewed energy and vigor after a year and a half of introspection while in the opposition, talked of economic reform and began to win over the electorate; the upper and middle classes were enthused and excited. Editors who had been disappointed with his performance predicted a comeback for him. Those who had lost hope began to believe in the Nehru-Gandhis once again.

Rajiv launched his campaign by flying himself and Sonia into Amethi in a light propeller aircraft on May 1, 1991. He had always been very physical with people, but this time around, he went at it with even more gusto—determined to shake off past criticism and present a new, better Rajiv. He was so keen to be accessible to the crowds that he would engage in a little bit of pantomime when they surged forward and surrounded his jeep. As the police tried to push the hordes back, Rajiv would pretend to get angry with his gatekeepers and play-fight with them using mock-blows to the wild cheering of the masses. When asked whether he was concerned about his safety, Rajiv told a magazine reporter that he always trusted the ordinary Indian and could not afford to keep worrying about it as he needed to "live life." Two personal security officers rotated duties so that one of them accompanied him in public.

In the forests of Sri Lanka, Prabhakaran, the Tamil Tiger leader, had his plans for assassination well advanced and had recruited his key players. Through his highly effective intelligence network, more precise than any opinion poll, he was tracking the likely outcome of the Indian general election and the possible consequences for his Tamil Tigers. It seemed most likely that Rajiv Gandhi would win. This might mean a reintroduction of the IPKF in Sri Lanka and certainly a crackdown on the LTTE infrastructure in Tamil Nadu. If Rajiv Gandhi was to be neutralized, he thought, then it had to be done while he was in opposition and his security was at its weakest. Once he returned to power, it would be much more difficult to kill him. Prabhakaran's scouts were watching Rajiv's movements; they found that his rallies and meets outside Delhi left him the most exposed. The elaborate Tiger network in Tamil Nadu was already in place, so in November 1990 Prabhakaran called in four of his trusted lieutants and instructed them on their mission. One, Baby Subramaniyam, was the owner of a printing press that published LTTE literature; he was tasked with preparing a backup team and safe accommodations for the assassins. The second man, Muthuraja, was to prepare a base in Madras (now Chennai), the capital of Tamil Nadu, for communication and courier facilities and to provide money for the killers. The third was Murugan, an instructor and explosive expert, and the fourth was Sivarajan, the Black Tiger who was assigned the actual murder.

By the beginning of 1991, the plan was in motion. The LTTE press owner had sold his printing company and premises, which could also serve as a hideout, at a ridiculously low price to a Tamil family in dire need. The mother of this poor family was a nurse, her son a political activist, and her daugher, Nalini Sriharan, a secretary. Nalini was persuaded to help her brother run the printing press and immediately became exposed to LTTE propaganda, which was heavily anti-Rajiv Gandhi. She was tasked with working on a book, a compilation of photographs, news reports of alleged misdemeanors of the IPKF, and negative stories about the government of the former prime miniser. Soon she was completely indoctrinated. The second LTTE insider needed to find a photographer and identified Haribabu, who was indebted to the Tigers as they had paid him well for previous assignments.

Safe houses and converts to the heinous cause were now all in place. Simultaneously, an electronics expert was asked to start to improvise an explosive made of grenades that could be detonated by a suicide bomber. Sivarajan, who was also an explosives specialist, examined the design for the human bomb and pronounced it satisfactory. Returning to Jaffna in northern Sri Lanka, he briefed Prabhakaran, who asked for a photographic record of the actual assassination—the Tigers maintained a gruesome visual archive of their most important murders.

Sivarajan brought two girl assassins, his cousins Dhanu and Shubha, back to Madras. They were already trained and ready to die for their cause, being shadow squad members of the Tamil Tigers. Then he explained the specifics of the bomb he required to the explosives expert. He wanted one that could be hidden under clothes and around the waist of a female. A belt bomb was designed so that grenades, placed in a series around the belt, could be connected with silver wire. Two toggle switches completed the circuit, and a 9mm battery charged the device. Blue denim heavy enough to support the two-pound explosive was used to carry it.[21]

Despite the years in public life, Sonia had never gotten used to the fact that Rajiv was always going to be at risk given the tensions in the politics of the subcontinent. She found it hard to come to terms with this stress point. She told a television interviewer 15 years later, "Both my children and I—when he'd go out in the morning, we were never quite sure if he would come back in the evening."[22] They would spend time together on the campaign trail but could enjoy little privacy. On April 24, Rajiv and his wife stood in an open-top car, Sonia gazing pensively into the distance as hordes crowded round, their hands reaching up to garland Rajiv. Sonia stood completely still, always looking in the right direction, yet her eyes had a faraway appearance.[23] It is a reminder of Indira, who had the capacity to temporarily enter her own space; an associate observed a silent gaze that would appear in the middle of meetings.

Rajiv and Sonia decided to split the campaign work; she had accumulated so much experience by this time that she could well handle the constituency on her own. Rajiv told Amethi voters that from then on, Sonia would be taking care of them while he would take care of the rest of the country. (Tragically, the first part of these last words he would ever say to them was prophetic.) There was now a strong bond between Sonia and Amethi's residents; they viewed her as one of their own, often referring to her as a daughter-in-law. She planned to spend three weeks campaigning there, the longest time she and Rajiv would ever have spent apart. On April 28, Rajiv and Priyanka saw Sonia off from Safdarjang airport.

Before he left Delhi for his tour, he sent his wife a rose with a note of affection attached. Sonia and her husband spoke on the telephone only once during the first week of her stay in Amethi. After that, her staff back home in Delhi gave her secondhand news of Rajiv, as did Priyanka when she joined her mother to canvass in the constituency. Sonia finished the Amethi leg and returned to Delhi on May 17, a day before Rajiv. When he returned he was exhausted, having spent up to 24 hours a day campaigning. He could hardly speak or walk. Always completely engaged with the masses, he gave himself to them to hold, to hug, to kiss, to shake hands, and to pat with affection and a great deal of vigor. They would pinch his cheeks. Occasionally, a baby would be handed to him to name. Rajiv, like his party, wanted to come back victorious and he was giving it everything. His hands were swollen and scratched; his body had bruises. The fierce desire for physical contact was not just one way, either; one journalist who had known Rajiv for a number of years said that when they were walking together, Gandhi would maintain a firm grip on his hand for as long as 300 feet—he'd have to ask him to let it go.[24] Rajiv did not mind his aching body, for it mattered more to him to feel the visceral affection of the public. He told Sonia about his tour and she spoke of what had been happening in his constituency. With the hectic campaign in its last phase, Sonia was starting to feel a sense of hope and relief. She and Priyanka were happy, expecting good election results, and Rahul would be coming home from the United States for the summer holidays. The family would be together again.

On May 20, 1991, in Delhi, Sonia and Rajiv went to the polling station at 7:30 AM, and she fretted over not finding the right tick box to cast her vote for her husband on the lengthy ballot paper with its numerous names. Sonia recalled that Rajiv had laughed and "held my hand with that gentle, reassuring touch which had always helped to dispel any feeling of anxiety or hurt."[25]

Rajiv was off on tour canvassing and was due to return to Delhi that afternoon in order to change from a helicopter to a plane to fly east then south, allowing him to cover three states on May 21. The last stop was a small town to support a candidate in Tamil Nadu. On the same day they cast their votes, Rajiv came back home around 4:15 PM to the Janpath house to spend a few precious minutes with his family. He wished his son well for an upcoming test over the telephone, and bade farewell to Priyanka. Sonia expected to see him in just two days, on May 22. The campaign would end May 24. In her photo-memoir she recalled, "I watched him . . . till he disappeared from view."[26] It was the last time Sonia would see her husband alive. She had been with Rajiv for 26 years, 23 of those in marriage.

PART IV

A BROKEN DYNASTY

15

THE LAST POST

> Living under terrorist threat . . . has never really bothered me; I've not let it interfere with my functioning or my thinking . . . if it comes to having to die for what you believe in—I don't hesitate.
>
> —*Rajiv Gandhi*

In the southern state of Tamil Nadu, Sivarajan, the Black Tiger charged with killing Rajiv Gandhi, had everyone and everything in place—a complete assassination squad, operators to support it, and several facilitators. The mastermind planner and head of the Tamil Tigers, Vellupilai Prabhakaran, now told him to test the physical logistics of his plan with a few dry runs. Sivarajan and some of the squad had already observed an April election rally headlined by Rajiv Gandhi in Madras. Noticing how journalists were always given close access to political speakers, Sivarajan decided that if he were disguised as one, it would help him get near enough to make sure that the Indian opposition leader was killed—by the human bomber Dhanu or by Sivarajan himself with a hidden pistol.

At their next dry run, the night of May 7, the rally was for another former prime minister. The squad was able to see how close to the potential victim it could get: Dhanu even managed to garland the chief speaker.[1] Sivarajan was caught on camera in a front-row press seat pretending to be a journalist (but without a notepad) less than 20 feet away from the stage, assessing security loopholes and signaling in silent code to his team with seemingly normal hand gestures. Because he could see only through his right eye, he swiveled and turned his head unnaturally. Noticing a real journalist writing in a notebook, he added that prop in for the next rehearsal on May 19,[2] so that he and his accomplices were completely ready for the main event. They were eager for it to happen as soon as possible—time was running out.

On the morning of May 20, 1991, in the house of one of his recruits, Nalini Sriharan, Sivarajan reexamined Rajiv Gandhi's election event schedule. The best opportunity for his squad was the last rally, set for May 21 in a small town called Sriperumbudur. His team assembled at Nalini's house and relaxed and watched a film that evening. Dhanu tried on her explosive belt as well as the glasses she would wear to conceal her features, which were too Sri Lankan to go unnoticed in a mainland state. She would become known as one of the world's earliest human bombers and the first to use a belt bomb (letter and transistor explosive devices had been popular terrorist currency hitherto).

On May 21, Rajiv had a three-state tour, the first in Orissa and the second in Andhra Pradesh in the south, north of and adjacent to Tamil Nadu. A ham radio enthusiast, he made a call between election rallies at Visakhapatnam, a coastal city in Andhra Pradesh. Visibility was starting to drop to a dangerous level, and the airport at Andhra Pradesh was bereft of night flight facilities, so he almost canceled the last part of the day's schedule in Tamil Nadu. It would mean postponing the program to the next day or scrapping it altogether. Suddenly, however, visibility improved and the original plan was back on; they were running only an hour late, not much during an election campaign.

En route for the deadly encounter with Rajiv Gandhi, on May 21 the photographer, Haribabu, was waiting near a bus stand with a sandalwood garland—a prop for Dhanu. At 4:30 PM he was joined by the other four members of the assassination squad for the bus trip to Sriperumbudur, where they arrived around 8. At the rally site, Haribabu, when questioned by a woman police subinspector, Anushya Kumari, told her that he was there to photograph Dhanu garlanding Rajiv Gandhi. He was immediately admitted to the press enclosure. Subinspector Kumari told Nalini Sriharan and another squad member, Shubha, to sit down as they were early. Sivarajan and Dhanu, wearing a shoulder bag, took up their positions along with others near the stage. When Rajiv arrived, he was mobbed; one party worker grabbed him so tightly he winced. Dhanu was held back by Kumari, but Rajiv said, "Let everybody get a chance." So the subinspector moved away, and Dhanu, having divested herself of her shoulder bag, closed in, bowed, and triggered the bomb. The blast was so powerful it not only killed Rajiv; it actually launched someone near him onto the canopy above the stage. Seventeen others died in all; body parts of many of the slain were found quite some distance from the explosion. The assassin's head was severed from her body and was hurled 65 feet away in the blast, to be recovered later more or less intact along with some limbs that were immediately assembled for evidence.[3]

Nalini and Shubha quickly walked to a bus stand and were joined by Sivarajan, who confirmed that Rajiv, Dhanu, and Haribabu had perished. But Haribabu's camera had been left at the site, and detectives soon recovered it. The ten photographs it contained provided vital evidence to the investigating team.[4] Nalini Sriharan and Murugan, by whom the former was now more than eight weeks pregnant, were arrested on June 14. In August 1991, tracked down to a house and surrounded by members of the Special Investigation Team, Sivarajan shot himself with his pistol; other Tiger suspects on the run with him bit into and swallowed their glass cyanide capsules, dying within minutes.

Over approximately 11 months, around 26 accused were rounded up and interrogated. Documentary evidence, wireless transmissions, and video footage were scrutinized. The LTTE and Prabhakaran were implicated. Four of those involved in the assassination, including Nalini Sriharan, were ultimately sentenced to death; the others received various jail terms.

Rajiv's death was the most devastating of the three Sonia had experienced in the Nehru side of the family. Yet she now had to lead, to handle the proceedings, and only managed it with the support of her equally devastated children. Rahul was 21; Priyanka was 19. Although Rajiv had been leader of the opposition, a panoply of world leaders attended his funeral. Those in Sonia and Rajiv's closest circle, friends and family, had to improvise and do their best to cope first with an unexpected tragedy and then with an unexpected number of mourners. Sonia, at the center of it all, had to respond immediately to console visitors, for Rajiv was virtually public property.

Rajiv lay in state at Teen Murti Bhavan. Sonia, the children, and close family sat on the floor to one side of the man they had all loved. After Indira was killed, her face could be seen by mourners, but Rajiv had had to be fully covered and his tall frame was now considerably reduced. His body was on a raised platform and a garlanded photograph of him stood at its head. He would remain draped with the Indian national flag until the time of his cremation when it would be removed.

Over two days, thousands of mourners filed slowly through the main hall of the home that Rajiv and Sanjay had lived in as children. The grand building where Indira had lain in state was once again filled with pain. Sonia, someone said, was like a fortress unto herself and for her family as she, Priyanka, and Rahul comforted one another while trying to deal with their individual devastation. One of the mourners who came to Teen Murti was Wajahat Habibullah. He had worked with Rajiv in the prime minister's office and was now commissioner for the state of Jammu and Kashmir, the conflict-ridden territory on India's border with Pakistan. The armed insurgency that had been raging since the late 1980s resulted in frequent clashes between Indian soldiers and militants, with civilians often caught in the crossfire. Habibullah, a high-profile Indian bureaucrat, had been a target for Kashmiri insurrectionists.

In April 1991 Wajahat had been shot at in Kashmir. Rajiv had telephoned his friend and said, "Wajahat, take care of yourself." Two days later the local Indian Airlines office had called him to say that they had a parcel for him from Mr. Rajiv Gandhi. When Wajahat opened the unexpected package, he found that Rajiv had sent him his own bulletproof vest. The commissioner, advised to move back to Delhi or else upgrade his personal security in view of the dangerous situation, decided to return to the capital "as the general expectation was that Rajiv would be back as prime minister. I hoped that if I came back to Delhi I'd be able to work with him again."[5]

On May 21 Wajahat's sister urgently telephoned him with news of the assassination. He immediately rushed to Delhi. Walking quietly into Teen Murti Bhavan's hall where Rajiv lay, he saw Sonia sitting on the floor, engulfed in grief but quite focused. "Her state of mind was not dislocated," he noticed, for she remembered that Rajiv's colleague and friend had also been attacked. "When I went toward her, I said, 'Madam, I'm so sorry.' She said, 'There was an attempt on your life. Rajiv was very worried about you. He sent you a bulletproof vest. Are you wearing it? I hope you're wearing it.'" Wajahat burst into tears. "She looked at me. She was obviously touched but didn't say anything. She didn't say, 'Get a hold of yourself.'" Years later Wajahat asked Sonia if she would like to have Rajiv's vest back, but she told him that he could keep it. He still has it.[6]

Sonia's primary concern was to make sure that her children did not collapse with the shock of the loss, and they had the same concern about their mother. It was the broken supporting the broken. Along with his wife, Sunil Nehru, from Rajiv's generation of the Nehru family,[7] joined the throng of grief-stricken people. "Rahul and Priyanka . . . were red eyed and drawn, but composed, solemn and dignified. Our hearts went out to them."[8]

While Sonia and her children were experiencing the most profound tragedy of their lives, some were concerned with their own political futures—even as they cried and commiserated in public. Rajiv's assassination left the Congress Party without a president; a new one would have to be appointed. Some worried that a headless Congress machine would now start pulling Sonia toward it in order to save itself. The sharks were waiting to pounce, someone noted, and Sonia had to figure out how to fend them off. Several people with eyes on the prime minister's job assumed that the party was now up for grabs, mistakenly thinking that the force of the Nehrus was extinguished forever.

It was not. Though Sonia was distraught, there was no thought of her ever abandoning her adopted country—going back to Italy was never an option. Priyanka had been fully educated in India, and Rahul had been predominantly educated there. The futures of all three lay in India—they were firmly and absolutely rooted in the Nehru-Gandhi homeland. It was the *only* place they called home. Sonia's subsequent actions would reinforce this view.

On May 24, the day of the cremation, the doors of Teen Murti Bhavan were closed for the family to say a private farewell. Afterward, Rajiv's body was placed on a pall, and Priyanka bent to touch her father's feet in reverence. Sonia, standing nearby and watching quietly, became tearful.[9] Still standing where a rose and jasmine garland had been placed, Priyanka said a silent prayer before moving next to her mother. From then on, she would be at Sonia's side whenever and for as long as she was needed. Mother and daughter leaned into each other, sharing a private moment of grief among the jam-packed throng. The bier was carried out of Teen Murti House by Rahul, close male family members, including some from Sonia's side, and friends.

Rajiv's body, placed on the same gun carriage that had been used to carry the bodies of Jawaharlal and Indira, was to be taken to Indira's cremation area, Shakti Sthal, to be placed on a funeral pyre with formal prayers. When the bodies of Rajiv's brother and mother were taken to their cremation grounds, Sonia was able to rely on Rajiv for support. This time there were only her children—a somber-looking Rahul and a seemingly calm Priyanka, the strain showing on both their faces. Sonia would have to perform public rituals for the death of the man she loved most in the world even as she absorbed the shock of losing that man. As Rajiv's body was taken out of Teen Murti, Sonia was escorted to a car with Priyanka. She managed to hold back her tears until the cavalcade moved off. Then she removed her dark glasses with trembling hands to wipe her eyes. Commandos walked alongside the car with automatic weapons at the ready. At a corner along Duplex Road, they allowed the throngs lining the pavements to join the funeral procession, and there were cries in Hindi of "Sonia, we are with you!" and "Rajiv Gandhi lives!" The excited masses crowded her car, and Sonia had to close the darkened glass windows.[10] In the next vehicle, Rahul rode with family friend, film star Amitabh Bachchan; their car came to a halt as some near-hysterical members of the public climbed up and over the car in order to catch a glimpse of both men. In India, where horn-blowing is routine, the sirens of the VIP vehicles stuck in the convoy behind the Gandhi vehicles wailed incessantly. Eventually, commandos, plainclothes police, Congress Party workers, and constables managed to contain the hordes.

Sonia's car broke down at the central avenue, Rajpath, which runs from the presidential palace to the memorial at India Gate. When she got out with Priyanka and proceeded on foot toward an air force staff car, the crowds converged on the women, desperate for a glimpse of them. As the motorcade had only covered half the distance it was supposed to, the pace was sped up, and commandos and those on foot had to jog the rest of the way under the blazing sun. Undeterred and bathed in sweat, mourners ran alongside, holding onto trucks and buses where they could. By now, the crowd exceeded that of Indira Gandhi's funeral procession. The cars arrived at the cremation site an hour late.[11]

Rajiv's Doon School and Cambridge friend Dalip Mehta was chief of protocol at that time and handled the arrival of the visiting dignitaries. Toothbrush in his suit pocket, he rushed into action, greeting the influx of world leaders who flew in from May 23 on to pay homage. He was on duty from the moment they arrived until the moment their planes left India. Some, like Yasser Arafat, did not announce their flight details in advance due to security fears, which certainly did not ease the situation. Mehta and his protocol team slept at the airport "standing on our feet."[12] They were expecting around 20 heads of state for the funeral and were unprepared for the 64 who arrived. "It was unprecedented. Normally such people come to attend the funeral of the head of state or a head of government, but Rajiv was only the leader of the opposition. It reflected the kind of stature he had attained and the kind of affection in which people held him," Mehta said. With no precedent or handbook for such an event, he found the funeral traumatic. "You don't normally as chief of protocol come across such terrible experiences. . . . I had to improvise everything . . . it was very poignant. There was an extra dimension of sadness because it was an old school friend."

There was also concern for the coming years. Wajahat Habibullah, worried about India's political future and its trouble spots in particular, remarked to the then chief minister of Kashmir sitting next to him on a special bus for close friends and relations, "All hope is lost."

Heads of state, presidents, vice presidents, and members of royal families sat patiently at the cremation site. Prince Charles was in a white naval uniform with medals and ceremonial sword. Prince Alexander, the crown prince of Holland, was similarly attired. Rajiv and Sonia's friend the fourth king of Bhutan was there, as was the German vice chancellor. According to tradition on such occasions, everyone was sitting on the ground in reverence, nothing between them and the sky, so there was virtually no protection from the blistering heat. But, says Mehta, the prime minister, Chandra Shekhar, did allow chairs for the foreign dignitaries, some of whom were infirm, while others, like the British and Dutch princes, might have had difficulty sitting on the ground in their formal regalia.[13] US vice president Dan Quayle, Prime Minister Nawaz Sharif of Pakistan, and that country's leader of the opposition, Benazir Bhutto, all paid their respects at Teen Murti Bhavan in the morning and also were present at the cremation. Yasser Arafat cried copiously when he saw Rajiv's covered body. He told Sonia later that he had warned Rajiv of threats to his life. In the United States, the House of Representatives stood in silence as a mark of respect, and US secretary of state James Baker spoke of a "rapid expansion of ties" between the two countries that Rajiv Gandhi had helped produce during his premiership. George H. W. Bush said that the killing was "a sad thing," especially as he and his wife Barbara had developed a personal relationship with Rajiv and Sonia.[14]

There were many at the funeral who had special links with the Gandhis. Tariq Karim, Bangladesh's High Commissioner to Delhi, describes how Sheikh Hasina's presence symbolized her heart-rending connection with Sonia. "The ties that bind them together are the emotional bonds of personal loss. Sheikh Hasina lost her parents, her brothers, even one who was ten years old was brutally murdered. Sonia lost [Sanjay, then] her mother-in-law and then Rajiv in very tragic circumstances. This loss of very near and dear ones gives them the empathy to bond with each other."[15]

At Shakti Sthal, Sonia kept her large-rimmed sunglasses on most of the time, shielding her eyes from the world and affording her some privacy. Amitabh Bachchan walked behind her as she entered the cremation site on foot at 4:35 PM while a helicopter dropped rose petals on the gathering. Ten minutes later, Rajiv was brought to the pyre platform and placed to the northwest side of the pile of wood. At 4:50, Rahul, Bachchan, and some priests placed Rajiv's body on the pyre. Sonia, Priyanka, and an uncle of Rajiv, Gautam Kaul, watched. Hindu holy men were joined by a Parsi priest to conduct the ceremony. Five minutes later, Rahul began the rites, scattering rose petals and sprinkling drops of water from the sacred river Ganges on the body of his father.

At 5:13 PM, Rahul, then Sonia, then Priyanka sprinkled offerings onto the pyre and placed sandalwood logs around him. Sonia gave a circular piece of thread to her son to place over Rajiv's head and gave a string of rosary beads to Priyanka to lay on the wood pile. Rahul began the final rite, somberly walking around his father's body seven times with a burning torch in his hands. He was following the instructions Rajiv had set out in November 1985, when he and Sonia wrote down what the children should do in the event of their deaths. "Our bodies should be brought to Delhi and cremated together, in accordance with Hindu rites, in an open ground. . . . According to our custom, our eldest child Rahul should light the pyre. . . ."[16]

The Gandhi family kept a dignified silence throughout the whole ceremony, not showing any discomfort. Wajahat Habibullah noticed that "there were a number of relations and others who were about them who tried to show that they were the actual heirs of the whole legacy. But this family just didn't [react]. . . . They were not looking about, seeing who's who or anything like that. They focused entirely on their father, on Rajiv. It was a moment of deep grief and silence for them. They communed with each other and with their father as he lay on the funeral pyre."[17]

Sunil Nehru felt a great sense of foreboding and worried for his country. He remembers, "Rajiv was basically honest. With his going, [I] felt that the country's leadership would now be seized by lesser men, even perhaps men of the Hindu right."

Some members of the Congress Party were already jockeying for influential roles. "They tried to get the cameras on them, to make it appear as though they were the managers of the whole show, pushing people here and pushing people there and saying, 'No, don't come here, go there, go this way and that way,' even though they had not been particularly close to Rajiv himself. They were trying to project themselves as that because it was known that his party had won the election. They were using it as a stepping stone for future elevation," Habibullah said of some unseemly behavior he noticed around the pyre.

At 5:25 PM Rahul set his burning flame to the sandalwood pile on which his father rested. Three volleys of gunfire followed, and bugles played *The Last Post,* the Commonwealth homage to those fallen in war. Silently, the world leaders stood to pay tribute. Many of them could be seen wiping their eyes. At 5:28 PM, Rahul poured oil and water from the Ganges onto the pyre, causing flames and smoke to billow. Two minutes later, the broken Gandhi family walked around Rajiv for the last time. As the flames climbed, Sonia's body seemed to half collapse as she folded at the waist, unable to deny herself any more pain.

Rahul put his right hand on her shoulder in a steadying, comforting move, while she clung to his elbow with her left hand for support. It was a flashback to when his father comforted his mother seven years earlier at the cremation of his grandmother Indira.

Rajiv's close friends sat in misery and watched his remains go up in flames. After the funeral of Indira, young Rahul, with his big spectacles, had clung to his father, who had comforted him. He was gone now, and just Rahul, Sonia, and Priyanka were left to hold each other. With his death, an era characterized by an easygoing style, a free and open relationship with the media, and, above all, complete access to the public suddenly ended. Sonia moved through the funeral rituals once again. The political vultures had closed in on her husband, and now she became their target. The Congress Party drum was already beating at her door, demanding that she take over the presidency.

16

DEFYING THE PARTY

> The dynasty cult . . . lives on in the minds of Congressmen. . . . The motive of the coterie is becoming apparent: Raise a sympathy wave in favor of the widow, get into power, and grab the administration.
>
> —Business Standard, *Calcutta*

Amid the horror of her loss, Sonia was, much to her dismay, thrust into the political limelight. The assassination of Rajiv left the Congress Party without a president, and immediately party factions began to fight for supremacy. India was in the midst of a general election; the first day of polling had taken place May 20, but the rest of the voting days were suspended after Rajiv's murder. Widespread violence was feared, but the type of riots that had occurred after Indira's assassination were quickly prevented by the government declaring a state of high alert and calling out the army immediately in and around Delhi. Some who were overwrought expressed their emotion by throwing stones at Bharatiya Janata Party offices. Meanwhile, a special police team under the Central Bureau of Investigation was feverishly ferreting out the names behind Rajiv's grizzly murder. Within 24 hours of his death, the Congress Working Committee (the decision-making core of the party) unanimously elected Sonia to the post of party president without her permission.[1]

Pranab Mukherjee, then party spokesman, later a finance minister, told the media that state units supported the election. The ailing party was again desperate for a Nehru-Gandhi to lead it and wanted Sonia. Abroad and at home, the move by party barons was seen as a cynical effort by those close to the family to retain their power. While one of the reasons for the decision to install Sonia was to prevent an internecine leadership contest, Congress's rivals exultantly sneered at the move as a sign of "cold-blooded calculation" on the part of a bankrupt party. It was accused of being willing to flog the personal tragedy of the family for immediate electoral gains. One opposition leader asked why a party several decades old could not find someone who had participated in the freedom struggle to lead it. Privately, Congress's enemies were restive; another Nehru-Gandhi could further shore up a vote already likely to be sympathy-led in the wake of the assassination.

For Sonia, there was no question of any leadership role at this stage, and Mukherjee announced that she "respectfully" refused because of the "tragedy which had befallen her and her children." The *Hindustan Times* reported that Sonia was "understood to have discussed the matter with her relations. They, especially her sister, prevailed upon her to decline the office for the sake of safety and security of Mrs. Sonia Gandhi and her two children."[2] In a 2006 television interview, Sonia stated, "I was shattered at that time so I couldn't even think about anything else."[3] Mukherjee explained that the Congress Working Committee did not discuss the matter with Sonia before electing her because it felt that consultations could be postponed to a more appropriate moment. But rumblings of disunity within the party persisted. One senior member said that imposing a decision on Sonia could be misunderstood and would prove damaging to Congress. Others felt that 23 years in a national arena were preparation enough for Sonia, and that she needed to think about the interests of the larger family of Congress men and women for the "safety" of Indian democracy. Critics acerbically noted that 1991 gave Congress a chance to emerge from the "protective shadow" of the Nehru-Gandhi family, to democratize a party that had developed into a court and retinue revolving around the wishes of its leader. If Sonia had taken the post then, she would have been the fifth member of the Nehru-Gandhi family to become president (and if Congress won the election as predicted, then as the head of the party it was assumed she would become prime minister). The umbrella-like Congress had been the country's main bulwark against political chaos during 44 years of a free India, the only national organization with the moral authority to hold together the competing forces of caste, regionalism, language, and religion. Though until the 1990s it remained India's foremost party, new groups representing a particular region, or the poor, or low-status citizens, were eroding Congress's dominant position. In the 1990s these groups became more assertive, more aware of their rights, and acquired more of a say in politics than at any time in the past. This devastated the upper castes, who at one time had controlled everything. Congress saw the political grid sliding away from it as power moved from New Delhi to the state capitals.

Some Congress leaders were interested in Sonia because of the dynamics of personal rule that are particular to South Asia. Political families like the Nehrus, who invested many years in working for the country (earning extra kudos if they were part of the freedom struggle), soon acquired a positive image and name recognition. By 1991 Nehru had been a household name for 70 years. The familiarity, even if it came with criticism, gave the family a head start as people had at least a rough idea of what they might be getting.

This branding helps the children of leaders, too; the public feels that they know them because of their name and heritage. Children of leaders are exposed to politics early on; they have the opportunity to develop contacts, which gives them an edge over competitors. Successors to political chiefs who are relatives by blood or by marriage are always more acceptable than rivals from outside the family. For if outsiders are not carefully integrated into the command structure, they tend to set up their own groups and divide the party (which is why there are so many factions with the word "Congress" in the name). Charisma plays a major part in Indian election campaigns. This was most obvious after 1971 when Indira Gandhi was at the height of her popularity after the Bangladesh war. Party men and women coined the phrase "India is Indira and Indira is India!" Former foreign minister Natwar Singh, who worked with the Nehrus for more than five decades, remembers, "When Nehru got up to speak, a million people came to hear him. When Indira Gandhi got up to speak, a million people came. Even when there were no microphones, a chap sitting half a kilometer away would be perfectly happy. He couldn't hear a word. 'I have seen *Pandit Ji* [a respectful form of address, meaning teacher, for Nehru]. That's all I need.'" Natwar says that now the common man reacts to Sonia in the same way, often with awe. "He doesn't necessarily want to sit down and talk to her. He thinks, 'I have seen Sonia Ji. That's all I need.' When Sonia enters a room, all eyes are on her; she is the center of attention. So it was with her husband, her mother-in-law and her grandfather-in-law before her."[4]

All eyes were and are on the Nehrus because of a special link. The bond between the party, the people, and Indira was obtained through personal rule: political authority flowing more from the leader than from codes of party procedures and constitutions.[5] In India when a strong ruler leaves office or dies, that ruler's party usually atrophies unless a dynamic heir or heiress takes over.

The attributes attached to the Nehru name provided unity, many thought. Congress was so desperate to have a Nehru in a leadership role that it even asked Priyanka to become leader of the Youth Congress. Unlike his mother, Rajiv had not formulated a succession plan so the party was at war with itself. It would not be the last time. It would take hard work over more than a decade for Sonia to win over the chattering middle and upper classes. At this point, having been only in a supporting role on the political stage, quietly working away in the constituency, she lacked vast public support. Her constituents were faithful; they came to see her, pleading with her to look after them now that they had lost their "brother" Rajiv. She reassured them even while she grieved, telling them that they were her people, and said, "I am with you."[6]

As speculation over the presidency of the party continued, it was suddenly open season on Sonia. There was a rash of articles, many of them dismissive. Because the media had hitherto not taken much interest in her directly, people didn't know what she stood for, so the overall tone varied from perplexed to downright negative. In a May 1991 sample survey conducted in the town of Chandigarh in the state of Punjab, a farmer commented that no one knew what kind of person she was and that she had no experience. A retired army general noted, "She is not a leader to take command of the country. We are in a mess. [The] economy is bad. Internal security problems are staring [us] in the eye. We need committed and experienced leaders. . . . But she is not the stuff of a party president or prime minister." One author declared, "Her selection in the name of consensus is a mockery of democracy. This would only strengthen the forces of masked authoritarianism. . . . The country is in need of some dynamic leader, from the soil of the country."[7] And in an insidious comment on the perceived hazards of trusting Sonia, which would be amplified in later years, a professor declared, "Okay she is an Indian citizen, but how much [does] she [know] India and how much do Indians know her. It is dangerous to entrust her with this responsibility. She would jeopardize many things."[8]

With Rajiv gone, the place of Sonia's residence could have become an issue. On May 29 the Cabinet Committee on Political Affairs (CCPA) decided that Sonia and her family could stay there, bearing in mind that a high level of security would be needed for them. The CCPA decided that the National Security Guard would handle family protection[9]; there was a precedent for widows of the country's leaders retaining government accommodation.

Also in late May, a commission of enquiry into the security of Rajiv Gandhi was charged with examining the adequacy of the security apparatus and determining whether those who had handled Rajiv's protection were in any way at fault. In 1992 the commission, under Justice Jagdish Sharan Verma, delivered the damning conclusion that throughout his premiership, Rajiv Gandhi had been the "most threatened person in the country" and that "this threat remained unreduced till his assassination. It is obvious that his security requirements did need the SPG cover or an equally efficacious suitable alternative, neither of which was available to him." The Special Protection Group had been removed from him in February 1990 "as a result of the decision of the central government," as directed in a January 1990 note from the Cabinet Secretariat.

Rajiv's smoldering ashes were being guarded at the cremation site by Indo-Tibetan Border police and the Army Engineer Corps. On May 26, in the midst of a dust storm that had hit the capital, a distraught Rahul[10] ceremoniously collected the ashes. It was still dark at 5:15 AM, as he worked diligently at the pyre with Amitabh Bachchan, close friends, and Congress leaders, placing the ashes in many copper urns covered by red cloths. As the only son, he had to lead the rites, which were overseen by the same 70-year-old family priest who had presided at the ceremonies for Sanjay, Indira, and Jawaharlal Nehru. Rahul's movements were slightly wooden, but he was calm as he performed his duties.[11]

In the early hours of the morning, the urns were placed under an Amaltus (Indian laburnum) tree's cascading yellow flowers on the rear lawns of Teen Murti Bhavan. Rahul walked in with one arm around his sister and the other around his mother. All three of their heads were lowered as they were escorted into the building by commandos.[12] The next morning brought strong winds and drizzling rain. In procession, Sonia, her dark glasses hiding her tear-swollen eyes, followed Priyanka, who followed Rahul carrying one of the urns of ashes in both his hands. They were on their way to a special train, escorted by platoons from the army, navy, and air force, for the journey from Delhi to Allahabad, to arrive there early the next morning. The remaining urns were to be ceremoniously escorted to all the different states and union territories of India by Congress Party state presidents and members. Just as at Indira's request Rajiv had scattered some of her ashes over the snow-clad Himalayan peaks of Jammu and Kashmir, now one portion of Rajiv's ashes was sent by an Indian air force plane to the state where he and Sonia had spent such happy vacations. Along with Sonia, Rahul, Priyanka, and some relatives and friends were senior Congress members and national and international media representatives. The 17-stop journey included the Nehru family constituencies of Rae Bareli and Amethi, allowing the grieving common man who had not been able to go to Delhi in the past few days to be part of Rajiv's last journey before some of his ashes were immersed at Sangam, the place where three holy rivers meet.

As the train pulled into each station, mourners stood on top of vending stalls, packing the platforms to catch a glimpse of the urn that was on a specially erected low platform in a marigold-and-jasmine-bedecked carriage. Sonia, Rahul, and Priyanka sat on white sheets; a garlanded portrait of Rajiv hung on the wall. At Rajiv's constituency, Amethi, thousands of people pressed forward from behind a cordon to sympathize with the woman they called *Bhabi,* the affectionate term for sister-in-law. Sonia seemed to feel the anguish of the constituents—many of whom she knew personally. She sat at the window of the train compartment with Priyanka, receiving flowers and garlands brought by mourners, a lot of them weeping Amethi women. One who had been waiting since 1 AM cried uncontrollably; as she passed Sonia's window, she asked her for a photo of Rajiv. Sonia looked at her with tears in her eyes. The emotion emanating from the Amethi women was so overwhelming that after a while she had to move away from the window and sit on the floor by the urn.[13] The Amethi stop was the longest part of the journey; the train arrived at 3:40 AM and stayed for 45 minutes. At the final destination, the Nehru ancestral hometown of Allahabad, hordes of people thronged the route into the city. Along the way, crying nuns sang hymns, and wailing Muslim women raised their hands to the sky moaning for "our son," Rajiv. At Anand Bhavan, the historic Nehru family home, retainers achingly drew on their memories as Rahul brought in the ashes. One anguished old woman cried that to see Rajiv come there in that form was heartbreaking because she could remember him playing there as a child.

With the main urn of Rajiv's ashes, Sonia and her children started a three-mile boat procession to the islet called Sangam while a helicopter sprayed rose petals on everyone. The river Yamuna—which runs alongside the cremation sites of Indira Gandhi and other leaders in Delhi—joins the mythical river Saraswathi at the sacred confluence of Triveni on India's largest and holiest of rivers, the Ganges. At this meeting point, Sangam, some of the last remains of Jawaharlal, Indira, and Sanjay were also given a home in the flowing waters.

Previously, the immersions of ashes had been conducted from a boat on the river, but for the Gandhi family, a jetty had been constructed. Standing with his mother, his sister, and several others, Rahul took the urn in his hands and got ready to overturn it into the river. Sonia had been relatively restrained in public for a whole week, but, watching her husband's ashes about to disappear from view forever, she suddenly burst into tears. She put her left hand to her face and her body bent, racked with sobs. Her eyes were hidden behind her sunglasses, but her body language said it all. She had to reach out and grip a wooden post with her right hand just as Rahul bent to her left, turning around and twice checking on the state of his mother before committing the vestiges of his father to the fast-flowing waters. He carried out the instructions Rajiv had written six years earlier: "It is my wish that our ashes should be immersed into the Ganga at Triveni, Allahabad, where my ancestors' ashes have been immersed."[14] Priyanka rushed to help her mother, holding her hand to lend her some strength. A hush fell over those watching from a distance in motor craft and on the riverbank. Buglers in a steam-powered boat played *The Last Post.* The rains that had hit Delhi the night Rahul collected the ashes and the milk that had been poured over the pyre to dampen and lower its temperature caused some of the ashes to stick to the copper container. Sonia put her left hand on Rahul's back as he reached into the urn to remove the remainder, her gold wedding ring glinting in the sun. Sonia took a glimpse of Rajiv's ashes and then turned away; she went and sat in an open motor boat. She turned around to take a last look at where her husband's ashes disappeared and bent her head, crying inaudibly. As they returned along the river, heartbroken, the children and Sonia dipped their hands in the sacred waters, watched by thousands from the riverbanks. Rahul cried into his mother's lap, and Priyanka placed her head on her shoulder.[15]

While this family said their tearful goodbyes, back in Delhi, the lions of Congress were waiting and scheming.

17

PRESERVING RAJIV'S LEGACY

> My mother's sole wish is to communicate to the world the true nature of my father's accomplishments . . . to preserve the things he left behind . . . and pass his legacy on correctly to future generations.
>
> —*Priyanka Gandhi*

A Hindu widow is expected to remain quietly at home for at least a year after her husband's death. But Sonia did not shut down completely; she occasionally engaged in very low-level activity at the Janpath house during the mourning months. Her mother, two sisters, and friends were a great support during this time, but the real source of strength lay behind closed doors, where the wounded Sonia and her children drew from and gave to each other. Priyanka later said that they explained Rajiv's murder to themselves by thinking that it was "for our country because he believed in something." But she had another reaction too. Although she didn't realize it at the time, she was "absolutely furious inside . . . not with particular individuals who killed him . . . but I was furious with the whole world."[1]

While the family was going through the various stages of grieving, the Congress Party would not leave them alone. Even though Sonia had already refused to be party president, many Congress members of parliament still wanted her to emerge on the political scene, and they would ask for meetings on the pretext of wanting to express their heartfelt sympathy at her loss. It got so irksome that in June she put her foot down and decided that if she granted a meeting, no one should talk politics.[2]

But politics was all around. The result of the 1991 general election was a hung parliament. In the lower house, the Congress Party emerged as the largest in a three-way fight—with the Bharatiya Janata Party coming in second—and would therefore choose the prime minister. The party's choice, Pamulaparti Venkata Narasimha Rao, would be only the second Indian prime minister who was not a Nehru. Rao was an Indira loyalist who had moved away from active politics; he was recovering from a quadruple coronary bypass operation and was looking forward to retirement and the peaceful pursuit of literary topics. Party seniors pushed for him because they thought that he might be a unifying and malleable candidate. According to author and former *Guardian* correspondent Inder Malhotra, Vice President Shankar Dayal Sharma would have been Sonia's preferred candidate, but he pleaded that he was too old and frail for the post, so Sonia reluctantly agreed to Rao.[3] The first national problem for the new prime minister was that India faced a balance-of-payments crisis; there was not enough foreign currency in India's national bank accounts to make payments on international loans. If action was not taken, the country might have to default, likely placing India's credit rating and future loan prospects in jeopardy.

As soon as he was appointed, Rao installed Manmohan Singh, a former World Bank official and former International Monetary Fund (IMF) governor, as his finance minister. Singh, who holds postgraduate degrees from Cambridge and Oxford, consulted with both of his former organizations and was advised to overhaul India's monetary policy. India, always cautious, began a slow economic reformation, but enough was done for creditors to allow the rescheduling of its debt repayments. Import restrictions were eased, more foreign investment was allowed in, and lengthy bureaucratic procedures were reduced where possible. State-run businesses were to be sold. The policies of Manmohan Singh and Narasimha Rao took hold, and the country started averaging an annual growth rate of 5 percent and more. There would be no turning back. The socialist nation that Jawaharlal Nehru had fathered had now turned toward a free-market economy. Pleased with the situation, Rao engaged with the country's economic reforms, gathered strength both physically and politically, and set up a rival power center to 10 Janpath, where a great deal of attention was focused.

Sonia was also going through a transition. It was to be a slow and steady ascent, one that those around her were more aware of than she was at this stage. It would mark the transformation from a person without much public responsibility to a weighty leadership role. She was learning to handle life on her own, just as Indira had before her. Sonia commented later, "For the next several years I withdrew into myself." She drew comfort and strength from the many thousands who grieved, who treasured Rajiv's memory, and who offered support and affection to Sonia and the children.[4] Cherry and Karma Topden had kept in touch with Sonia and Rajiv since their Cambridge days, and Cherry recalls that when they went to see Sonia to express their sorrow, the bright and happy person they knew from Cambridge two and a half decades earlier now looked completely lost, her legs tucked up under her on her chair, small and lonesome.[5]

Indira Gandhi was described as having an ability to disassociate herself from her surroundings and commune with her inner voice. Indira spoke of being able to "retire into yourself"[6]—she could access her internal resources to renew herself and used the technique to generate long-lasting energy.[7] Mahatma Gandhi, too, often spoke of the still small voice within, or his inner voice. Sonia now turned within to find her fortitude.

Sonia was rarely among people outside the family at this time, but a big part of her way of coping with the tragedy was to create a roadmap to complete her husband's unfinished dreams. They had shared ideas, values, and Rajiv's program for the country. With one half of the couple gone, it was left to the other half to take the project forward. Sonia's commitment to India is that unfinished agenda. One writer says that Rahul and Priyanka have that passion too, a restlessness to complete it.[8]

In central New Delhi, the building called Jawahar Bhavan (Jawahar House) was designed to house a foundation and a research institute for contemporary studies, a kind of think tank, in Jawaharlal Nehru's name. A meeting was called, in which it was decided to rename both institutions after Rajiv: The Rajiv Gandhi Foundation (RGF) and the Rajiv Gandhi Institute of Contemporary Studies (RGICS) were thus born.[9] Now Sonia needed the right people to run the foundation, which was established as a nongovernmental organization.

Sunil Nehru, whose grandfather, Brij Lal Nehru, was a first cousin of Rajiv's grandfather Jawaharlal, was then a senior manager at Max India Ltd. in Delhi. He was invited to be a founding trustee of the RGF by Sonia in 1991, as a representative of the family. Apart from Sonia, there was no other senior member of the family involved. Nehru readily agreed, for he felt "a sense of protectiveness toward Sonia in her hour of need. . . . She came across as someone in deep pain, bearing her anguish with courage and composure, but vulnerable and alone."[10]

Others who were deeply distressed by Rajiv's passing also wanted to do their bit to help; a set of guardians was gathering around Sonia to perpetuate Rajiv's memory and formalize the ideals he stood for. Venkataraman

Krishnamurthy, later chairman of the National Manufacturing Competitiveness Council, had known Rajiv Gandhi well. He says that Sonia trusted him "instantly" because her husband had. But Sonia, only four weeks after his death, did not want take a central role. He observed that she assumed that those who had worked with Rajiv Gandhi could lead the RGF, but *they* all thought that Sonia, as the guardian of her husband's legacy, was needed to set the foundation in motion, so she became its chairperson.

With everything in place exactly one month after Rajiv's assassination, on June 21, 1991, a Deed of Declaration was published, which dealt with objectives, the names and functions of the initial board of trustees, the executive committee's formation and functions, voting rights, the appointment of a secretary who would run the foundation, and the status of the chairperson (Sonia Gandhi) who, the document stated, would continue in the position "during her pleasure and not be liable to be removed."[11] Reimbursements and allowances were also covered, and on the last pages, an appeal for funds was made by the vice president, Shankar Dayal Sharma. The first eight trustees included Sonia, Rahul, Priyanka, Sunil Nehru, Shankar Dayal Sharma (later to become the president of India), and Amitabh Bachchan. In addition, intellectuals, industrialists, and journalists worked with the RGF in various capacities. Abdul Kalam, a rocket scientist who would also later become president of India, joined the board. Like Krishnamurthy, most were people who had worked closely with Rajiv. Rahul and Priyanka were still young and not active in the meetings, but giving them a stake in the foundation at this stage prepared them for involvement in carrying forward the Rajiv Gandhi legacy.

The Foundation Deed of Declaration set out objectives and purposes based on Rajiv's ideas: the development of science and technology to be used in the service of the people; literacy development; national integration, communal harmony, employment skills for the young, and the protection of the environment; supporting the underprivileged, women, handicapped, and elderly; and development of the highest standards in the aviation field. The RGF now had specific goals shaped around many programs and ideas that Rajiv had initiated and were also close to Sonia's heart; every government bill that she would later advocate for had been conceived in Rajiv's game plan for India. The foundation would eventually have subdivisions for such areas as local self-government and nuclear disarmament.

In a meeting at her home, Sonia asked Wajahat Habibullah to set up the foundation and become its first secretary. Because he had worked closely with Rajiv, he was concerned about Sonia and felt a sense of duty. "She seemed so completely out of place in her surroundings. An innocent in the wilderness. Can you imagine? Today she's regarded as one of the most powerful women in the world, and then I, poor puny fellow, thought that I might be able to stand forth and protect her! And the roundabout of politics in India can be quite harsh."[12] Habibullah was willing to give up his Indian Administrative Service salary, retire, and go to work for the foundation, but Sonia did not want him to make this or any other sacrifice. She wanted him to become secretary of the RGF only if he could retain his income—and the government agreed. He was aware of the political sharks circling Sonia: "I was terrified that because she was so innocent, because she was so reticent, because she was not assertive, there would be those who would want to exploit her, [who] would want to take advantage of her."[13] He recalls that her being this "terribly tragic figure" brought out the best in him and the others; he felt that he *must* help and protect her.

Sonia was indeed reserved and not assertive. At the first executive meetings, Sunil Nehru recalls hardly any debate at all; discussions were mainly handled by Sonia's friends. "The early meetings were gentle affairs, with business conducted in quiet tones. Sonia attended but scarcely ever uttered a word, except for constant concern about the welfare and comfort of those present. Her demeanor was always very composed and formal, but she occasionally would let slip a shy smile."[14] Aside from the raw feeling of loss, it appears that Sonia was fully aware of her vulnerabilities and limitations. Krishnamurthy recalls that Sonia questioned the value and necessity of her presence in early sessions: "'My contribution is not that great . . . why don't I leave it to the professionals?'"[15] she asked. But there was another agenda at work. Krishnamurthy and others, acting as her angels, "insisted that she *should* come, not only for that but for the purpose of understanding the ground realities of the situation."[16]

She understood the point. Wajahat Habibullah was part of a core group that would assemble every Tuesday at Sonia's house in her book-lined meeting room. Sonia was the perfect hostess under all circumstances, serving the finest tea and making sure the essentials were all fulfilled. The members of the board would discuss and then decide on schemes and projects to be supported by the foundation. He too noticed that Sonia was fairly passive; she did not interfere with the workings of the foundation and said very little at this stage. "We would speak among ourselves—we should do this, we should do that—and decide what we wanted to be done, but it was always under her chairmanship."[17]

At the same time, huge amounts of money were pouring into the RGF—from Reliance Industries and Tata Group,[18] the biggest companies in India, among others—so the person who managed the accounts also needed to have a sense of commitment to Sonia and the memory of Rajiv. Palaniappan Chidambaram advised on investing the money and how it should be properly looked after. Prime Minister Narasimha Rao set aside money in the national budget for the foundation, but Sonia refused it because, she said, the foundation must be self-sufficient and stand on its own feet. This policy has kept it a fully functioning independent entity.[19]

Rao and Sonia were both quiet, retiring individuals who communicated mainly through their intermediaries: the principal secretary to the prime minister and the secretary of the Rajiv Gandhi Foundation. Habibullah describes the relationship between the two principals as "cordial and very respectful."[20]

But Sonia was in a lot of pain, and some recollections were just too much to bear. Under normal protocol, meetings involving the premier could have taken place at his office or at his residence at Race Course Road, where Sonia had spent some happy years with Rajiv and the children. "She said she did not want to have the meetings of the board of governors at Race Course Road, it brought back too many memories of her time as a prime minister's wife." Habibullah conveyed the message through the prime minister's principal secretary, and Rao agreed to hold meetings at the vice president's house or at 10 Janpath. The RGF team wanted the Indian ambassador to the United States to head up the think-tank wing of the foundation, and Rao readily seconded him.

Krishnamurthy described how Sonia showed an important quality in meetings as the RGF took shape: "You can't get a better listener. There was no flippancy in anything she did. She listens and comes to the right conclusion. That's her trait."[21] Though empathetic listening is a hallmark of any successful chief executive, she does not use her authority to behave autocratically. She did not *actually* ask Habibullah, for instance, to do anything. He learned how to read her and instinctively knew what to do; voluntarily supplying her with notes, for instance (although she likes to write her own notes, too). He found her artless: "The years that I was there, the RGF was a nascent stage of her political growth. She was really questing. She felt that she needed to do it for her husband. But how she would do it, I don't think she was very sure. She was not really very assertive, saying this is how it should be done, or that is how it should be done. She didn't do that. She was very much open to guidance. She *wanted* to be guided."[22]

She may have been seeking help, but Sonia was always the most important person in the room. The strong, silent woman who had remained behind the scenes was now center stage. Habibullah recalls an ambitious RGF program on nuclear disarmament in which several nations participated; Sonia was always on standby to help and make arrangements for guests, she was the hostess at the dinner, and she chaired the session. Despite the fact that people of both Indian and Italian origin tend to be physically and emotionally expressive, Wajahat noticed that Sonia does not readily show her feelings either on her face or in her body language. "It's very difficult to tell how she's feeling . . . you have to understand. If she doesn't like something, she might wrinkle up her nose. She won't say no. If she likes something, there may be a slight smile. She won't say, 'Oh, how nice!' There'll be nothing of that kind. She's very subdued in her reactions." Later on, his fears about Sonia being exploited by those around her proved unfounded. "None of that happened. Which is actually a tribute to her sensibility and the fact that she was more astute than I thought. It's all for the good of the whole Nehru tradition which otherwise would not have survived,"[23] he said appreciatively.

On June 17 Rajiv was posthumously conferred the nation's highest civilian honor, the Bharat Ratna (Jewel of India). Less than two months after his assassination, on July 6, 1991, a somber award ceremony took place in the President's Palace. He would have been its youngest-ever recipient, taking his place alongside such elders as Nelson Mandela, Mother Teresa, Jawaharlal Nehru, and Indira Gandhi. In a high-domed hall, Rahul and Priyanka sat straight, dignified in their sorrow, while their mother, immaculately dressed in a light-colored sari, received a medallion and scroll of honor on behalf of her husband. The hall was very quiet; instead of the customary applause after the presentation, there was a pin-drop silence loaded with emotion. Sonia was slightly hesitant and walked slowly to her seat, set a little apart from the distinguished audience and to the right of the president.

Sonia had been part of other committees mainly related to cultural legacy for some years, but the Rajiv Gandhi Foundation could be described as something of a political training ground for her, even though it was not a political body. There she learned how to run a more high-profile committee, more personal to her, guided gently by the top experts from different fields. Krishnamurthy, who is on the executive and investment committees as well as being a trustee, noted that though in the beginning she did not participate much in discussions, as time went by she was more active. Sitting through three-hour meetings was excellent preparation for the mandatory four-hour political sessions she would chair in later life. When the RGF held sessions with experts, he said, "She was proactive in meeting the highest of the professionals and discussing with them the greatest problems of this country. So over a period of time she gained confidence because she was a person who never thought she was going to be grappling with this type of a problem." Krishnamurthy and the other trustees were conscious that Sonia needed subtle coaching, and they sensed that in the years to come the demands on her would increase.[24]

In November 1992 she sat in the center of a panel to listen to the first of the Distinguished Speaker Series with the late John Kenneth Galbraith, organized by the Rajiv Gandhi Institute for Contemporary Studies at Teen Murti Auditorium, which is situated next to Teen Murti Bhavan. His talk was called "The World Economy: The Larger Perspective." Galbraith, the chairman of the US Chapter of the Rajiv Gandhi Foundation, gave a Rajiv Gandhi Golden Jubilee Memorial Lecture a couple of years later. Titled "The Imperial Syndrome: Then and Now," it touched on the collapse of colonialism. In November 1994 Senator John F. Kerry also delivered a Rajiv Gandhi Golden Jubilee Memorial lecture in Delhi, stressing the value of Indo-US cooperation and emphasizing the importance of the host country as one of the top ten emerging markets for America. Sonia would willingly appear at launch events, interact with important people, and give speeches occasionally, right through the years, when required. By 1997 she was highly practiced and delivered a welcome address for a speaker from Thailand on family welfare programs, citing her late husband's support for public involvement in family welfare policy. She described how better health care and education, especially for women, a lowering of infant mortality, and vaccinations could all help speed up these policies.[25] With the Congress Party's support eroding over the years and coalitions now a major factor in the Indian polity, the RGICS held a seminar on coalition governance in 1997, which resulted in the courageous though somewhat surprising conclusion that one-party government was still possible.[26] It was through her chairing the RGF that the trustees tried to help her bring her leadership qualities to the fore, to a strength from which she would be able to lead the party. Krishnamurthy observes that the first RGF years were therefore important for "the maturity level, the understanding level, the quickness with which she was able to absorb, the way she was able to appreciate the problems of the people of this country. That was the learning period."[27]

In February 1992, nine months after Rajiv's assassination, the founder of Tokyo Fuji Art Museum, Daisaku Ikeda, who had known Rajiv, met with Sonia at her home. Ikeda is president of the Soka Gakkai, a branch of Nichiren Buddhism based on the teachings of a thirteenth-century Japanese monk. He said that he had felt compelled to try to relieve her suffering, even if only by a "smallest iota." He told her a story from The Lotus Sutra, one of the most sacred scriptures of Buddhism, in which the daughter of a dragon king attains enlightenment, just as Buddha did, demonstrating that fathers and daughters have unbreakable bonds. He explained, "Your daughter's life is indivisible from the life of your husband. They are eternally father and child.

Eternally you are a family. Please believe in this eternity."[28] He said that if she could withstand the pain and the suffering she was going through, after the dark nights, one day a dawn of happiness would finally arrive and she and her family would be victorious. Ikeda then gave Sonia a custom-made wind-up music box that played tunes called *Mother* and *Human Revolution*, with lyrics he had composed. He explained to Sonia that the title *Human Revolution* represents a key concept for Nichiren Buddhists who encourage people to take responsibility, to live with courage and conviction, and to transform their lives. When a father dies young, he said, Buddhists pray that his unlived span of years will be passed onto his family. A Soka Gakkai member who was present at the meeting, Akash Ouchi, said that the conversation between Ikeda and Sonia helped her to understand that the spirit of Rajiv lived, guarding and protecting them, and that it was up to Sonia to carry forward the Nehru legacy. He found that Sonia "loved the music" and became more positive, brightening up during the conversation, and was "quite clear" on what she had to do from then on.

In 1994 Sonia traveled to the Tokyo Fuji Museum to open an exhibition, taking with her the treasured music box (it had broken and could not be restored in India) that was immediately replaced by Ikeda.[29] Around this time, she talked to him about her concern for thousands of deteriorating photographic negatives from Rajiv's collection; in response, the curator sent a team to Delhi to clean and digitize them. Out of that yearlong conservation project arose a collaboration between the RGF and the Tokyo Fuji Museum to show, for the first time ever, an exhibition of Rajiv's work.[30] Sonia told Daisaku Ikeda that opening up a part of her life she had kept closed until now was not easy for her; but once it had happened, she knew it was the right thing to do.[31]

Mrs. Sonia Gandhi and Mr. Rajiv Gandhi in Salang, Afghanistan, June 8, 1969. Prime Minister Indira Gandhi was on a six-day state visit to the country.

Courtesy Photo Division, Ministry of Information and Broadcasting, Government of India

Prime Minister Rajiv Gandhi consoles Rahul Gandhi after the urn containing the ashes of Indira Gandhi was brought from the cremation site to be placed next to the urn of her father, Jawaharlal Nehru, in the garden of Teen Murti House, November 5, 1984.

Photograph by Debatosh Sengupta. Courtesy Photo Division, Ministry of Information and Broadcasting, Government of India

Pallbearers carrying the body of Mrs. Indira Gandhi to the cremation site near Raj Ghat after it had been brought there on a gun carriage. The president of India, Giani Zail Singh, Prime Minister Rajiv Gandhi, Rahul, and Mrs. Sonia Gandhi can be seen. November 3, 1984.

Photograph by Debatosh Sengupta. Courtesy Photo Division, Ministry of Information and Broadcasting, Government of India

(next page) Prime Minister Rajiv Gandhi and Mrs. Sonia Gandhi acknowledge the warm greetings of the residents of the northeast state of Mizoram during a tour in July 1986.

Photograph by Debatosh Sengupta. Courtesy Photo Division, Ministry of Information and Broadcasting, Government of India

Mrs. Sonia Gandhi paying respect to the urn containing Indira Gandhi's ashes with flower petals in the garden of Teen Murti House, New Delhi, November 5, 1984. Prime Minister Rajiv Gandhi, Priyanka, Rahul, Vice President R. Venkataraman, and President Giani Zail Singh are also seen.

Photograph by Debatosh Sengupta. Courtesy Photo Division, Ministry of Information and Broadcasting, Government of India

K. STORE

Mrs. Nancy Reagan with Mrs. Sonia Gandhi at a dinner hosted by President Reagan in honor of Prime Minister Rajiv Gandhi and Mrs. Sonia Gandhi at the White House in Washington, June 12, 1985.

Courtesy Photo Division, Ministry of Information and Broadcasting, Government of India

The US secretary of state, Mrs. Hillary Clinton, meets the UPA chairperson, Mrs. Sonia Gandhi, in New Delhi, July 20, 2009.

Photo by Dinesh Sharma. Courtesy Photo Division, Ministry of Information and Broadcasting, Government of India

The prime minister of the Russian Federation, Mr. Vladimir V. Putin, meets the UPA chairperson, Mrs. Sonia Gandhi, in New Delhi, March 12, 2010.

Photo by Asish Maitra. Courtesy Photo Division, Ministry of Information and Broadcasting, Government of India

18

NOT JUST TEARS

> At this time of anguish, we must remember Gandhiji's message of tolerance and non-violence, and the struggles of our nation's builders, who strove and sacrificed to create an India in which all its citizens could live together in harmony, as one big family.
>
> —*Resolution of the Rajiv Gandhi Foundation*

December 6, 1992, is a day Sonia has said she will never forget. More than 2,000 people were killed in the worst interreligious violence since the partition of the country in 1947. The city of Ayodhya in the state of Uttar Pradesh was the scene of the Hindu-Muslim hostility and the longest running legal dispute in Indian history. Hindu extremists had been campaigning to demolish a sixteenth-century mosque built by the first Mughal emperor of India, Babur. The Bharatiya Janata Party (BJP) wanted to build a temple in its place, claiming the location was the birthplace of Prince Ram, a Hindu warrior king and hero of the *Ramayana* epic. The Babri mosque was protected by a court order.

On that day Hindu groups, vowing to stay within the law, raised a demonstration that they had promised would be limited to a religious ceremony symbolizing the laying of the first bricks of a temple. Before the rituals could even start, a crowd of 200,000 surged forward, breaking flimsy police cordons. Quickly some of the crowd demolished the domes of the building with hammers, and then, with their bare hands, people tore down the bricks of the mosque until it was reduced to rubble. Eyewitnesses reported that the extra police brought to the site stood by and did nothing to stop the carnage.[1] The hordes turned their venom on both Indian and foreign media recording the mayhem before attacking Muslim homes, shops, and assets. Muslims in other parts of India were targeted as well.

The secular reputation of the Congress Party, seen until that day as the protector of all Indians, including every minority, lay in ruins among the rubble. BJP member and opposition leader L. K. Advani accepted "moral responsibility" and resigned. M. J. Akbar, an adviser to the Human Development Ministry, also resigned his post immediately. He explained that "The attack was in a sense expected. The movement for the construction of a temple had been going on for some time . . . what was unexpected for me was the manner in which the legitimate authority of India, which is the government of India, abandoned its responsibilities, its commitment to protect the mosque. You can't . . . be betrayed by your enemy, you can only be betrayed by somebody you trust. I was the only one to resign from the government and the party. No one else from Congress resigned. No one."[2]

On December 9, 1992, Sonia chaired a meeting with other senior members at the Rajiv Gandhi Foundation (RGF) headquarters in New Delhi. Sonia was furious[3] that the authorities had let the violence happen. The carnage "brought not just tears, we were all distraught," she recalled.[4] She and her RGF team worked on a strong statement condemning sectarian mob violence. The resolution, widely publicized in the press and later referred to by Sonia in interviews, began, "The outrage at Ayodhya and its appalling consequences elsewhere since Sunday are a tragic repudiation of the faith that inspired and guided the great sons and daughters of this ancient civilization. . . ." It quoted Rajiv Gandhi's words: "Secularism is the bedrock of our nationhood. It implies more than tolerance. It involves an active effort for harmony. No religion preaches hatred and intolerance." It said that those who had been inciting violence did "not have the welfare of the Indian people at heart. Their ends are selfish and they must be vigorously resisted." It called for repair to "the grievous damage inflicted on our nation's identity."[5]

Sonia, apparently frustrated by inaction on the part of any authority, organized emergency relief through the RGF, sending tarpaulins, blankets, medicines, and cooking utensils to families affected by the riots. In Delhi, the secretary of the RGF, Wajahat Habibullah, personally led a team that provided blankets to more than 250 families whose homes had been burgled or destroyed in the riots. In the state of Bihar, 500 blankets were distributed (just under 500 families had been affected) while further relief was provided in Calcutta.

The center of government in New Delhi, often just referred to as "the Center," headed by Congress prime minister P. V. Narasimha Rao, was responsible for national security and seemed enfeebled in the face of the violence. In Ayodhya, law enforcement agencies could have stopped the carnage immediately if the will had been there. Sonia was shocked and later commented in a television interview during the 2004 election on the appalling lack of government response: "The Congress was in power in the Center but don't forget there was a BJP government in UP [Uttar Pradesh] . . . we [the party] have always said that this has to be resolved through the court. And if there is an understanding between the concerned parties (Hindu and Muslim) even that has to have the sanction of the court."[6] The statement condemning sectarian mob violence was taken seriously by the Congress Party. Akbar observed, "The Congress Party tends to be very obedient to every prime minister or whoever is in power. You don't find much by way of dissent. Those who had kept their dissent silent knew that there was some pillar in the party which would represent them. That became Sonia."

The party was now confronted with serious problems. Sadia Dehlvi, Muslim author and commentator, said that the demolition of the mosque and the subsequent failure of government to take effective action caused the Muslim minority, previously attracted to the Congress Party for its liberal, inclusive agenda, to suddenly drop away. It marked a decline in Muslim support that has not yet been fully reversed. "The spirit of the Indian Muslim was deeply wounded. It exposed how vulnerable we are in this country. There was a secular facade we wanted to believe in. Muslim hearts were bleeding. That's what moved the Muslims away; they did hold the Center guilty and ineffective."[7] And most ineffective was Prime Minister Rao. The destruction of the mosque had sharpened the battle lines nationally; the Hindu right—in the form of the Bharatiya Janata Party, its youth wing, and its affiliates—was a force that much of India feared. Eighty percent of India is Hindu, and of the remaining minority religions, Muslims make up 14 percent. Political parties in India frequently use the notion of "vote banks" or communities of people in adversarial speeches to imply that their opponents are just playing to certain groups for votes rather than to the actual interests of that particular community.

In Uttar Pradesh, the location of the Nehru-Gandhi constituencies, the Muslim disaffection with the Congress Party was pronounced. The Muslim vote evaporated as the community started to feel that *dalits* (untouchables) and OBCs (other backward castes) were now their kindred spirits, so they started mending fences with people who would treat them as vote banks in the string of north Indian states that includes Uttar Pradesh. No one did anything to appease or support the Muslims; many Indians blamed Rao for behaving impotently in the matter, and by now Sonia had expressed her feelings in plain words through the Rajiv Gandhi Foundation. Akbar comments that by the time of the Babri mosque attack, Sonia "had been . . . isolated by Narasimha Rao. She was not much in the power structure either in the party or in the government. I suppose her helplessness and the way she saw the party drifting away added to her anger."

In 1992 Wajahat Habibullah was serving a second term in Kashmir, as divisional commissioner in the state of Jammu and Kashmir, at the request of a new governor there. He had been keen to go. Sonia "was not at all happy"[8] about her trusted adviser's departure to the strife-torn valley but had reluctantly agreed to release him. The last time he had been in Kashmir there had been an assassination attempt on him. This time around, he nearly lost his life.

Since the late 1980s, India had struggled to contain an ongoing armed militancy fighting for the right of Kashmiris to self-determination. Militants in the Muslim-majority state had taken over the most important Islamic shrine for Jammu and Kashmiri Muslims and were under siege from the Indian army. Habibullah had been working toward a crisis resolution by peaceful negotiation. In 1993, on the final day of the siege, a military truck rammed his car (an inquiry later deemed this to have been an accident). His skull was fractured and the bones in the right side of his body were shattered. It took him many months to recover from these very serious injuries, which had damaged him psychologically as well as physically, for he was no longer the "self-contained, independent sort of person" of before. He was brought back to Delhi and found that Sonia was sensitive to his loss of confidence, his greater need for care and concern, "and was not to be found wanting." He was told that "the day I'd had the accident and the news came in that I might be dead, she was aghast. She felt very sorry that she allowed me to go. . . ." The man who set up the Rajiv Gandhi Foundation for Sonia and for the memory of his deceased friend found that when he returned to the capital, "it was her office and her staff that saw to it that I got the best treatment that could be had here." He was hospitalized for more than three months while the doctors "put my bones together. When I came out of hospital, I couldn't walk unassisted, I had to use a stick, but I couldn't lie about at home because I was suffering from post-traumatic stress disorder." Wajahat felt restless and ill at ease. The psychological impact of the accident could not be treated by doctors, but he wanted to feel useful. He talked to Sonia: "I want to be of service. Can I come to work at the Foundation? She saw to it that I did. She saw to it that a room and staff were assigned to me."

After a couple of months, Habibullah was posted to the Ministry of Urban Development, where he looked after projects close to the Nehru-

Gandhis amongst other portfolios. He ran poverty alleviation programs and was responsible for the memorials to Rajiv in Delhi and Sriperumbudur. For Vir Bhumi ("land of the courageous"), Rajiv's cremation site in Delhi, Wajahat says that Sonia had a clear concept of what she wanted and, apart from the structure itself, put an emphasis on the landscape. He describes her vision for this site as being a celebration of Rajiv's life, so there are carved friezes of familiar images—Rajiv with one of the hundreds of garlands he was always given when on tour; Rajiv speaking at the United Nations. The central piece is made of gray stone, a large single sculpted lotus raised above a square pool of 46 lotuses; one for each year of his life. The theme of the lotus was Sonia's idea. At Sriperumbudur the theme is the perpetuation of Rajiv's legacy—his commitment to technological progress and the unity of India. A narrow walkway, known as the "path of light," traces his final steps. Seven giant cream-colored pillars, headed by dark brown sculptures, guard the site of the actual blast, where a gray stone mural of Rajiv marks the spot of his death. Wajahat notes that while Sonia was planning the memorials, designers went to her home to present their ideas for her to choose from; to select the sculptors, she visited studios and examined their works. He says that when matters of culture and tradition were concerned, she absorbed facts and information rapidly. If she wanted something, she would say so, but only after hearing an exposition. Later, the rear portion of Safdarjang Road was converted into a museum to Rajiv. In a glass case, painstakingly sewn onto a white cloth background, every shred of the white clothes he died in, blackened, charred, and tattered, hang above his shoes, the only part of his clothing to remain intact.

In those days, due to his skull fracture, Habibullah said, "my mind was not working to its full capacity." He had an appointment with Sonia to discuss the designs and plans for Rajiv's cremation sites. "I remember going to a meeting with her one day to discuss this and all the maps that I produced were the wrong maps. I hadn't taken the precaution, which I normally would have done, of having checked the maps that I was taking to the meeting. She said, 'It doesn't matter, it doesn't matter at all.' She was extremely kind, extremely gentle, I would say even effusive, which I had never known her to be earlier."

Sonia has a way of looking after those she likes.[9] She helped her husband's friend silently, almost without his knowing. By October 1994 Wajahat took a post that the government had passed orders for at the Indian Embassy in Washington, DC, as minister for community affairs. He worked hard at his job, piloting a bill through the US Congress to obtain clearance for the establishment of a Mahatma Gandhi Memorial in Washington. He later discovered that it was through Sonia's "office and her staff that I was given this posting to the US, where I could get the best treatment for post-traumatic stress disorder anywhere in the world." Throughout this harrowing period of recovery, he "took inspiration from the fact that I and my family were not alone. That there was this pillar and that was Sonia Gandhi. I could turn to her if anything went wrong. . . . I felt that I could depend on her."

Habibullah commented that the care shown to him was symptomatic, that Sonia was protective of all those she cared about. Rahul was in America, still studying, so before Wajahat took up his American posting, he asked his boss about Rahul's whereabouts. Sonia replied, "'You know, I feel very bad about this, but I've been told by the security people not to divulge Rahul's address and location to anyone, even to my family.' She was so apologetic about the whole thing." Mindful of what had happened to Indira and Rajiv, Wajahat urged her to observe the advice that she had been given. (Rahul had been at Harvard when his father was assassinated and moved to Rollins College in Florida before taking a master of philosophy degree in Development Economics at Trinity College, Cambridge.)

While Sonia was perfectly comfortable making decisions in matters such as the design of the memorials to Rajiv, Wajahat says she preferred the guidance of her chosen advisers on government policy matters that interfaced with the crafting of RGF programs. One of the earliest programs, Project INTERACT, provided education and rehabilitation to assist those who suffered the psychological effects of a traumatic experience. At the time, militancy and agitation in the disturbed states of Punjab, the heartland of the Sikhs, and in Kashmir had resulted in many casualties, mental as well as physical. The project for child victims of terrorist violence, especially the destitute who had lost their family's breadwinner, was set up within RGF's first year. Sonia provided initial finance to the project by donating the money awarded posthumously to Rajiv for the Indira Gandhi Prize for Peace, Disarmament and Development. Dr. V. Krishnamurthy, an RGF trustee, asserted that "the maximum amount of money" was spent sending orphaned children to public schools.

Project INTERACT, which has supported more than 1,600 children since its inception, now has a higher education wing, Project INTERACT II, that finances young people through college and university. Victims of riots that took place in 2002 have been helped, as have children who lost one or both parents in areas hit by the tsunami of December 2004. In addition, there are programs for street children and for the training and education of women. In 2000 the RGF, in collaboration with the National Book Trust of India, organized a workshop of writers and illustrators to develop comic books for neo-literates in Hindi on subjects Rajiv cared about: village councils, respect for the elderly, the eradication of superstition, women's empowerment. In 2004, recognizing that bookshops in Delhi and other cities tend to be located in upmarket shopping malls and clusters of shops that cater to the middle and upper classes, Sonia supported the foundation on a literacy initiative for urban dwellers. The foundation gave a nongovernmental organization money to set up two libraries in slums on the outskirts of Delhi, where people had no access to books. RGF funds paid for someone to run each library and buy books. In 2009 two more library projects were provided to the same NGO.[10] This enterprise falls under the RGF strategy of improving literacy and education in the most deprived areas, setting up libraries and informal education centers.

Sonia also encouraged initiatives for the physically challenged. As chairperson of the RGF she spearheaded a campaign for the enactment of a disability law that would affect the 7 percent of Indians who suffer from a disability. But Sonia was disappointed that it took nearly three years after the Disability Act was passed in 1995 for a chief commissioner to be named. At a 1999 RGF seminar on employment for people with disabilities, she decried the lack of progress and spoke of the "shocking absence of political will," reminding the participants that "employing the disabled is not an act of charity" for they "constitute a valuable, talented and constructive segment of our society."[11] Every year on Rajiv's birthday, August 20, specially modified cars and three-wheel scooters are presented by the foundation to individuals from various places in India. Sonia is noticeably relaxed with the newly mobile vehicle recipients with whom she exchanges hugs. Unlike many native-born Indians, who boast of their regional differences and the north-south divide, Sonia's behavior is not governed by prejudice, observed Krishnamurthy: "Having adopted India, every Indian was close to her . . . she judged everybody and every issue on its merits."[12]

Her responsibilities at the RGF gave her good training for entering politics, observed Krishnamurthy. He found that as Sonia Gandhi discovered that she was benefiting from an expansion in her knowledge, she became proactive about connecting with seasoned professionals at the top of different disciplines, discussing with them the most important problems concerning India and absorbing much general knowledge about the economy. As chairperson she met with diverse people, NGOs, statesmen, and intellectuals. Nelson Mandela delivered a lecture to the Rajiv Gandhi Institute for Contemporary Studies (RGICS) in January 1995, in which he quoted the fiercely antiapartheid Rajiv's words: "Our freedom will not be complete till South Africa is free." Mandela observed that his country could learn about the rights of the citizen and democracy from Jawaharlal Nehru and broached the idea of an Indian Ocean rim of socioeconomic cooperation.

He talked about a joint commission that had been established on this visit and emphasized the importance of closer bilateral ties. At Sonia's request, Hillary Clinton delivered a lecture, which was quite emotional, just three months later. America's First Lady rewrote large parts of it after being handed a poem by a female student from Delhi University about the silence of women. Clinton read the whole poem aloud, her voice catching at one point, adding that women's voices needed to be heard, not only in their own lives but also on the world stage. It is a feeling that she and Sonia share.

Acquiring more knowledge, Sonia was developing exponentially into a politician, for those who have the aura of knowing a little more than anybody else are respected by people who are involved in the affairs of state.

PART V

SONIA'S REBIRTH

19

UNDERSTAND MY ANGUISH

> My grief and loss have been deeply personal. But a time has come when I feel compelled to put aside my own inclinations and step forward. The tradition of duty before personal considerations has been the deepest conviction of the family to which I belong.
>
> —*Sonia Gandhi*

While Sonia was avoiding the public political scene, she was nonetheless very much a presence with an indirect influence on it. A constant stream of visitors—chief ministers, their deputies, and politicians—would call at her Janpath home as "a matter of courtesy," providing her with intelligence on what was happening in the Congress Party and in the country. Sections of the grand old party also had plans for her. They felt that if she could revive its fortunes, their own political careers would be made. Their survival was at stake, for Prime Minister Rao was getting mixed reviews and the party was losing strength.

In June 1991 a commission had been set up to investigate the identities of the conspirators and their motives in the May assassination of Rajiv Gandhi. Headed by a retired judge, Milap Chand Jain, the commission was going nowhere fast. At least 12 extensions gave it extra time to wander up and down blind alleys and to ruminate on an interim report about Indian government policy on Sri Lanka, the operational strategies of the intelligence agencies, or the fanciful conjecture (sometimes based on unverified reports) of plots by, variously, Nepali groups, Sikh extremists, and Kashmiri militants, some of whom were said to be working in collusion. There were also tussles with investigating agencies. One writer suggested that Justice Jain would happily examine any affidavit presented to him simply to prolong the length of his own contract; the net result was that the commission eventually turned into a saga of truths and half-truths.[1] The government would occasionally fiddle with the scope of the inquiry, even toying with the idea of winding it up, but there seemed to be no political will to move swiftly or efficiently. The hopes of the Gandhi family for concrete findings as to what lay behind Rajiv's murder faded as the years went by. Meanwhile, Sonia was responding to some very persistent requests.

The most important large forum of the Congress Party, the 1,000-plus strong All India Congress Committee (AICC), holds periodic conclaves, and Sonia, even though she was not even a primary member of the party, was always asked to attend as a "special invitee." Each time Sonia arrived, a crowd of enthusiasts and sycophants would start shouting and interrupt proceedings, sometimes for more than ten minutes,[2] once right in the middle of one of Prime Minister Rao's speeches. He was forced to stand and wait on the stage while delegates chanted for Sonia and pleaded with her to come to the aid of the party. She would go and sit in the audience, but she was not oblivious to the message.

The Congress Party was slowly falling apart. Although India continued to grow economically, allowing more groups and communities to take part in the democratic process, there was a disturbing trend toward right-wing ideologies that was dividing the country along religious lines. The principal view that disturbed Sonia was the notion that the country, with its dominant Hindu population, could be hijacked by those who believed that other religions—Islam, for instance—should take a subordinate position. Nationalist politicians were campaigning using evocative Hindu motifs, symbols, and deities to arouse the passions of the people, and religion was now firmly established as a political tool in the hands of the right. Sonia objected strongly.

In May 1995, mainly because they were disillusioned with Prime Minister Rao's ineffective response to the interreligious violence in the wake of the December 1992 demolition of the Babri mosque, two senior leaders split from the party and formed their own group, naming it the All India Indira Congress (Tiwari) after one of them, N. D. Tiwari. Both leaders looked for signs of Sonia's implicit or explicit support, which she carefully avoided giving. On the other hand, she did not try to dissuade them from dividing the party. The All India Congress (T) started to gather others around them.

And, four years from when the Jain Commission was first set up, there were still no answers.

There was apparently something on Sonia's mind that she wanted to let people know about. On August 23, 1995, she took a 5 PM Indian Airlines flight with Priyanka and her secretaries from Indira Gandhi Airport in Delhi to Lucknow, the capital city of the state of Uttar Pradesh. She was on her way to flag off the Lifeline Express train, a mobile hospital facility initiated by the Rajiv Gandhi Foundation. To the consternation of the prime minister and his friends in Delhi, more than 15,000 Congress Party workers crowded the tarmac, lounge, and surroundings of the airport to meet Sonia and Priyanka at Lucknow. The two women were mobbed as the Special Protection Group tried to keep a tight cordon around them both. Sonia's convoy began the 93-mile drive to Amethi at 6:30 PM, stopping along the way as she was enthusiastically greeted by party workers and constituents. A journey that should not have lasted more than three hours took almost double the time, and it was just before midnight when Sonia and Priyanka arrived at Amethi. Prime Minister Rao's acolytes in the constituency were in continuous telephone contact with New Delhi, reporting on Sonia's movements and the reception she was getting. No one could figure out what she was up to.

Her itinerary for the next day contained only two events. After the flagging-off ceremony for the medical train, Sonia Gandhi was to address a public meeting in a large venue called the Ramlila grounds. Sonia began her speech in a soft tone, describing how important Amethi was to her and her family. She then moved on to the rise of antisecular forces in India. "The principles and ideals to which Jawaharlal Nehru, Indira Gandhi, and my husband devoted their lives are being tested today, divisive forces are gathering strength." Then she turned to the subject of the probe into Rajiv's assassination. "You can understand my anguish. My husband has been dead for four years and three months, but the inquiry into his assassination is moving at such a slow pace."[3] The heartfelt speech, taking direct aim at the prime minister, was well received. *Outlook* magazine said that Priyanka was the one who prompted Sonia to lash out at Narasimha Rao.[4] And it got worse for the beleaguered man. In 1995, the Congress Party lost two important state elections: Gujarat and prosperous Maharashtra. In a general election called the following year, the party suffered its worst ever electoral defeat. Though Rao's government suffered heavy losses, no party could claim a strong enough majority. Congress was disintegrating; it was no longer even the largest party in parliament, and many stalwarts had quit. "Everybody started leaving. . . . After the 1992 Babri Masjid [mosque] riots we felt that . . . Congress had lost its ground, its ideology," the party's Uttar Pradesh state unit president remembered bitterly.[5]

A hung parliament was in place again. During the two shaky years that followed, there were three prime ministers; the first, and shortest, of the governments lasted only 13 days. A 13-party United Front coalition took power, and a new Congress Party "provisional president," Sitaram Kesri, was appointed in 1996. Kesri was in his eighties, but within the party many were snapping at his heels, hungry for the title. One writer suggested that the party thought "Kesri was a candidate favored by Sonia. In this perception was hidden a hope that in time Sonia Gandhi would enter active politics and soon progress to becoming party leader herself."[6] To fend off the sharks, Kesri aimed to demonstrate to the party not only that he had Sonia's backing, but also that he controlled her access to the top party position. The party defections, the insistent calls for her to come forward, and the dismal showing in the 1996 elections were leading Sonia to consider that she could perhaps have a part to play in restoring Congress's strength. By now, she was completely immersed in the Nehru legacy, and so, quietly, in March 1997 she took the first step and became a primary member of the Congress Party. Sonia supporters were thrilled.

By now, two governments had collapsed and a third one was in place with the Congress Party supporting it from the outside. Sonia was hugely troubled that the investigation into Rajiv's assassination still had not drawn any conclusions. The Congress Party threatened to withdraw its support of the coalition government if presentation of its findings was delayed further. By the end of November 1997, an interim report from the Jain Commission was tabled on the floor of parliament. It indicted one of the partners in the ruling coalition, the Dravida Munnetra Kazhagam (DMK), for supporting the Liberation Tigers of Tamil Eelam (LTTE), who were held responsible for Rajiv Gandhi's assassination. The Congress Party demanded that DMK ministers be dropped from government, which the ruling coalition refused to do. The party saw the opportunity to use Sonia's personal tragedy to seize a political advantage. On November 28, Congress withdrew its support from the government, the prime minister resigned, and midterm elections were announced for February–March 1998. Furthermore, if Sonia could be persuaded to campaign and bring some Nehru-Gandhi luster to a party whose star had dimmed badly, Congress members who had lost their seats in the 1996 election hoped that the result would be their own comeback.

Sonia now faced the same dilemma that had troubled her so much when Rajiv had been asked to switch careers. It was difficult. She was not pushy, not by nature a politician, and not used to handling the hustings alone. In a later television interview, she explained what had gone through her mind:

"Many of my senior colleagues asked me to come and help the Congress . . . there was a conflict within me. . . . I have photographs of my husband and my mother-in-law in my office . . . each time I walked past those photographs, I felt that I wasn't responding to my duty, the duty to this family and to the country. I felt I was being cowardly to just sit and watch things deteriorate in the Congress for which my mother-in-law and the whole family lived and died. So, at that point I took the decision."[7] On December 29, 1997, an announcement was made that Sonia would campaign for the party in the forthcoming election. Immediately Congress workers were energized; they thronged her home, set off fireworks, and danced in the streets deliriously. Their political messiah had arrived. Rivals poured on the scorn; one whom Sonia had almost coaxed into an alliance described her decision as being like the arrival of a doctor after the patient is dead.

Anti-Italian comments echoed from the rooftops; the rightist Hindu nationalists described the forthcoming battle as *Ram Rajya* versus *Rome Rajya* (the rule of the legendary Hindu God Ram up against the rule of Rome, the center of the Catholic faith). Her children, as always, were a vital source of support and part of the process. "She was shy, it was hard for her, public speaking was very difficult for her and both of us had to really be there for moral support, for everything . . . the fact that duty was such a powerful pull, also means that is a part of her, that is also who she is."[8] Sonia's sense of duty propelled her to a strong start in an evocative location. Suddenly the woman whom the public had hardly heard speak was shooting from the hip. The years of silence quickly turned into a torrent of unleashed emotional assaults as she addressed topics that had the potential for exploitation by the opposition.

Sonia began her energetic campaign with a speech at Sriperumbudur, where Rajiv had been violently assassinated seven years earlier. Her head modestly covered, she declared, "I stand here today on the soil made sacred by the blood of my husband who died a martyr to the cause of the nation's unity and integrity. I stand here today, surrounded by security, where he stood valiantly facing his assassins, unprotected and alone."[9] And she was not afraid to level veiled criticism at Congress Party controllers while campaigning in south India. She declared in a speech in Bangalore on January 15, 1998, "I am deeply disturbed when I see the future of India and its stability and prosperity threatened by those who put their narrow self-interests and ambitions before the interests of the people they should be serving."[10] She passionately defended the name of her murdered loved one, devoting the last part of her speech to a topic that had rocked the last years of her husband's premiership: Bofors. She declared stoutly that he had been the victim of "malicious" slander, reminding all those watching and listening that "six governments have come and gone—five of them from opposition parties yet the complete truth has still to be revealed." She declared that she would "be the happiest person the day all Bofors papers are made public because on that day my husband will be vindicated, because on that day it will be proved that this campaign was nothing but a vicious attempt to destroy his reputation."[11] Though in later years others wrote her speech drafts for her, her daughter was providing the hard-hitting rhetoric; Priyanka said that she wrote all her mother's speeches in her first campaign.[12]

On January 16 in Hyderabad, Andhra Pradesh, Sonia talked about how "devastated" she had been at the 1992 demolition of the Babri mosque. She also reinforced the popular theme of dynasty, which resonated with the ordinary Indian. She continued with her themes throughout the campaign, adding details to suit the location. When the results of the 1998 polls came in, analysts noted an increase in female and in Muslim voters, though the number of seats won by Congress, at 141, was just one up on the previous election tally of 140 in 1996. But party morale had shot up, and Congress had suffered in so many ways through the previous years that its leaders looked at Sonia as a career-saver. She had stopped the hemorrhage and had given confidence to the party, which now got so excited that it immediately decided the time had come to get rid of the dead wood at the top.

Unlike Sonia, Sitaram Kesri did not photograph well and had no voter appeal. But he jealously and carefully guarded his position, as he knew that many were lobbying for Sonia to become party president. He was right; party officials were trying to persuade her to stand for election while working hard on Kesri to step down. Unwilling to do so, Kesri fired a shot across the bow to any group that would seek to replace him with Sonia or another candidate. At a meeting attended by Sonia, he stated, "You have come as a symbol representing the family. I am aging and if the Congress collapses, the responsibility will be yours."[13] The inference was that Sonia could only replace him if he died or if the party disintegrated. The most important decision-making body of the party, the Congress Working Committee, passed a resolution on March 5, 1998, asking for Sonia to feature more heavily in the party organization.

On March 10, 1998, Kesri issued a cunning statement, foreshadowing a hesitant "decision to resign" with the caveat that his reasons would be announced at a special meeting of the AICC. There was no meeting of the AICC scheduled; Kesri was determined to hang onto power for as long as he could. But most politicians are not slow to send lambs to the slaughter when their own careers are on the line; the Working Committee wanted Sonia in and Kesri out. They thought she should head the AICC *and* the Congress Parliamentary Party as Indira had done. An unhappy Kesri chaired a Working Committee session on March 14.

It was a stormy meeting, and rumors were flying about a change at the top. Major Dalbir Singh was in the next room at party headquarters. There were a couple of hundred excited party men and women in the compound; everybody was expecting Sonia to come in and take over after the meeting. Some wanted to make reference to newspapers that had reported Sitaram Kesri publicly stating that he would make way for Sonia, so the papers were sent inside and the Working Committee read them out loud. Kesri's innings were over; his belongings were already being packed and sent to his house. The deposed party president and a close associate, a party general secretary, came out in a huff, rushed to Kesri's office, and then left. Not a moment was wasted. Major Singh, at that time the national convener of a department at the AICC, was asked to have Kesri's nameplate replaced with one for Sonia Gandhi. He was also asked to work through his guest list and make arrangements for 80 to 90 senior Congress figures to be invited for an early evening welcome reception. There were a lot of enthusiastic people gathering in the compound in an atmosphere of anticipation and euphoria. Around 6 PM Sonia, the new Congress president, arrived to graciously meet her new team. After five or ten minutes, she left with a few leaders for Kesri's residence in order to make peace with him, a diplomatic gesture he remembered for a long time.

After the party's swift coup, Sonia made the move into her new role and crossed over to what she used to think of as the dark side. She quickly settled in, coming to 24 Akbar Road, the headquarters of the Congress Party, three or four times a week around 10 AM, according to Major Singh, who ensured the smooth functioning of her office there. In India, it is routine for there to be endless streams of people waiting to meet even the humblest of politicians, let alone the party president. Appointments would run right through from 10 AM until around 1:30 PM, and Singh recalls there always were people who had come from all over the country hanging around the compound, wanting to meet her. It might be someone in need of financial support; it might be someone who felt that they should be included in the organization of the party at a particular level—state, district, block, or village; or someone seeking justice, feeling wronged by a particular official. Or it might be someone wanting her backing to run for election at assembly, corporation, or local body level. Or some member from what India, with its plethora of bureaucratic institutions, calls civil society, seeking Sonia's intervention if they had been wronged by a government agency. Or it might be a resident welfare, trader, community, charity, or society group inviting her to one of their functions.[14] She would take three or four more people out of the 200 or more waiting outside and would walk past and greet everyone. People coming to meet with politicians often carry something that they wish to present—a letter, a representation, a book, a flower, a painting, a handicraft, or an idol of an Indian God in wood or metal.[15] Sonia would give Singh the items to hold but would never disappoint those who had traveled sometimes thousands of miles to meet her. She reads every scrap of paper that is given to her; even in meetings, she likes to be given a note of the points raised. She receives reams of paper, and she reads it all at her leisure.[16]

In September 1998 Sonia presided over a three-day brainstorming retreat for the party at Pachmarhi, a hill station and former British cantonment in the state of Madhya Pradesh. There, in her inaugural address as Congress president, Sonia laid out her policy statement. On housekeeping matters, she announced that she would like camps of this kind to be organized regularly at the national and other levels as the party had "little scope for looking back; do serious thinking and self-introspection. We need all those three things."[17] She also launched a regular monthly party journal, called *Congress Sandesh*, which would contain articles and opinion pieces from a cross-section of party workers as well as comment on events, performance, and schemes at all party levels. Today, the party president's message published in the magazine is seized on by the media as one of the few official indicators to her point of view. In her 1998 Pachmarhi address, she questioned the New Economic Policy that had helped India to development and an expanding middle class but had done little to alleviate real poverty. It was a salute to economic growth but also a slingshot at former prime minister Rao for ignoring the class divide. "Many of us thought that economic development and progress would roll back the spread of communal ideologies and put an end to the politics of hate. This has clearly not happened . . . we must constantly reinterpret our economic philosophy in the light of changing circumstance. . . . Our economic policy will have to be multidimensional to meet the needs of our people at various levels . . . we cannot spend our way to prosperity." She said that a fundamental objective needed to be the abolition of poverty over the coming 10 to 15 years, and that a higher level of growth in agriculture was needed. She pointed out that inflation needed to be controlled, "since inflation hits the poor the hardest."[18] One of the conclusions of the Pachmarhi camp echoed the Rajiv Gandhi Foundation seminar on coalition governments; it was decided that a coalition would only be entered into when "absolutely necessary," and that the difficulty of forming a one-party government was just a "transient phase."

Congress officials speak of a cultural change in the party that began around then. Editor in chief at the *Indian Express*, Shekhar Gupta, said that Sonia has the "sorted out, uncluttered mind of a European, she doesn't have the cluttered spaghetti mind of a South Asian."[19] The Indian disease of sycophancy, mind-numbingly endless speeches, and convoluted discussions to some degree was reduced. Her trademark punctuality came as a bit of a shock to some people. Former foreign minister Natwar Singh commented, "Sonia is punctual. Nehru was punctual because he'd spent so many years in England. Mahatma Gandhi was very punctual. This appeals to the average Indian. We are not punctual."[20]

In the 1998 retreat, she also spoke of wanting to enhance the standing of the party with the young and the educated. Noticeably, to the present day, the faces of the party are more educated and more articulate, often coming from professions outside politics such as law. On foreign policy, Sonia spoke of the recent nuclear tests conducted by India as well as Pakistan, adding, "We must now consolidate our technological capacities for defense and deterrence, avoiding . . . provocative gestures." Here, she maintained the stand of her husband on becoming "part of the international mainstream on disarmament without . . . jeopardizing our society's options."[21]

Sonia had seen Rajiv carefully build bridges with China and regretted that in a matter of a few weeks the coalition government destroyed what the Congress had achieved over a ten-year effort to normalize India's relations with its neighbor. On the western border, she added, "Our policy toward Pakistan is also confused and unclear." She also mentioned that it was important to "repair our relationship" with previously friendly countries that opposed the nuclear tests India conducted. A declaration was produced covering the major issues in the presidential address as well as women's rights, population control,[22] water policy, the northeast, the Jain commission, and local self-government. It was an important statement of intent; Sonia was getting down to business.

She had undergone quite a transformation from the time when she set up the Rajiv Gandhi Foundation. Dr. V. Krishnamurthy, RGF trustee, noted with satisfaction that she had graduated from her own leadership training school. The two years that Sonia had taken to recompose and enter the type of management role she played later was, he notes, less than the orientation period and training undertaken by "the best people selected for the highest of services."[23] Krishnamurthy and others around her foresaw the potential hazards and challenges she might face in public life, so they worked hard to develop her confidence during the two years after Rajiv's assassination when she first became chairperson of the Rajiv Gandhi Foundation. It helped her to prepare for the rough and tumble of being Congress president and to take on an adversarial role as opposition party chief. "In about five years she was a tremendously mature political leader," notes Krishnamurthy.

20

AKBAR ROAD

> While we make every effort to come back to power both at the Center and in various states, we can also enrich the political, economic, and social life of this country, even by being in the opposition. There are many tasks we can and will take on apart from the most fundamental task of exposing the government in power.
>
> —*Sonia Gandhi*

In 1997 Sonia presided over a happy occasion: the wedding of her daughter Priyanka to businessman Robert Vadra at Sonia's home, 10 Janpath. Vadra first met Priyanka when she was 13—he was only a few years older—and was completely unfazed by her background: "Robert treated me just like anybody else when I first met him. I liked that," she told an interviewer in 2009.[1] According to the headmaster of the exclusive New Delhi British School, where Robert studied, Priyanka and Robert met through the school's social network, an "established formal social club."[2] Priyanka was not studying there, though among the children of other families from around the world were the offspring of some Italian friends of the Gandhis,[3] and a decade later Maneka Gandhi's son Varun attended the school. The wedding was a two-hour-long Hindu ceremony, presided over by Kashmiri priests, followed by dinner. No high-profile Indian wedding can happen without press cameras, and for the photos, Sonia stood beaming on the steps outside her house, holding quite protectively onto Robert's arm, even allowing the media a minute's encore. Rahul stood on the other side of

Priyanka. Among the guests were her cousin Varun Gandhi, Sonia's mother and an uncle, and others from the Maino family.[4]

Through the 1990s and the early years of the next millennium, Priyanka received endless calls to become a politician. She said that from around the age of 14 to 16 or 17, she thought that politics was "absolutely" what she wanted for a career, for she knew that she found public speaking easy, she could connect with people, and she liked the attention.[5] But she also felt that she would not go into it out of a sense of duty, as her mother had. Before the 1999 election, she went away for ten days of Vipassana meditation, a specific, nonreligious technique introduced by Buddha 2,500 years ago. She told her interviewer, "I just disappeared . . . so that I better know what my own mind is, rather than what other people want of me."[6] She called making the decision "growing up."

Sonia was settling into her job as Congress Party president; her staff was getting used to her style. Major Dalbir Singh, secretary of the All India Congress Committee, headquartered at 24 Akbar Road, New Delhi, maintained her office. The party building is adjacent to her home, so one of his first jobs was to have a connecting gate installed between the two compounds so that Sonia could walk from one protected area to another. The central office of the Indian National Congress is a set of one-story buildings with some extra offices tacked on, and inside the complex, there is a large room in the main building used for press conferences and meetings. At least once a day a throng of press people gathers, waiting for some Congress luminary to emerge and give them a sound bite. To the left of the colonial building, on one side of a garden, there is a billboard with a large photograph of Indira. A phrase from her last speech, "Every drop of my blood," is a chilling reminder of the fragility of the lives of Nehru-Gandhi political leaders.

While Sonia generally had her first appointment at the Akbar Road office at 10 AM, Major Singh would be there at 8:30 AM getting the place ready. "She likes everything orderly. She's fastidious about cleanliness. She didn't want a fancy office," he explained.[7] Singh often asked Sonia if he could change the tapestry on the chairs. "She would say 'No, get them dry-cleaned, it'll be cheaper; why should we spend money on changing the fabric of the chairs?'" In the mornings, Singh would see to security clearances for visitors, to housekeeping details such as flower arrangements, "stationery, her pen, making sure that a timepiece is working, that the battery isn't dead, that the air conditioner is working, and that the temperature is OK." Major Singh said that certain conditions must be observed in her office due to her mild respiratory problems—no room sprays, for instance. "She wanted the room to be vacuumed nicely, no dust; I made sure there were no carpets there."

Sonia meets visiting dignitaries and delegations, chief ministers, and members of parliament at her home in a large, book-lined room with a light-colored set of sofas, a glass coffee table, and a long wooden table for formal meetings. It was Rajiv's meeting room and study.

With a country the size and geographical scale of India, when natural catastrophes like floods, drought, earthquakes, and cyclones strike, leading politicians are expected to visit the disaster zone. Indians take note of how quickly the powerful move to be at the side of the bereft. In 1999 there was a cyclone in the state of Orissa; after a Congress Working Committee meeting, Sonia tasked Singh with sending 100 truckloads of relief material to the affected area. In 2001 there was an earthquake in Bhuj in the state of Gujarat; tens of thousands died and many more were left homeless. "The national leadership is expected to respond spontaneously; you can't go there days later. We were in opposition; the BJP was in government at the Centre and in the state. No one had gone. Madam said, 'I want to go right away.'" Sonia arrived there before anyone else, before Bharatiya Janata Party leader Lal Krishna Advani, Singh remembered, bursting with pride.

Singh said that if Sonia had an encounter before she came to the office for her regular meetings, it might affect the way she felt for the rest of the day. He would gauge Sonia's frame of mind, which could be "OK, quite pleasant, or very good," by the way she responded to his "Morning, ma'am"—whether she nodded her head or said, "Morning" or "Morning, Dalbir." The former soldier took pleasure in working with Sonia: "If I saw her once a day, if I gave her some papers and she felt good reading them, if she said 'You did well,' or if I did something good in her office and she said 'Thank you,' if she smiled, that was a reward." Army officers are straight-talking, so Singh did not shield his boss from unpleasant truths.

Now that her life is more public, even more discipline is required. He said that she eats regularly and is "very strict" about her diet. On campaigning days, on board a helicopter, Singh said, "we used to have a food packet loaded for her, very light food." While traveling, she prefers "soup and sandwiches." According to him, Sonia gets up fairly early in the morning, goes to bed late, but by following a strict regimen, she remains "absolutely fit." Sonia told one of her state presidents that she lapses sometimes and does not always follow a physical routine regularly, but that Rahul reminds her that she must exercise to maintain her energy levels, and she practices yoga.[8]

Something rarely mentioned is the Sonia spine. Indian political party meetings usually take place on a raised platform, as in the West, but Indian leaders very often sit on white sheets on a dais, with white covered mattresses and white cushions discreetly placed around the stage for comfort.

Major Dalbir Singh has been at party headquarters for more than 21 years and has attended a good many of the meetings in the capital and elsewhere. As the age spectrum for Indian politicians tends to be top-heavy, there is a plethora of the elderly on stage, and Sonia herself is now in her sixties. Sessions start around 9 or 9:30 AM and go until lunchtime. On the dais, there may be as many as 70 or 80 leaders. One by one, Singh has observed, each of them droops and starts looking around for the cushions, pillows, or the small mattress. "The older ones would give in a little earlier than the younger ones, but all of us, after a couple of hours, we're shifting from side to side, and we're twisting." Sometimes, those sitting behind Sonia might fall asleep. "I've seen the most responsible of leaders doze off and she would tell me or anyone sitting next to her, 'Just go and nudge that fellow, he's sleeping and the media will take a shot.'" Sonia, however, always sits upright and listens carefully to everything. "She'll put to shame even the youngest member of the party. You'll see her sitting motionless for four hours without a cushion. . . . I've never seen Madam Gandhi doze even once during sessions and proceedings."

In 1998 Sonia visited the Nehru ancestral home, Anand Bhavan in Allahabad. The Bharatiya Janata Party was riding high on its promulgation of Hindu nationalism. A BJP titan known for his lethal tongue, Dr. Murli Manohar Joshi, was the sitting member of parliament. Meanwhile, a Congress activist turned independent mayor, Dr. Rita Bahuguna Joshi (no relation), was making her mark in politics. Sonia immediately set about getting Rita to return to the Congress fold. She wanted to see if Rita "could defeat such a strong leader in his own constituency. Then she asked me point-blank to join the Congress Party," explained Joshi. Six months later Sonia met her again. Sonia wanted her to contest the election against the BJP incumbent. Rita Joshi was reluctant, pointing out that it was just three weeks away. "I'm going to lose," she said. Sonia replied, "Never mind; I want to contain him in that seat so that he cannot campaign outside Allahabad, and you're the only one who can keep him entrenched there. Give him the run around, that's all I want."[9] As predicted, Rita Bahuguna Joshi lost, but Sonia was very happy because it was only by a very small margin. She awarded her national posts in the women's wing of the party and finally the position of state unit president, a competitive job rarely held by women. Sonia was developing an ability to strategize. The state unit chief finds that in meetings, her party president tends to give her full attention to a solution-oriented approach and says that Sonia Gandhi reacts to trivial complaints by being "cold, looking down, or she'll start writing."[10]

After the 1998 election, then Congress Party spokesperson Najma Heptulla gave a tea party in her garden for the media personnel who had followed the campaign. Heptulla encouraged her senior politicians to have some one-on-one time with the media. It was, Heptulla says, "the first occasion where she [Sonia] was able to directly meet the press. She was the main attraction."[11] The political editor of the *Hindu* group, Smita Gupta, interviewed Sonia about a year into her new role. Because Sonia talked so little to the press, Smita went in with "very low expectations"[12] but came away "fairly impressed." Experienced politicians evade or refuse to answer awkward questions, but at that time, Sonia did neither. She talked frankly about problems within the organization of the party with a clear awareness of what was happening around her. Gupta felt that her views on foreign policy were "very considered, that she knew a great deal about relations with other countries and discussed her husband's international efforts in fine detail. On economic issues, Gupta had the impression that "someone else had explained to her what to say," but on secularism Sonia addressed the issue "straight from the heart."

The year 1999 marked Sonia's public entry to the media, for she started allowing journalists more access. Vir Sanghvi, adviser to the *Hindustan Times,* persuaded her to give her first television interview. He said to her that it was "All very well for you to say you hate the media and not to give interviews, but if you are in politics, then there *are* issues, such as the foreign origins" and why she had come into the profession, that people wanted to know about. He told her, "'I think you're obliged to provide some answers.' . . . She conceded that principle quite quickly, but her own nervousness kept her from fixing a date even when she'd agreed to the interview, until we finally pinned her down."[13] What surprised his crew was that Sonia was perfectly calm about the team making a mess with lights and equipment in her meeting room; she took it all with equanimity, making sure everyone had something to drink. Rahul and Priyanka were there to help their mother through what was going to be a "bit of an ordeal." Sanghvi recalled that every time she started answering, she would burst into giggles, until she relaxed and ignored the camera.

Like Smita Gupta, Sanghvi noticed that Sonia felt obliged to answer a question directly, something her husband also did, "even if the answer did her no good." When he asked Sonia about people attacking her on account of her foreign origins, she said that she understood the reasons for their objections—which was "not tactful, but honest." He grilled her mercilessly, asking her about her accent, whether she felt Italian or Indian, and how she felt about her party losing the election as the polls were predicting. At the end of the hour-long recording, his crew noticed the hugs shared between the children and their mother; they all seemed to be relieved that it was over.

Former minister of state for external affairs Natwar Singh had by now firmed up a system whereby important foreign visitors like prime ministers always made sure to pay a visit to Sonia Gandhi. "It didn't take long to send the word round to the embassies informally that she is the president of the Congress Party and Rajiv Gandhi's widow," he remembered.[14] Britain's Tony Blair, US secretary of state Colin Powell, Chinese and Russian leaders—all paid courtesy calls.

And in 2001 Sonia presented a talk to the Asia Society and the Council on Foreign Relations in New York City, demonstrating just how far she had come since the days of simply standing or sitting beside another member of her family. With warmth, confidence, and charm, she spoke of how a meeting between her husband and Vice President George H. W. Bush in 1985 had resulted in the Indian city of Bangalore becoming an international information technology hub. She joked that with the numbers that India had to deal with at election time, the country could easily offer the United States advice on electoral technology, as well as support with how to deal with power cuts. Speaking proudly of India, she said that her country was very used to what India called defections and what America called "shifting political alignments." She tackled relations with Pakistan and China and was unequivocal on Jammu and Kashmir, rounding off a well-delivered, accomplished speech before taking questions from the audience. That same day, Sonia Gandhi addressed the United Nations General Assembly on HIV/AIDS. On this trip, she also gave a speech to the Congressional India Caucus. It was 16 years since her husband had made his first speeches at the UN General Assembly, the Council on Foreign Relations, and addressed the US Congress.

Sonia's international appearances went down well at home and abroad; she was getting used to the limelight, and the public was getting used to a talking Sonia. There was an upbeat mood in the air. Sensing a new wind blowing in the Congress Party, the opposition parties prepared to hurt Sonia in the most brutal public battle she would face since she adopted India as her home.

21

THIS IS MY LAND

I chose India as my country. I am Indian, and will remain so till my last breath. India is my motherland, dearer to me than my own life.

—*Sonia Gandhi*

Sonia Gandhi needed to be removed from the political scene, or so the ruling coalition, known as the National Democratic Alliance (NDA), of which the Bharatiya Janata Party (BJP) formed the largest of the right-wing groups, decided in 1998. The NDA realized that Sonia, the keeper of the Nehru-Gandhi flame, was someone Congress supporters could rally around and subjugate their own competitive instincts to in hopes of securing their own political futures. So the BJP-led coalition talked up the economic progress of a resurgent, nationalist, Hindu India, under the slogan "India Shining," while trying to take Sonia apart.

The NDA laid into her foreign origins, endlessly making fun of her accent, and the more she campaigned, the more she spoke, the more they ridiculed her. This was at a time when she was also struggling with her inhibitions about interacting with the media. But she soldiered on, determined to do her duty. In April 1999 some partners of the NDA government of Prime Minister Atal Behari Vajpayee, feeling ignored or left out, began bickering within the coalition before turning toward the Congress Party. The NDA started to look shaky, and some Congress Party leaders scented blood. Sonia Gandhi, cautious at first, advised that Congress was not going to "jump to anything"; it would watch and wait and "act when necessary."[1] Some NDA allies withdrew their support from the ruling coalition, and when challenged with a confidence ballot, the coalition lost by one vote. President Kocheril Raman Narayanan was weighing the options—dissolving parliament or exploring the possibilities of an alternative government. Members of the Congress leadership had been having discussions with potential allies—one of whom was Mulayam Singh Yadav, head of the Samajwadi or Socialist Party—and concluded that it would be possible for the Congress Party, with allies, to get a majority tally of 272 of the 543 elected seats in the People's House (Lok Sabha) and to form a government. They conveyed this information to Sonia, who met with Yadav for 45 minutes at Janpath a few days after the Vajpayee government had fallen. The next day, after meeting with President Narayanan, she stood in the forecourt of the President's Palace to announce to the media that the Congress Party had achieved the 272-seat tally. But Yadav would have none of it, denounced her as a "foreigner," and wrote to the president of India that he would not be supporting the Congress Party. As one party member put it, there was "a fair amount of egg on everyone's face when this fiasco took place."

In a 2004 interview with Vir Sanghvi, advisor to the *Hindustan Times*, Sonia was asked why she had made the statement. She explained, "I obviously didn't mean that I, Sonia Gandhi, had 272. For God's sake, grant me a little more sense than that! What I meant was the opposition now constituted a majority of the House because the government had just been defeated in a confidence vote." She had prefaced this with, "It was a miscalculation on our part. We were depending on assurances given by certain persons and those assurances were not fulfilled."[2] In a 2006 television interview, pressed by Vir Sanghvi to say whether or not she would have become prime minister if Congress *had* been able to form a government in 1999, Sonia replied, "Most certainly not. . . . I didn't even have the mandate of a constituency, how could I do so?"[3] The 272-seat incident is often described as one in which Sonia showed some naiveté; she claimed that there was simply a lack of clarity of meaning. Dileep Padgaonkar, consulting editor with the *Times of India*, describes it as the "only . . . instance where in front of the media she botched it."[4] Author Inder Malhotra said that the incident taught her the importance of acquiring knowledge directly.[5] Sanghvi noted, "it came back to haunt her."[6]

While the press was convulsing over the 272-seat incident, it completely missed a significant meeting that showed that Sonia had not only decided that her party would return to victory one day, but also who would be premier when that happened. In her television interview with Sanghvi, she confirmed that she went to visit the president twice, once on her own and once with Dr. Manmohan Singh, to say that he would lead a Congress-majority government should such an entity come to pass. This would have been around 1999, during President Narayanan's tenure. In the early years of her active political career, Sonia had already made up her mind that she would not accept the post of prime minister. A decade later, Priyanka told an interviewer that long before the 2004 election, her mother made it clear that she did not want to be prime minister.[7]

A national election was called for September 1999, and Sonia contested two parliamentary seats: Bellary in south India and Rajiv's constituency in Amethi—which had been represented consecutively by family friend and former pilot Satish Sharma and Dr. Sanjay Sinh. The BJP placed one of their toughest-talking orators, Sushma Swaraj, against her in Bellary.

Sonia won both seats and chose to represent Amethi, resigning from Bellary. Sushma Swaraj and her other opponents inside and outside the party simply waited for the next opportunity to train their sightlines on her—next time they would use bigger guns. And while the mocking continued, Sonia honed her skills on the public campaign stage. Tarun Tejpal, the editor in chief of the investigative weekly *Tehelka*, which published an exposé of the NDA government, had a few short one-on-one meetings with Sonia. He said that someone sitting in her position would have had to "declutter a lot to arrive at the right course. For years [this] 'India Shining' nonsense had been going on"—the elite of India, who had benefited from the whole opening up of the economy, in tandem with the media had taken public discourse to a level of "high commerce, high gloss." Economic growth and a "shining India" were just one aspect of a larger, more troubling picture of the country, and Sonia drew the curtain back on that scene. "She took the discourse a little away from the noise, the money, and the gloss and reached back for those . . . wellsprings of India, she just began to repeat and rearticulate those . . . that itself began to reshape the public tone."[8] Human rights activist, author, and former high commissioner to London Kuldip Nayar, who had been jailed during the Emergency years, saw Sonia for a solo meeting at Janpath around this time. He wanted to assess the views of the Congress president for himself. They discussed pluralism, and he "found her very committed to the concept of secularism which is . . . part of the spirit of our constitution."[9]

The coalition NDA government was riding high and benefiting from a spike in national pride after India won the Kargil war fought around the Line of Control between India and Pakistan, in the mountainous state of Jammu and Kashmir. Prime Minister Vajpayee was seen as the defining politician of the "India Shining" years, from the late 1990s to the early 2000s. He had a fierce attack dog: Amar Singh, the bald and bespectacled spokesman for the socialist Samajwadi, who would say that to progress in politics you cannot "be the sidekick of a sidekick, you need to be the sidekick of a main person."[10] In the 1990s he addressed 150 meetings criticizing Congress and notoriously scorned Sonia as "a reader, not a leader."[11]

Tejpal describes these "bad" years of BJP muscularity as "hysterical, the amount of Hindu shrillness in the public space. . . . She was under daily attack from the BJP. They used to trash her accent, they used to trash her Hindi, they used to trash her every day."[12] Just over a decade later Singh justified his verbal attacks by saying that they had nothing to do with Sonia; they were made because the leaders of the Socialist Party he spoke for had been jailed during the Emergency for 19 months: "So their political DNA was bitterly opposed to Congress." On the "reader, not a leader" line, he is remorseful and admits that "I feel very embarrassed for Sonia Gandhi, and L. K. Advani [a former BJP deputy prime minister[13]] . . . irrespective of practicing different ideologies. I did not know Sonia Gandhi at all, so I had no feelings, good or bad, toward her. So I had no qualms about saying what was fed to me to say against her."[14] Singh claimed that he was given his lines by a Socialist Party stalwart. "It might have been my lip movement, but it was somebody else's thoughts. . . . I was used by the party," he claimed.

Amar Singh was not the only one of Sonia's former opponents to hurl insults at her. In India, the gap between innuendo and slander is quite wide and leaves plenty of scope for the nuanced comment. In such an ethnically diverse country, sexist and racist remarks flow across the political spectrum—online and off—unchecked. NDA minister Pramod Mahajan, for example, told a rally, "If we are so keen on having a foreigner as a prime minister, why not have Tony Blair or Bill Clinton . . . ?"[15] Other enemies referred to Sonia as a *vidayati murgi* (a foreign-bred hen) and spoke of "spaghetti English." Italian-ness, Christianity, and Catholicism seemed to be easy targets for them. Opponents also spoke of Sonia casting a "widow's shadow" on her party. Among the anti-Sonia slogans was "*Congress Party ka ek hi raasta, bolo Italian, Khao pasta*" (the Congress Party has only one route option: speak Italian and eat pasta).

Some Indian politicians do not enunciate clearly in English or Hindi, yet Mulayam Singh Yadav would ridicule Sonia's accent, making out that when she said the "Dal" in Janata Dal, the name of a political party, the last word came out like the Indian word for lentils, *dhaal,* with a long "a." The attacks by politicians were just verbal, but it appears others had more sinister intentions. Around this time, threats to Sonia's life increased, so senior Congress leaders sent a letter to the president of India, and the BJP government tightened her security.[16]

The abusive, anti-Sonia arguments cut no ice in rural India, where she was accepted for who she was. While villagers marveled at her fair skin, they told her and anyone who asked them that, as far as they were concerned, Rajiv Gandhi had brought her to India, she was his wife, she had borne his children, there was no other issue. The foreigner label did not apply in their minds, nor in hers: In 1999 she said that she didn't feel "one bit Italian," she felt *completely* Indian: "I love India, I love the people, India is in my heart."[17]

Sonia never once reacted publicly to the insults tossed at her, even though much of India was shocked at the onslaught. In fact, the BJP's negative campaign became counterproductive and began to rebound on the right-wingers. It was putting people off, especially when contrasted with the quiet, well-mannered Nehru-Gandhis. Some of Sonia's friends, like interior designer Sunita Kohli, said that the Gandhis are stoical about untruths. "They never gave a retort. One certainly feels incensed on their behalf."[18] Tejpal observed that Sonia was strong enough to take the blows: "I remember a very close friend of hers . . . telling me, 'You're wrong if you feel that's kind of crippling her, or destroying her, or diminishing her personally. She's very, very tough. She can take it.' Anyone who could take that daily thrashing, that daily humiliation . . . that [ability] comes from moral clarity, from knowing the difference between right and wrong."[19]

There were some in her own party who also were ready to knife her politically, combining arguments spouted by the NDA with her perceived inexperience in a frontal assault. In 1999 three Congress leaders—Purno Agitok Sangma, Sharad Pawar, and Tariq Anwar—decided to highlight the foreign origin issue. In a Congress Working Committee meeting, one of the three announced that the BJP might have legitimate areas of concern with regard to Sonia's Italian origins. After the meeting was over, they wrote a letter to the party president: "We accept with interest and humility the best which we can gather . . . and we absorb them into our soil. But our inspiration, our soul, our honor, our pride, our dignity, is rooted in our soil. It has to be of this earth."[20] They wrote that the ordinary Indian expected the prime minister to have a track record in public life; the overall inference was that Sonia did not fit the bill. She had never said that she wanted to be prime minister, but they made the assumption. The move from *within* the party astonished and saddened her. She responded in a letter on May 15, 1999: "At this morning's meeting of the Congress Working Committee, certain of my colleagues expressed views to the effect that my having been born elsewhere is a liability to the Congress Party. I am pained by their lack of confidence in my ability to act in the best interests of the party and the country. In these circumstances, my sense of loyalty to the party and duty to my country compel me to tender my resignation from the post of the Party President."[21] Immediately, ordinary party workers rushed from all over the country to Sonia's home and office. These were the rank-and-file Congress diehards, the unacknowledged, often from rural heartlands, for whom the Nehru-Gandhi legacy meant a great deal. Some workers threatened to kill themselves with cyanide capsules, a symbol of the mass hysteria that can spread when an iconic personality is under threat. Sonia was moved by the support and so nine days later, on May 25, she told an audience at a stadium in Delhi: "A few days ago, I submitted my resignation to the Congress Working Committee. I did so that day with a heavy and burdened heart. . . . The very people who had come to me with folded hands to plead that I emerge from my seclusion to save the Congress began to question my patriotism. They sought to sow seeds of suspicion about me in the minds of my fellow countrymen and women." She described herself as "deeply pained. It seemed to me I had been abandoned on my own in this great struggle. Those whom I considered my own appeared to have been overcome by their greed for power and position." She said they were consumed with "their mean intrigue and petty conspiracies against each other."[22]

Sonia then rescinded her decision to relinquish the party presidency. And she sent out the message that those who were not on her side could leave the party: "Let those with the slightest reservations . . . go their own way. We have neither fear nor concern. We are not lusting for office." Then she asked, "What is the meaning of their questioning my patriotism? . . . Every second of my life has mingled with this land. It was here that I married, here that I became a mother, here before your eyes that I was widowed. The greatest daughter of this country, Indira-Ji, breathed her last in my arms." In a clear echo of Indira's last speech, Sonia said, "Each drop of blood in my being cries out that this is my land. This is where I belong, this is my country."[23]

Despite his actions toward Sonia, Pawar, who formed his own party with Sangma, has been a coalition partner of both United Progressive Alliance governments, and in 2009 Sangma's daughter was sworn in as a member of parliament under the same party banner.

Though the Golden Temple at Amritsar, the scene of pitched battle between militants and the army in 1984, had been repaired to a great degree, the Sikhs felt they had grievances that needed attention. Victims of the 1984 Sikh riots would organize demonstrations outside party headquarters every couple of months. Many hardcore Sikh Congress families became BJP sympathizers. *Tehelka* editor Tejpal, who refers to the days after the storming of the Golden Temple as "one of the lowest points in the history of modern India," has said that Sonia "knows it's a huge blemish on the history of the Congress."[24]

Major Dalbir Singh, national secretary of the All India Congress Committee, was approached by a group of Sikh leaders once Sonia took over as

Congress president. In 2002 a group of these leaders met with Sonia to ask her to visit the Golden Temple and to talk to her about other outstanding issues to keep in mind should Congress return to power. No president of the party had been to the Golden Temple in 16 years. The meeting started, but the leader of the Sikh delegation, sitting next to the Congress president, was star-struck and just stared at her, his jaw dropping, overcome with awe, as some Indians are when they meet her. Sonia looked at Dalbir. Dalbir looked at Sonia, then quickly listed the requests the leaders wanted to make.[25] Sonia responded positively, and about a month later she went to the Golden Temple. Inside the complex were 10,000 people, and another 25,000 stood outside. There is a narrow walkway across the lake from the inner perimeter of the temple to an inner sanctum. As Sonia was walking toward the inner sanctum, a stampede of Sikhs knocked over Major Singh, who sprained his ankle. Sonia, inside the holiest part of the temple, was greeted and honored before being whisked away to attend a meeting at a nearby site, Jallianwala Bagh, where thousands of people were once massacred by the British. Singh tried to follow, limping, but was stopped by overzealous security men. Sonia was on the dais, looked around and asked for the major, having seen him fall. With a fixed smile, he hobbled at double speed toward the platform; an army man likes to be in place and on time.

Sonia's visit to the Golden Temple sent a message out to the community. Later on, when the party came to power, a 100-acre landscaped memorial to one of the Sikh gurus was constructed in Delhi. Some political observers, especially Sikhs, believe Sonia sowed the seeds that led to India's first Sikh prime minister in 2004, even though it was the *personal* attributes and abilities of Manmohan Singh that attracted her. But a shift was taking place, for the second largest standing army in the world acquired its first Sikh chief of staff in 2005. These actions encouraged minorities to feel that Congress was their home and enabled them to slowly return to supporting the party.

22

THE PEACE DIVIDEND

Our social systems have been subject to many fissures. The feeling of alienation has grown. Violence has become endemic in many parts.

—*Sonia Gandhi*

In jacket and sari, Sonia sat among the crowd on the ground outside parliament, protesting by practicing *dharna*—the demonstrator sits outside the door of the offending party and fasts until justice is obtained.[1] They were symbolically opposing the recent events in the western state of Gujarat. A few days earlier, on February 27, 2002, a train was traveling from Ayodhya, the site of anti-Muslim riots in 1992, to the capital of Gujarat, Ahmedabad, with Hindu passengers. Just after dawn, as the train left a railway station at Godhra, someone pulled an emergency chain and a horde of Muslim attackers hurled bottles of gasoline, setting the coaches alight. Many managed to scramble off the train, but the nearly 60 charred bodies found in the remains were women and children, who were slower to react to the flames leaping through the compartments.

In retaliation, Hindu mobs fanned out across Gujarat. They targeted Muslim neighborhoods, raped women, and burned entire families in their homes. It was the worst outbreak of sectarian violence in a decade. Police and bureaucrats were slow to react; the pro-Hindu BJP government in Delhi led by Atal Behari Vajpayee delayed several hours before sending in the army to quell the rioting. Within a few days, 300 people, mostly Muslims, had been killed.[2] On the television program *Walk the Talk,* Sonia described how she "was absolutely distraught, and immediately I asked my office, the SPG, to arrange a trip because I wanted to be there. But the SPG said there was absolutely no question that they would allow me to go."[3] The government explained that if Sonia were to travel there, security resources would need to be deployed that could be used elsewhere. As soon as she was allowed to go, she did. "I visited some of the hospitals and I can never forget the horrible sights." She also traveled there with a delegation from parliament. "We went to Godhra and saw the train and what happened there, as well as the areas in Ahmedabad and around where atrocities had been committed on minorities." Sonia was so struck by what she saw that five years later, campaigning during an election in the state, she referred to "those running Gujarat" as "merchants of death."[4]

Sonia knew all about the rituals and manners of Indian politics, and that the nation's leaders excelled in the symbolic: marches, sit-downs, fasts. The Nehru-Gandhis reign supreme in the well-placed moral protest and she was clearly able to move fast when she believed action was needed. Sonia's *dharna* echoed many scenes from the past, such as Indira's sit-down on the outskirts of Delhi, surrounded by supporters, when she was being harassed by the government and arrested by police in 1978. She might have been proud to see her daughter-in-law attacking the government with gusto.

Nandini Mehta, at that time an editor with Penguin Books, said that she saw Sonia Gandhi two or three times on a Saturday afternoon or evening about the condensation of the volumes of Indira–Jawaharlal letters she was working on, and observed that though Sonia had gone into "a bit of a shell" after Rajiv's assassination, Mehta felt that she had now "flowered, had come into her own, in a very quiet way."[5]

Although the fallout of the violence of 2002 is still felt today, eight years after the event, and with the United Progressive Alliance in power at the center, there was a different mood in the country—a desire for inter-religious tranquility that seemed to cut across the political divide. Though not completely eliminated, the violent attacks of 1992 and 2002 seemed to be too awful to be given a chance to be repeated. Toward the end of September 2010, ahead of a long-awaited ruling on the Hindu-Muslim dispute over the religious provenance of Ayodhya, there was a strong determination to maintain harmony. Sonia Gandhi, in a message to the nation, asked it to "keep faith in the Indian judiciary"[6] and appealed to "all sections of the society to maintain peace and calm and accept the verdict graciously whatever it may be."[7] The call for restraint was across the board, with a Hindu leader saying that his organization's response would be "within the limits of law and constitution"[8] and a Muslim representative saying that his community would try to remain unprovoked. The message was very different from the insipidness of the authorities in 1992 and 2002, but the UPA government took no chances; a crisis control room was set up in the home ministry, 190,000 security personnel were on duty in the state of Uttar Pradesh, and group mobile phone text messages were blocked to stop any exhortation of violence. The Indian air force was on standby, helicopters kept watch overhead, and the judgment, which ruled that the site should be shared between three groups, two Hindu and one Muslim, was passed down without major incident. The case went to appeal and was suspended, but analysts agreed that this time around, political leaders of all shades were proactive in ensuring Indians were kept safe when emotions were running high, providing some reassurance to citizens. Commentators wondered if a page had been turned on interreligious violence in India.

Protests aside, in 2002, Sonia was used to going in and out of Parliament House as leader of the opposition, and there were many formalities that came with the job. She received delegations, such as one from the Mongolian parliament, and in the same year addressed a gathering at a commemorative function to mark the golden jubilee of the Indian parliament. The building she was now visiting regularly is circular with an open verandah supported by 144 sandstone columns. Throughout the interior are paintings and large statues of key leaders in Indian history, exhorting members to respect the legacy of their political forbears. Outside, among neat gardens, more such statues strike typical poses: Both sixteen feet tall in bronze, Mahatma Gandhi sits cross-legged on a platform, meditating, a shawl draped around his shoulders; Indira Gandhi stands on the lawn, her gaze alert.

Outside parliament, Sonia also was proving herself an able player on the talk circuit.

It is an established tradition in Delhi for the leading journals to organize annual conclaves or summits to which world leaders and statesmen are invited to speak. Once Sonia had stepped onto the national stage in politics, she became part of this cast and was invited, as leader of the opposition, to speak at the first *Hindustan Times* Leadership Initiative summit in 2003, chaired by Vir Sangvhi. The prime minister of India generally is one of the speakers—that year it was Atal Behari Vajpayee—along with former US secretary of state Madeleine Albright, former Pakistani prime minister Benazir Bhutto, and Richard Haass, president of the Council on Foreign Relations. The theme of the conference was the *Peace Dividend: Progress for India and South Asia.* The subject for speakers at the *Hindustan Times* forum was peace and prosperity in a region that is predicted to accommodate a third of humanity by the year 2050.[9] In the coming decades, South Asia is set to become both one of the globe's greatest markets as well as one of its largest production centers. It is likely to be producing a quarter of the planet's economic output. So Sonia's first *Hindustan Times* summit was an outing placing her with some of the best and the brightest to discuss global issues. More confident and strategic than before, when she accepted the invitation to speak at a large seminar, she would speak only at a plenary session. By talking to a large group, it was guaranteed that there were enough people receiving her message at the same time, so that any one person's interpretation could very easily be confirmed by others who were present.

Her speech at the conclave was clear, idealistic, and comprehensive. Sonia spoke of "economic development that is both efficient and equitable" and highlighted her stand against economic development as an end in itself, while accepting the need for growth. "Our economies have performed well . . . but not well enough to deal with the huge backlog of poverty, malnutrition, disease, and unemployment. There is no alternative to faster economic growth. . . ." She spoke of the need for "institutions of dialogue," and in a clear reference to Pakistan, said that "we have every right to expect that our neighbors will not allow themselves to become sanctuaries for those who unleash their deadly tools of terror against innocent men, women and children in our country."[10] Given the sometimes prickly nature of the relationship between India and her two immediate neighbors, she suggested that China, India, and Pakistan "should evolve a credible and transparent mechanism to manage the consequences of a nuclear South Asia." She equally stressed the importance of India, Nepal, Bangladesh, and Bhutan in developing the large east Himalayan river basin. Sonia proposed a South Asian Free Trade Area that "ought to be in place by 2005, and an economic community by the middle of the next decade." She asked rhetorically why a South Asian parliament (it is thought that she meant perhaps along the lines of the European Union model) could not be formed. She spoke of the ethnic tensions in Sri Lanka, calling for "power-sharing and devolution" on the war-torn island. Mentioning that India's relations with China had improved since 1988 (the year her husband went there, though she did not talk of the visit itself or, indeed, Rajiv in this speech), she said that "a deeper Sino-Indian relationship has a positive impact on our immediate neighborhood." In passing, she mentioned the South Asian diaspora, saying that while it had done well, it had its "dark side . . . dangerous long-distance offshore nationalism"—most probably a reference to the funding of right-wing Indian parties by wealthy business people abroad. When asked, "How often and how effectively are you consulted in the formulation of our national foreign policy?" she replied, "We are consulted at times, but not always." Pressed with, "Are you consulted more often or not consulted more often?" she answered, displaying a polite assertiveness, "I would say that perhaps more often we are not consulted. Or, let us say we are consulted when decisions have been taken. . . . Yes, we are more informed but it is not always so. Let's not be too harsh."

At the summit it appeared that Sonia had sharpened her claws and was ready to take on the ruling BJP-led coalition in the 2004 election. It was going to be a hard fight as the BJP was firmly entrenched, and no one except Sonia thought that Congress had a chance of regaining power. It was now, too, that the family decided that Rahul would enter the political arena and contest the Nehru-Gandhi seat of Amethi, in Uttar Pradesh. Rahul was 33 and not long out of his job managing an engineering and technology outsourcing firm called Backops Services Private Ltd., which he started in 2002 in Mumbai. Before that, he had worked for three years for the Monitor Group in London under the assumed name of Raul Vinci.[11] The seat had been represented at various times by Sanjay, Rajiv, and Sonia, so it was a good bet that Rahul would win. Sonia took on a constituency nearly 50 miles away, Rae Bareli, once held by her mother-in-law. Priyanka would help manage the campaigns for her mother and her brother, but commentators in the Indian media still saw Priyanka as the anointed one, running will-she-or-won't-she columns almost daily, asking if her campaigning signaled her definite political entry. She responded by saying that if she was really interested in national politics, she would be in the fray and not campaigning at a local level.

But Sonia was the one who took on the battle to save the party from yet another election defeat.

A politician is reported to have said to her at this time that when deciding what to do in politics, it was much better to hit the road and connect directly with the people rather than talk to advisers. She apparently took that counsel, using every ounce of energy to engage with the masses.[12] Major Dalbir Singh coordinated her election tours and would prepare daily assessment reports on the campaign for the Congress president and strategists like Manmohan Singh. "If we were to lose, the initiative would have gone to the BJP for many years," Dalbir Singh noted.[13] The government, led by Prime Minister Vajpayee, feeling that turning the economy around would ensure an appreciative and supportive electorate, brought elections forward by six months, to May.

Political journalist Neerja Chowdhury commented on the BJP ruling coalition, "There was an arrogance creeping in there. They talked about 'Shining India.' They talked *so* much about 'Shining India' that it became counterproductive, because India was not shining for large sections of people."[14]

PART VI

CONSOLIDATING POWER

23

AGAINST THE ODDS

This is no time for petty and destructive criticism, no time for ill-will or blaming others. We have to build the noble mansion of India where all her children may dwell.

—*Jawaharlal Nehru*

Photographs of Sonia walking with long strides ahead of a pack of Congress men and women appeared frequently in the news. The press still had her on trial; dramatic shots of her accompanied articles asking if she was ready to lead a government.[1] The Hindu right-wing of the ruling government coalition was keeping up the pressure, pounding away on the issue of her foreign origin and her inexperience. The Congress Party realized it would need to form alliances for a coalition; the days of preeminence, when the party could easily reach the 272-seat tally alone, had died long ago.

In state-level elections in India, the vote is for the chief minister and members of his or her own state government (*state* cabinet, members of the *state* legislative assembly). In five-year national elections, such as 2004, Indians over the age of 18 vote for candidates running for seats in the Lok Sabha (House of the People).[2] Major parties will sometimes name their candidate for prime minister in advance, in the event their party wins the majority and is asked to form a government. The Congress Party had formed some successful, winning coalitions in certain states. Sonia decided to repeat the experiment at a national level and set about making political friends.

On February 16, 2003, Sonia invited some opposition leaders to dinner. One of these was Sharad Pawar, the same former Congress leader who had opposed Sonia as Congress president on account of her "foreign origins" and was summarily ejected for his audacity. Pawar and four of the other guests had their own parties and their own followings.[3]

As well as forming strategic alliances, she was bringing younger blood into the party. Sachin Pilot, with a newly minted MBA from Wharton, remembered Sonia asking young Congress Party workers like him to a meeting in 2003 as she and her team were in the process of preparing the party's election manifesto. She said, "'I want to hear what it is you want this party to do, what are your needs and aspirations and expectations from the Congress Party."[4] Pilot, along with 15 or 20 others from different states around the country, provided ideas and were sent to campaign across India. The son of a former Congress minister, in 2004 he became a first-term—and at that time the youngest—MP at 26. He was appointed minister of state for communications and IT in the United Progressive Alliance's second term. "She spots talent and she gives you the pen with the power to sign off on things," Pilot observed. "Very few have exercised that discretion, that liberty, that faith."[5]

The move to absorb young talent into political life and to talk about issues that mattered to the majority of Indians has had a broad effect. The BJP also is fielding younger candidates, choosing for its president, for instance, a man in his fifties. The right wing, badly burned, has also started to change the nature of its own discourse, talking about development and corruption rather than concentrating on personal attack. It has, says Dileep Padgaonkar, a *Times of India* consulting editor, turned into the B-team of Indian politics, which he views as no bad thing for the country.

Minister Sachin Pilot represents the Indian politics of tomorrow. A part of Rahul Gandhi's age cohort, he and his inducted peers are serious individuals, frequently from political, royal, bureaucratic, or business backgrounds, often with MBAs or some other degree from an American or European university. They are driven, focused, and have an earnest desire to put something into their country. While upper-middle-class Indians over the last few decades have sought foreign educations as a stepping stone to the world, their modern counterparts, just like Nehru, Mahatma Gandhi, and other founding fathers who went to university in the United Kingdom, bring back what they have learned abroad to help the motherland. They feel a strong spirit of national identity and want to make a difference. Their style is almost uniform; most of them are in good physical shape, exercise regularly, talk softly and quickly, and are careful with their time. Of the main political groups, the Congress Party has the highest number of bright younger people led by Rahul. In stark contrast to the wrinkled old-boys who dominate parliament, their faces reflect the growing demographic of the country. Another example is industrialist Naveen Jindal, in his forties, who runs one of India's largest business conglomerates based around steel. After observing his classmates at the University of Texas in Dallas proudly displaying their national flag, on his return to his country after his degree, he began a successful legal campaign for Indian citizens to be able to exhibit and wear *their* national flag—a move supported and cheered on by Sonia. Now a member of parliament, inspired by his party president, he says that he feels a sense of responsibility toward India and wants to "give the best years of my life to work on building the country of my dreams."[6]

In 2004 Sonia still had to build unity in her own factionalized party as well as consensus among other opposition groups. The party mood was low and demoralized after some state election losses. With few options, the various groups accepted Sonia as a possible coalition leader. The media and the public were not yet fully convinced that the Congress Party believed in an antipoverty agenda and that it had no right-wing leanings of its own. Sonia needed to get the message out; she prepared and campaigned on a war footing with military precision and relentless energy. From December 2003 on, there were about a dozen major preelection meetings, and during the actual intense three-week campaign Sonia logged nearly 30,000 miles, addressing a total of 148 rallies.[7] Major Dalbir Singh, who planned and coordinated her tours and itinerary, noted that Sonia studied each aspect of the fight, every "phenomenal detail of the political constituency/segment." She would work late into the night, waking up early to catch a flight. Sonia liked to return home at night, however short the stay might be. Often she would get to New Delhi at 9:30 PM and stay up until 2 AM, hardly sleeping more than three hours a night during the campaign, absorbing briefings and preparing speeches, sometimes through all the hours of darkness. If she wanted an extra fact or data point, she would phone her team "around the middle of the night" and get the necessary information. A 24/7 war room was set up in which party strategists worked nearly 20 hours a day.[8]

With the 28 states of India each having different identities, problems, and electoral patterns, Sonia studied indigenous issues from inflation to climate control. Singh wrote background notes, others would prepare her speeches. "But she would still go through those drafts herself, add, subtract; finally it was her word as to what she would say and her own comfort with the draft. . . . She'd rehearse for the next day," he said. There was another reason that she would return to base daily if possible. With competing party factions still needing a firm hand, two or three days away from headquarters could be dangerous. Singh explained that "pending files, people needing attention, would be at the back of her mind. It was difficult to handle matters from a remote area like the northeast." The party, however, was highly skeptical, and Sonia had yet to produce a tangible election result.

A media strategy committee handled the public relations agencies for campaigns. The party core group, the key decision makers, worked out which resources would be deployed where. They knew that the party's prime asset was (and is) Sonia. The core group decided that narrow-margin constituencies, where the party may have lost by three or four thousand votes, were suitable for her to visit, as she energized local workers and poll managers.[9] The party machine was behind Sonia, but her drive to lead from the front made the difference in 2004. It was time to give Indira's "Remove Poverty" slogan a contemporary feel. "The common man," typified by the skinny basket-carrying mango man, *aam aadmi,* became the mascot of the Congress campaign. All India Congress Committee secretary in charge of Uttar Pradesh and member of the upper house, Parvez Hashmi, explained: "We needed to build confidence at a grassroots level and get the message out that we are not caste-based. We held corner meetings; we made contact with remote areas, the villages."[10] The Congress Party hammered away at the need for better governance, an improvement in health care, and more employment and development.

If several election contenders needed attention at the same time, Sonia would be flown to a nodal point for a rally. The work rate meant that there were no Sundays and no Mondays. Bad weather on one of the working days meant another meeting would be planned to compensate. Sonia performed *yatras,* an ancient tradition of journeying, engaging with people by holding small meetings along the way. Journalists vividly remember Sonia often putting her arm around some old woman or holding the hand of an ill person. Some upper- and middle-class Indians refuse to touch sick people, considering them unclean, but Sonia has no such inhibition. While Sonia was going to the people, the BJP leaders sat atop their rafts in processions. The BJP (known as the saffron brigade because Hindu priests wear orange) had more money and more resources than the Congress. They continued to attack Sonia personally whenever they could, calling her "that woman." In 2004 opposition groups again scorned the "bankrupt" Congress Party having to provide dynastic candidates from a foreign mother—a veiled assault on both Rahul and Sonia—as evidence that the party could find no worthy Indian leaders of its own. Sonia ignored the personal attacks and continued to work most closely with Priyanka and Rahul. Sonia was much more politically mature than before, but the troika was (and is) very much in place. Rita Bahuguna Joshi, Uttar Pradesh Committee Party president, said that they are three persons with one soul, and they talk to each other every day when possible.[11] Author Sadia Dehlvi observed that they think alike and take collective decisions, and editor Tarun Tejpal said, "I wouldn't be surprised if they were not on some sort of daily consultation with each other."[12]

The troika also makes strategy decisions on public relations. One PR consultant who presented to Sonia on grand design described the Congress president as "very careful, very cautious, tending to be correct rather than adventurous." According to him, Sonia, Priyanka, and Rahul looked at the big ideas and the messaging points, wishing to know what kind of themes the party spokespersons and leaders were going to be using in their speeches and their press bites to television. The family's emphasis, he said, was on making sure the big picture was going in the right direction while avoiding anything provocative or damaging. Across the board, Sonia is described as a restraining hand, so the campaign was not allowed to become too aggressive, for instance. While the pro-poor stance was resonating with the ordinary Indian in 2004, Sonia knew it was important not to alienate the growing middle class, so Congress Party leaders also talked about the need to promote India's spending and growth. Sonia herself described the party campaign this time around as more structured than before, highlighting farmers, young people, women, and the middle classes.[13] This kept the base of constituencies broad and therefore harder to attack.

The logistics of moving the party president around a country of extreme terrains and weather conditions are calculated second to second. Air journeys taking an hour and a quarter can be managed by a helicopter for four or five people; for anything longer, Sonia flies the distance in a fixed-wing aircraft, as it is safer and faster. In mountainous regions, where there are no airfields, the only accessibility is by helicopter. In Himachal Pradesh or elsewhere in the snow-bound northern peaks of India, the last meeting had to be at 3 PM. Any later than that the chopper couldn't return—they could not afford for Sonia to get stuck anyplace, as she would be covering three or four events the next day. Speaking events varied from 40 minutes to an hour: garlands and bouquets to begin, Sonia's speech, a vote of thanks, and, if time, a talk from the local candidate. But occasionally the best-laid plans can be derailed.

On one occasion in Himachal Pradesh, a venue was on the far side of a shallow stream. Everything was ready for Sonia to fly in. Unfortunately, unseasonal rains quickly turned the stream into a river, rendering it impassable. People were traveling from far-flung hamlets and villages to hear the party president. There was talk of having a bridge built overnight, but this was rejected in favor of switching the venue to a dry location where she would be able to address a full rally. Another time, Sonia was supporting a candidate in the eastern state of Bihar. The stage, backdrop, barricades, bunting, flags—"all the paraphernalia of war, was in place."[14] Suddenly the candidate, who was sulking for some reason, disappeared. Six, then eight hours passed. Searches were made. The Congress Party president was due in a couple of hours. The candidate finally surfaced just before the meeting. Anything can and does happen in Indian elections, but as Singh explained earnestly, "You can't fool around with the Congress Party president's meetings."

The Congress Party candidate for prime minister was not announced during the campaign, so candidates and voters assumed that as head of the party, this would be Sonia. She remained silent on the subject, which allowed the assumption and hopes to gain credence. The Congress's focus on the poor versus the BJP's focus on the big-business-is-best attitude paid off. It also allowed left-leaning parties to gain confidence, crucial in making the numbers. On May 13, as the results came in, most people—except for Sonia Gandhi—were fixated on their television screens. She said that she would rather not spend "hours of tension so I just busy myself" reading or doing "other things, I tend to be cautious."[15] However, her son, daughter, and others could not wait to tell her that the Congress Party, at 145 seats, with allies on board, had a slim majority of 278.[16] The support of the smaller parties was needed to get it up past the halfway mark of 272 seats (out of 543 in the lower house). The country was astonished; the Gandhis were thrilled. Major Dalbir Singh says that "the electoral triumph of 2004 bore her personal stamp."

Rahul happily told reporters in his constituency, "I said some time ago that my father is my hero. Today, I have another hero. She is my mother. I have seen my mother fight when my grandmother died. I have seen my mother fight the day my father died, and I have seen her fight with her back to the wall. And she has won." She had won "against the odds."[17] Sonia and Rahul had both triumphed in their individual campaigns as well.

On May 15, Sonia was unanimously elected leader of the Congress Parliamentary Party. The headline in *Outlook* magazine summed up much of the media's sentiment; it read "Tortoise Troops In," referring to the Congress Party.

On May 16 coalition partners met at Janpath and Sonia was given responsibility for chairing the new government, to be called the United Progressive Alliance (UPA). Over the next few days, groups of Congress leaders collected letters referring to the formation of a secular government under the leadership of Sonia Gandhi from groups prepared to buttress the Congress Party. With these promises in place, there followed an invitation from the president of India to Sonia to explore ways of forming the next government. At the 2004 *Hindustan Times* summit held in November, six months after the election victory, Sonia declared, “I bet none of you expected me to be here today as part of the establishment rather than the opposition.”[18] Congress leaders now all expected Sonia to announce her candidacy for the post of premier. So the BJP opposition, smarting from its unexpected defeat, sharpened its claws.

24

MY INNER VOICE

> You have unanimously elected me your leader, in doing so, you have reposed your faith in me. It is this faith that has placed me under tremendous pressure to reconsider my decision. Yet, I must abide by the principles which have guided me all along.
>
> —*Sonia Gandhi*

In 2004 India and the rest of the world firmly believed that Sonia was poised to become prime minister now that the United Progressive Alliance, the coalition group that the Congress Party was leading, had won the election. It was one of the assumptions of that year's election campaign, and Sonia had at no point issued a statement saying that this tacit understanding was misplaced. She had spoken to her children about it; indeed, Priyanka later told a television interviewer, "Rahul and I would have these discussions with her where we would say: 'Why don't you just say so now?' But she didn't. . . ."[1]

On May 17, 2004, the entire euphoric Congress Parliamentary Party, consisting of all the lower and upper house members of parliament, waited patiently outside the Janpath house while inside Sonia remained ensconced with aides. The press was there too, eagerly expecting the announcement of Sonia's candidacy for prime minister, but the only information released was that Sonia would meet with the president the next day. Excitement turned to anxiety. On May 18 Sonia met with the president, then addressed the press pack. All she said was a summary of the conversation, that the president had called for a preliminary discussion on the formation of the government, a little more about who was supporting the party, and that they would meet again the next day with letters of support from coalition partners.

The opposition had been busy firing political salvos at Sonia and it was a time of high uncertainty in the country. While the Bombay Stock Exchange Sensitivity Index, the Sensex, plummeted, nationalist rallies took place all over India, protesting the idea of an Italian-born woman becoming prime minister. Bharatiya Janata Party leaders threatened to activate anti-Sonia cells, a right-wing priest urged his disciples to agitate, a BJP offshoot urged the recruitment of Mahatma Gandhi doubles to denounce Sonia, and a Hindu fundamentalist businessman killed himself as the ultimate method of protest.

Sonia's 1999 political foe in Bellary and former Bharatiya Janata Party minister, Sushma Swaraj, appeared outside parliament. Her hair scraped back from her round face in a customary bun, dressed in a sari, and looking like a homely Indian mother, she spoke emotionally to the waiting press in impeccable Hindi. Her words shocked the nation and are vividly remembered today. She claimed that if Sonia were to become prime minister, she would go into mourning for the nation. She vowed, "I will wear a white sari [the hue of sorrow for Indians], not colored clothes, I will cut my hair [a ritual attached to death in Hinduism], I will sleep on the floor, and I will eat *bune chane* [roasted chick peas, a food associated with sad times]. So long as she remains prime minister, I will not wear colored clothes, I will not grow my hair, and I will continue to eat *bune chane*."[2] India gasped.

The vicious message coming from the BJP was that the opposition was prepared to go on strike. The noncooperation would start with a boycott of any swearing-in ceremony of Sonia as the new prime minister, and opposition state ministers would refuse to work with her or even receive her whenever she made an official visit. Sonia's position was untenable, said political columnist Neerja Chowdhury.[3] The Congress Party was not in a majority, even though its coalition partners had accepted her, and the country could have been on the brink of violence. The opposition would raise the issue of her foreign origins over any decision she might take. Sonia recoiled at being the cause of such discord.

There were also security jitters. An Intelligence Bureau[4] report stated that the perception of threat to Sonia's personal safety had suddenly risen dramatically, given the feelings stoked by opposition groups around India. In addition to the level of protection afforded the premier of the country, Rahul and Priyanka would also have needed "enhanced security. . . . The SPG top brass had been told of this new threat appraisal and this would have been unofficially communicated to Ms. Gandhi."[5] Sonia was not fazed; the increased security threats were not the reason she turned down the premiership. Fears of an assassination did not worry Priyanka and Rahul either. Despite being prime targets on many terrorist hit lists, neither Sonia nor Rahul wear bulletproof vests.[6] *Tehelka* editor in chief Tarun Tejpal reported, "I've heard her friends say . . . that she thinks that she'll be assassinated one day. She lives with a very clear sense of danger. I don't think she's fuzzy about that at all. She expects the worst for herself all the time."[7] This does not stop her from going among the people, campaigning or visiting. The Gandhi family is so familiar with sudden death that it now ignores the constant menace. But despite Sonia's bravery, Priyanka is at times concerned for her mother. One time during the days of high drama in 2004, Priyanka peeped into Sonia's office and saw "everybody surrounding her and saying 'You have to be prime minister.' I had this one moment of complete terror, and I burst out crying." Priyanka ran to her brother. "I was [thinking] 'She's going to die' . . . you are scared of losing someone else you love."[8]

On May 18 the entire media corps again pitched camp at the Janpath house while United Progressive Alliance (UPA) chiefs were once more ensconced with their president. Other anxious leaders were in the garden. All sorts of rumors were flying around; some supporters, heading for the BJP offices nearby, carried stones, and in the midst of the hysteria, one man climbed on top of a car, held a gun to his head, and threatened to pull the trigger if Sonia really was going to forego her right to be prime minister. Television played the images, and the nation was hooked to its collective screen. A crowd of about 20,000 gathered around the residence. Inside, Sonia was telling eight people—six from the Congress Working Committee (including her political secretaries Ahmed Patel and Ambika Soni) and two All India Congress Committee secretaries—that she was not going to become prime minister. "We made an impassioned plea to her,"[9] Major Dalbir Singh recalled. He and the rest of the group told her that they could take care of the BJP or any other hard-right forces if their threats were bothering her. Sonia simply replied that it was "a decision of my conscience"[10] and asked for it to be respected.

Around 5 PM the members' discussion ended, and a Congress Parliamentary Party meeting was held in the central hall in parliament. Millions watched the proceedings via state television and heard the excited commentator describe the unfolding drama. As party men and women shouted *"Sonia Gandhi zindabad!"* (Long live Sonia Gandhi!), their party president, looking focused, entered and sat at a table at the end of the room. With her were other Congress leaders and Dr. Manmohan Singh. A light at the lectern threw her face into dramatic relief as she urged her noisy party to quiet down. "Friends," she started, but the group was hysterical, shouting and gesticulating. She started again. "Friends, throughout this past six years that I have been in politics, one thing has always been clear to me and that is, as I have often stated, that the post of prime minister has not been my aim. I was always certain that if ever I found myself in the position that I am today, I would follow my inner voice. Today that inner voice tells me I must humbly decline this post."[11] Uproar erupted in the hall. Sonia remonstrated in Hindi, "Let me say what is in my mind, otherwise I will leave. Let me speak! I will not reverse it."[12] There was further commotion as Sonia pleaded, "Please sit down and listen to me!"[13] To those who asked her about threats from the opposition, she responded, "There is no blackmail from anybody."[14]

Rahul, Priyanka, and her husband, Robert, all looking anxious, entered the hall to watch the proceedings. There was tension in the air, mainly from the emotional Congress members, and the trio was there to give support to Sonia. She continued: "We have waged a successful battle. But we have not won the war. That is a long and arduous struggle, and I will continue it with full determination. But I appeal to you to understand the force of my conviction. I request you to accept my decision and to recognize that I will not reverse it." She sought to reassure her party with the words: "As one of you and as president of the Congress Party, I pledge myself to work with you and for the country." She had no intention of giving up her post. Members thumped the tabletops in front of them. Again, they rose from their seats while Manmohan Singh sat impassively.

Disregarding protocol, one member addressed Sonia as "Madam Prime Minister" before remonstrating that he and others had sought votes on the basis that Sonia would become prime minister if the Congress Party won. The member said that they could not betray the people of India whose inner voice said that Sonia *had* to become prime minister! Sonia listened intently while another legislator, Kapil Sibil, ignoring Manmohan Singh, said that "not a single person in this hall believes that anybody else is entitled to be prime minister . . . we want to finish these fundamentalist forces in this country forever. . . . Nobody else will be able to do it." Now they were all queuing up to proclaim their loyalty. Another lawmaker, A. K. Anthony, asserted that the inner voices of those present "are not to be subordinated . . . to your, madam, inner voice."[15] There was more rowdiness and angry gesticulating. The party was scared for its own future more than anything: How would a resurgent Congress with its returning minorities stay afloat with someone else at the helm of government? Manmohan Singh, occasionally holding a pencil to his mouth, was quiet and still.

To some journalists, Congress leaders appeared to compete with each other to cry for the cameras,[16] and one tearful member, Renuka Chowdhury, beseeched Sonia, "We all remember . . . when selfish Congressmen . . . pulled you out of your home for our self-serving purpose and used you . . . dirty politics abused you . . . I'm only making one more selfish request: that you continue to lead us, because it is the need of the hour."[17] Sonia, clearly moved, looked straight at the woman speaker. But she held fast. Her officials were surprised. Some days after the event, one of her state committee presidents asked for an explanation. Sonia told her, "'Look, I want the nation to progress. I want things to stabilize. I want communal forces to lose. I do not want the BJP to harp on an agenda of the foreign origins of the prime minister; I want them to discuss developmental issues.'"[18] At the *Hindustan Times* conclave later that year, Sonia reiterated that she had already made her mind up, "Right from the beginning," that she would "never occupy that chair" in any event. She joked with the audience by smiling and shaking her hand in a wavering gesture: "But sometimes the flesh is weak."[19]

With one quiet thrust, Sonia confounded her critics and silenced her fiercest opponents. Even Sushma Swaraj, now leader of the opposition and a tornado on the parliament floor, has somewhat mellowed toward her former archenemy. Seated in her spacious office in the Lok Sabha of parliament, a low lamp lighting her face, she tacitly admitted that they are no longer in the boxing ring together. She said that she does not now see Sonia as a challenge, noting that the latter has "defined her role for herself" as the "guide and mentor of the Congress Party" and chairperson of the UPA. "I don't see any challenge from her as a person. . . . The BJP and Congress will challenge each other where the strengths and weaknesses of the party will matter, and because her party is ruling, her government's governance and policies toward the common man will matter more. So it will be the BJP versus Congress, not Sushma versus Sonia."[20]

The hubbub in parliament over, on May 19, 2004, Prime Minister Manmohan Singh and Sonia Gandhi emerged from a formal meeting with the president at his palace. Sonia, now looking benign and stress-free, stood to one side while Manmohan Singh talked. "I am happy to inform the nation that the president has invited me to form the next government. . . . I feel humbled. . . . The mandate was for Shrimati Sonia Gandhi." (Shrimati is a Hindi version of Mrs.) A reporter asked Sonia why she was looking more relaxed than she had in days. Sonia replied that it was because a final decision had been taken. "I had been under tremendous pressure from my colleagues and my party workers and many, many people throughout the country. So, naturally, being under such pressure, sort of . . . takes you down a bit. But now everything is over I am very happy. I think our country will be safe in Dr. Manmohan Singh's hand[s]." Singh modestly ended with, "I know my limitations but with Madam's guidance and the support of the country, I am sure we are going to make the future happen."[21]

They were to form a strong duo. Sonia Gandhi's powerhouse support of Manmohan Singh in the professional arena, one commentator thinks, echoes the reinforcement that Sonia gave to Rajiv. Though she is still Congress Party president, with more authority vested in her than ever before, "you can see in her equation with Manmohan Singh, she's giving him the same strength she gave to Rajiv . . . it's very much in tune and in the same vein. Her persona and her strength, she knows it lies in being the person behind—it's a straight continuation of that."[22]

Sonia's choice of Manmohan Singh—a talented economist, not a politician, free of taint and corruption—was farsighted. His calm presence alongside her was an indispensable neutralizing agent on the public mood in a period of high strife. She is comfortable with him, and he poses no threat to her. Tarun Tejpal says, "Manmohan Singh cannot be shrill. She [Sonia] brought in a man who was personally honest . . . so the tone was moderated."[23] Sonia had worked with Singh for a number of years; he was a member of the Congress Working Committee, and when Congress was not in power, he was leader of the opposition in the upper house. Sonia felt that Singh was the best candidate for prime minister from early on because of his "great integrity" and experience, which she valued, adding that "ours is a relationship of mutual trust. . . . We are not competitors. We work together."[24] He would never be what one writer called "a cuckoo in the nest."[25] The fact that Manmohan Singh is Sikh is not consequential. The understated bureaucrat was a highly experienced manager, and his economic reforms had brought years of growth to India. He was (and is) seen as the cleanest politician in the country (in inverse proportion to his charisma), with a dislike for ostentation, living quite an austere lifestyle—insofar as an Indian prime minister *can* live an austere lifestyle. With much more direct experience of government bureaucracy than Sonia, he was ideally suited to counterbalance her. And without having ever won a seat of his own, he had no political platform, no mass base, which rendered him dependent on her patronage. They make a good team. He is measured, sensible, and highly respected by world leaders; she manages party matters with a collegial attitude and still looks good in a crowd of largely elderly male politicians. They both have a dry, gentle sense of humor. And she is a stickler for protocol, courteous to the premier at all times, standing up when he enters the room, standing behind him if they are together at the microphone, and going to his offices for meetings rather than having him come to her. She does not leave a function before he does.[26] Her children show a similar Indian politeness to their elders, including to their staunchest political opponents.

Giving away the prime minister's chair to Dr. Manmohan Singh caused Dileep Padgaonkar, consulting editor of the *Times of India,* to describe Sonia as "the great renouncer." He said that relinquishing treasure when you are at the height of your powers is in the tradition of Prince Siddharth, who experienced enlightenment to become Lord Buddha, and of Prince Ram, who gave up his right to his kingdom and went to live in exile in a forest for 14 years. Jawaharlal Nehru's father, Motilal, gave up a successful legal practice to join the freedom movement under Mahatma Gandhi. Padgaonkar said, "When you give up power, wealth, prestige, this endears you to the people of this country more than anything else. One value that Indians cherish most is the value of renunciation. This adds to the mystique of the family."[27]

In fact, Sonia did not renounce everything. In a master stroke, while she allowed Manmohan Singh to essentially run the government, she did have the last word on important policy decisions. She was also about to create an instrument through which she could pursue her aspirations for empowering the poorer sections of society: her own policy unit.

25

I AM HAPPY

The service of India means . . . the ending of poverty and ignorance and disease and inequality of opportunity. The ambition of the greatest man of our generation has been to wipe every tear from every eye. That may be beyond us, but as long as there are tears and suffering, so long our work will not be over.

—*Jawaharlal Nehru*

Sonia Gandhi's project for India is grand social legislation, and it's driven by gut instinct more than calculation. For this purpose, she has created bodies entirely new to the Indian polity, made up of outspoken academics, former bureaucrats, and social activists. Rajiv Gandhi had been interested in the views of nongovernmental organizations (NGOs), independent bodies concerned with social welfare, and Sonia too recognized the need for the government to "create an institutional framework for the involvement of a diverse array of civil society groups . . . in both the democratic and developmental process."[1] She set up the first National Advisory Council (NAC) with experts from civil society to look at ways of devising policy that could then be presented to the government for implementation. The panel, which she chairs (giving her the technical rank of a union minister), is outside the government, so the group is not beholden to the United Progressive Alliance. Yet, it has devised policies that, when fully matured, could change the face of democratic India. Through this powerful body, Sonia promotes reforms that she would like to see made into laws. It has given her the image of a do-good legislator who spends her time with social activists and charity workers and the moniker of being "an NGO politician." *Tehelka* editor in chief Tarun Tejpal notes that "a lot of her fundamental DNA is connected to the idea of social legislation. . . . I don't think economics or the idea of the global economic machine is what turns her on or is her area of expertise."[2]

NAC member and former secretary of the planning commission, Naresh C. Saxena, a tall, soft-spoken man, is committed to the invisible India that has not seen any of the trickle-down effect much vaunted by advocates of the economic reforms of recent years. Even as India's economic growth leaves Western countries gasping in astonishment, eight Indian states have more destitute people than the 26 poorest African nations combined, and a 2007 World Bank report put a third of the world's poor, 80 percent of Indians, living on less than two dollars a day.[3] One of the United Progressive Alliance (UPA) government's own commissioned committees on poverty levels found that the poor and vulnerable, those living on 20 rupees, or 50 cents, a day—enough to buy a bottle of mineral water and a cup of tea—rose from 811 million in 1999 to 836 million in 2004–2005.[4] Though literacy levels have slowly risen, the country still has the largest number of illiterates in the world.[5] *The Hindu*'s rural affairs editor, Palagummi Sainath,[6] points out that actual indicators of poverty levels can be adjusted and figures massaged, but what has *certainly* gone up more than at any time in independent India's history is inequality. "Life has gotten much worse for hundreds of millions of people in this country," he says.[7] One NAC member calls the gap between India's rich and its poor "the biggest threat that we face."[8] M. J. Akbar, editorial director at *India Today*, agrees: "The trickle down theory, foist upon us by the World Bank and [people] of that kind is not going to work." Akbar finds the rationale faulty: "What is the trickle down theory? That there shall only be a trickle for those at the bottom end and there shall be a gush of water for you and for me? That those who have swimming pools will get a waterfall, and those who are dying of thirst will get a trickle? The way to save India is to be inclusive. You cannot have a democracy run by an English speaking oligarchy."[9]

Agriculture, too, has been severely hit. More than 50 percent of India depends on farm work for a livelihood, but Saxena notes that growth in this sector has dropped from 4 percent to 1 percent over the last 15 years. According to Saxena, many of India's 28 states are plagued with corrupt bureaucrats, mafia gangs, contractors, and criminals at the local implementation level. Even if directives come from New Delhi, they can be sabotaged before they get anywhere. Sonia is concerned that any policies made into law must reach the ordinary Indian. A woman's right to inherit agricultural property, rural employment, and meals for poor children are some of the subjects she cares about. She has sought to link policies of economic growth to social reform, with one not excluding the other: Growth is needed to generate revenue, and that revenue can be used for the benefit of the socially disadvantaged. Saxena recalls discussing with the panel how, on average, Indian bureaucrats earn seven times as much as the average citizen, compared to Western bureaucrats, who typically earn around twice as much as the average worker. This financial gulf was raised at the NAC, but Sonia understands the limitations of Indian politics and was, he felt, not at that time in favor of reducing either the salaries or powers of civil servants, whom she sees as agents of development and change, critical for getting help to where it is needed.[10] Sonia and her children know that winning over the Indian people is about earning the trust of the poor. Agriculture, clean, safe water, schools, roads, and employment: These issues matter more to most of India than trade or political relations with other countries.

Saxena says that Sonia made use of the early days of NAC to learn a great deal. She would look at presentations made very carefully, take notes, and ask questions—but not too many. Her focus was to translate the work into policy and action. Sonia's listening trait is much admired by Indians, for the more silent you are, the wiser you are perceived to be, remarks Dileep Padgaonkar, *Times of India* consulting editor. Once ideas had taken shape in the NAC, a letter would be sent by Sonia to Manmohan Singh with the findings. Panelists prepared draft letters that were sometimes quite strident, and Saxena would frequently discover that Sonia had adjusted the tone so that the final version would have a moderate pitch while retaining the essential ideas. At times, she would reorder the recommendations, perhaps with an enclosure, so that the letter that went from her to the prime minister was short and readable.[11]

Placing herself at the helm of the NAC gave Sonia some distance from the government while allowing her to speak on matters that the government does not address comprehensively, such as the right of every poor person to secure food. The party and the government can have separate identities in the public mind, and by not being part of the government, Sonia did not have to become entangled with the cogs and levers that get in the way of reform. It was a canny political move, for it allowed the breadth of concerns of the UPA to widen and embrace many more sections of society. It covers those buying into a free-market, new Indian economy and others sympathetic to the renowned social activists on the NAC capitalistic economists holding hands with bleeding-heart liberal thinkers.

Gone were Sonia's early hesitant days at the Rajiv Gandhi Foundation when she left the decisions and discussions to others and struggled with bureaucratic formulations. In chairing the NAC, she absorbed material much more easily and was well briefed by her secretariat.[12] She was happier in her role, more at ease running a committee.

Sonia made sure that as soon as the NAC was formed, it started work on formulating landmark legislation to bring transparency to the closed world of government. The right to freedom of speech and expression, cited in the constitution,[13] was to be supported by the right to unlock information from government, especially with funds often being misdirected through rampant corruption. Picking up on the empowerment of the village council and the protection of the citizen, causes supported by Rajiv Gandhi, Sonia saw to it that a Right to Information bill was drawn up by the NAC. So that it was not the "child of bureaucrats," it was devised by the department of personnel and training, scrutinized, analyzed, torn to pieces, and put together again.[14] She then made sure that the Right to Information Act (RTI) was passed in June 2005 and enforced just four months later. According to Wajahat Habibullah, India's first chief information commissioner, India's information law has influenced policy at the World Bank and differs from that of many countries by insisting that all government records are computerized. Though the RTI has a way to go in terms of uniform implementation and consistency, it has the capacity to attack low- and high-level corruption across the board.

At one point the government sought amendments to the RTI that Sonia disapproved of, as she indicated to Habibullah.[15] He wanted her to be the chief guest at the first annual convention on the law and asked her, "If you disapprove of the amendments why don't you say so?" She replied, "I can't."[16] And rather than say so directly to the prime minister, she simply refused to attend the convention[17]; her silent absence demonstrated her dissatisfaction. When the amendments were on the anvil from her own government, she let the game play itself out without interfering overtly. Eventually, the prime minister, sensitive to public reaction, dropped the amendment idea.[18]

Sonia uses reticence or silence to express disapproval, just as Indira Gandhi often did. (According to Padgaonkar, Indira's favorite answer was "Perhaps.") But when Sonia does proffer an opinion, there is no ambiguity. This has changed public debate, for as Padgaonkar comments, "the enemy of a great deal of thinking in India is clarity." Where Jawaharlal and Indira could ramble on, Sonia and her progeny get to the point. Sonia likes her speeches to be concise, be easy to understand, and to include a hard punch or two. But she does not ignore the family history; she likes to keep it as part of public discourse, and she often invokes memories of Rajiv and Indira. When she talks of Rajiv's interrupted promise of a modern India, it comes from the heart. After more than 20 years, Sonia still gets emotional at the mention of her husband's name.

With agricultural workers left sadly behind by the accelerating Indian economy, Sonia refocused on their plight. Many in the rural community commit suicide when they are unable to feed their families after drought ruins their crops or they cannot repay loans. Over a quarter of a million Indian farmers took their own lives in the 15 years from 1995 to 2010,[19] the biggest number of recorded suicides in human history—and the number is rising. One group of despairing farmers wrote to the president of India in 2010, asking for her permission to kill themselves.[20] Though the media currently has correspondents covering fashion, entertainment, business, environment, and politics, they barely give a thought to the farming sector, let alone appoint dedicated rural affairs editors—the only one in the whole of India is Palagummi Sainath. The situation was graphically demonstrated in the hard-hitting documentary, *Nero's Guests.*[21]

What the rural worker wants most is guaranteed employment. With the increase in urbanization, laborers are increasingly migrating to towns, breaking up the family unit. Through the National Advisory Council, Sonia worked to promote the National Rural Employment Guarantee Act (NREGA),[22] which guarantees 100 days of paid work to one unskilled volunteer adult worker from each rural household. The NREGA decrees that recipients should work a maximum of eight hours a day, as opposed to the 12 hours that they might have to in a factory. Though there are abuses, with some people not receiving their wages on time or even at all, and malnourished workers very rarely able to complete the physical work quotas set by the scheme,[23] there is a general acknowledgment that it has brought benefits. Fewer villagers face the trauma of having to migrate up to 300 miles from their homes in search of a living, as some can now find work in their own villages. More than 80 million[24] bank accounts have been opened under the scheme so that unskilled workers can be part of the banking system rather than using post offices. Still, as the number of farmer suicides continues to grow, NREGA is not free of the taint of corruption and is far from being uniformly implemented throughout the country.

When the draft of the NREGA came out, Habibullah went to see Sonia to request that village councils be incorporated into the act so that NREGA could be implemented through these village units. He says that she used her influence to ensure that they were; after a meeting with Habibullah, the law minister asked the ministry of rural development to make the necessary adjustments.[25]

On the political front, BJP member of the lower house Maneka Gandhi describes the Sonia story as "Amazing. It must be the only case in the whole world of somebody coming in from outside and being accepted. And there are one or two really good ideas: RTI, NREGA, at least she had the sense and the wisdom to know which ones were good and which ones were bad." But she expresses an opinion on the general state of India that is shared by some others on the opposition benches; that "there is still lots of bad that goes with that good: our inability to take terrorism seriously . . . our inability to take home security sensibly."[26]

In 2006 public and political attention focused on members of parliament who were deemed to be holding additional roles that could be described as offices of profit. The opposition group led by the BJP suggested that as chair of the National Advisory Council, Sonia might be holding an "office of profit." The day the BJP was due to petition the president to have Sonia disqualified from the Lok Sabha, the House of the People, Sonia resigned from both the chairmanship of the NAC and her parliamentary constituency in Rae Bareli. In a statement she read to reporters outside her home, with Rahul at her side and Priyanka observing, she said, "This has hurt me very much. I have stated it earlier also that I am in politics and public life not for my selfish ends. I have taken a pledge to serve the people of the country and to protect the secular ideals."[27] Just as she had resigned as Congress president when attacked over her foreign origins, she resigned from the NAC—plus "all social, cultural organizations including those connected with the Nehru-Gandhi family that have been receiving government funding." In a 2006 television interview, *One on One,* Sonia explained, "Because of me, the government found itself in a very awkward position, and I didn't like that feeling." She consulted her son and daughter and took an instant decision: "It was like that [snapping her fingers]!"[28]

In 2008 a parliamentary joint committee ruled that "advisory offices in Union or States" are not deemed to be offices of profit, and therefore Sonia had committed no violation in 2004. "I don't want to sound arrogant," she said in her *One on One* interview, "but in this case I was quite sure the people of my constituency would support me again." Within 90 days in a by-election in Rae Bareli, she was reelected with an overwhelming majority. She formed NAC2 a year after the 2009 general election, with many of the former panel joined by new names. NAC2 immediately started drafting policy aimed at ensuring that food reaches those below the poverty line at minimum cost, amid arguments about what really were the minimum poverty line and nutritional requirements in India. The NAC2 looked at a communal violence bill, among other social issues. Its updates provide a clear insight into the concerns of the Sonia Gandhi-led panel.

Sonia made it clear that she fully intended to carry out her late husband's mission to facilitate women's empowerment. She was determined to have a bill passed seeking a 33 percent quota of parliamentary and state assembly seats for women. One of the hopes behind the bill was to push forward into the national debate the issues of infant mortality, malnutrition, child care, and education.[29] The 2009 elections in India saw 59 women win seats in the 543-member lower house, little better than 10 percent. In state assemblies, the percentage of women members is significantly smaller. A Women's Reservation Bill was to be introduced into the upper house on International Women's Day, March 8, 2010. It had been gathering dust since 1996 when it was first proposed, but now it had the support of the main parties. A prominent few, such as the Socialist Party (Samajwadi), had opposed it in 2009 on the grounds that the Muslims and low-caste groups needed quotas set for them so that they would not be cut out of the legislative process. They feared that whatever happened, it would still be the wives and daughters of political families who would be elected.[30] As the ranks of both Congress and its chief national rival, the Bharatiya Janata Party, drew from the upper classes, the rich, and the upwardly mobile, those lower down the social scale would be disadvantaged, and those who represented them would therefore have their electoral prospects affected, the bill's opponents argued. There was also the suspicion that many female names would simply be proxies for male members of their families.

On the day the bill was introduced, Mulayam Singh Yadav, who heads the Socialist Party, and Lalu Prasad Yadav, another party group chief, protested the bill in the upper house. A third Yadav, with 20 members of his party in the lower house, aligned himself with those opposing it. Fourteen members of the upper house from the Yadavs' political parties forced an adjournment half a dozen times, snatching the bill from the chairman's table and tearing up copies of the proposed legislation, fragments of which could be seen floating around the head of the speaker as he tried to call the house to order. Congress Party floor managers, who had not taken adequate precautions to make sure the vote went their way, panicked.

On the evening of International Women's Day, President Pratibha Patil held an event for women at the President's Palace. There was a feeling of excitement in the air. Despite all the noise in parliament, it seemed that having the bill debated in the upper house was at least some sign of progress for India's 600 million females. President Patil said passionately, "Women's empowerment is a national mission . . . but we mustn't forget about the men. They will be empowered too. . . . A chariot needs wheels on both sides of it to move along; if one side's wheels are missing, the chariot cannot move. You cannot have one side without the other."[31] Pratibha Patil, who took office in 2007, is a Nehru-Gandhi loyalist. She was Sonia Gandhi's choice for president and the country's first woman to hold that position.

Even while guests were leaving the president's function, the media was speculating that the Congress Party was in a huddle, that discussions were going on late into the night of March 8, and that Sonia had let it be known that she wanted the bill to be passed the next day. Tuesday, March 9, when parliament reassembled, the speaker evicted seven of the upper house members who had disrupted the previous day's proceedings. The bill went through by 186 votes to 1. The effect of the bill, when it passes in the lower house, is that a third of the 543 seats will be ceded to women. Dileep Padgaonkar comments, "I'm not sure if the bill would have been passed if the leadership of Congress and the BJP had not issued the whip and had left it to the conscience vote."[32] There are a few more processes for the Women's Reservation Bill to clear before the Congress Party is able to make good on its manifesto pledge that the next general election will be held on the basis of a one-third reservation for women. In a speech called "Women as Agents of Change," the fourteenth Commonwealth Lecture delivered in London on March 17, 2011, Sonia Gandhi sounded very determined when she said that her party would persevere to get the bill approved by the lower house. The 37-minute wide-ranging talk was one of her strongest; it was delivered for the Commonwealth Foundation, an intergovernmental organization, and organized by the Commonwealth Secretariat. In her speech, she pointed out that both the chief minister of Uttar Pradesh and the leader of the opposition in the lower house are women.

Future hurdles notwithstanding, on March 9 female MPs of both houses were jubilant. Brinda Karat, the only female member of the Polit Bureau of the Communist Party of India (Marxist), says that the bill's passage through the upper house represents the possibility of fundamental social change, and that Indian women need to be helped through affirmative action. Looking as though she had just stepped out from an Indian miniature painting with her high forehead, a prominent *bindi* mark at its center, and long dark hair, Karat appreciates the "tremendous courage" with which Sonia came into politics, facing a "horribly slanderous campaign with a lot of dignity."[33] The media, which had been in a frenzy for two days, proclaimed Sonia Gandhi the heroine of the hour. Newspaper front pages showed photos of female members of both houses, such as Karat and opposition leader Sushma Swaraj, ecstatically hugging each other.

Sonia met with journalists to answer questions in the parliament building and later that evening gave television interviews. To one TV host she said that the ruckus on March 8 "was not at all the right thing to do" and that everyone needed to think of the "larger picture" of women's empowerment, which had been "a dream, a vision of Rajiv-Ji." But she was "relieved" and "very happy." Sonia explained that the resolution to take the risk "is not just me or my decision; I couldn't have taken this decision on my own. All of us, the PM and others, together came to this decision."[34] Padgaonkar explains that "she used these interviews primarily to say, no, it was a collective decision . . . you want to take your colleagues along with you so you share in the success, and if, unfortunately, things go wrong, then you're not alone to take the blame."[35]

The week the bill went through the upper house, Sonia held a dinner for parliament members. To one of those who opposed the bill, whose wife was a former chief minister and had seven daughters, Sonia joked that she now had a huge number of Trojan horses in his family.

26

THE NUCLEAR ISSUE

> What this agreement will do is free our nuclear establishment from the shackles and give our scientists an opportunity to create wonders and open up our energy sector to the rest of the world.
>
> —*Rahul Gandhi*

In 2008 Sonia, as chairperson of the United Progressive Alliance, was managing a coalition of which the Indian National Congress Party was the largest group. She was heading coordination meetings with the prime minister, coalition leaders, and supporters from the "outside," such as the left-wing parties. As chair of the alliance, she needed to talk with everybody, and one of the principals she met with was Brinda Karat, the only female member of the Polit Bureau of the Communist Party of India (Marxist). Karat found Sonia accessible, and they engaged in "convivial discussions" over social bills. "She was aware of all the issues and had a very firm view," says this Marxist member of the upper house.[1]

But there were rumblings from the left, which was threatening to pull away from the ruling United Progressive Alliance over a proposed India-US nuclear deal known as the 123 Agreement. For 30 years India had been denied access to foreign civil atomic energy because of its weapons program and its refusal to sign the Nuclear Non-Proliferation Treaty. India had limited coal and uranium reserves. By 2050 nuclear power is expected to provide around 25 percent of the country's electricity, up from the roughly 3 percent it uses now. India owns about a quarter of the world's total thorium reserves, which could ultimately fuel its long-term nuclear program.

The prime minister felt that nuclear power was the best way for India to meet its increasing energy needs and maintain its economic growth, and he had already met twice with President George W. Bush, after which joint statements were issued. A deal designed to end India's nuclear isolation was first announced in 2005, and in 2006 both the US House of Representatives as well as the US Senate approved it. Under the deal, India could keep its nuclear weapons as well as buy nuclear fuel and technology for its civilian energy requirements. India's record of nonproliferation, its growing energy needs, and its rising prominence in Asia—plus the fact that nuclear energy is seen as a cleaner alternative to other forms—helped garner support from the 45-nation regulatory group for nuclear trade. The deal, which China and Pakistan opposed, represented something of a paradigm shift; as India stood to gain more strategic and economic space, for Washington it meant that China might not be quite such a dominant power in Asia. Leftist parties, upon whom the government depended for parliamentary support, were against any deal with the United States, claiming it would damage the strategic sovereignty of the country. A few Congress Party members also had doubts. In 2007, with the Bharatiya Janata Party opposing the nuclear deal (even though it had proposed a softer version earlier on), the topic began to dominate public discourse. There was a growing sense of confrontation as the government dug its heels in, an indication that it was prepared to stake its own survival on the deal.

In August, when Prime Minister Manmohan Singh sought to defend his stand on the subject in parliament, he was shouted down by some allies and opposition parties. On August 14 Sonia leaped to his defense at a meeting of Congress Party MPs, saying that "technological self-reliance and national sovereignty have been and will continue to be fully protected."[2] The face-off continued through September, but by October Sonia and other leaders were in a conciliatory mood, as evidenced at the *Hindustan Times* leadership summit titled *Imagine the India that Can Be.* Both Manmohan Singh and Sonia Gandhi spoke at the conclave, appearing far from belligerent; Sonia stressed that an early election (the next was due in 2009) was not in the cards and that the position of the government as well as Sonia's own standpoint was that "we are working in a coalition," therefore "we will work toward bringing about a consensus with the left." When the chair, Vir Sanghvi, pressed her, saying that the government seemed to have changed its stance during the course of a week, she reiterated that "we are not looking for a confrontation" and that the *dharma* (or code of coalition—literally, that which holds) was "to try and understand each other's views and positions and that is what we will do."[3]

Sonia's and Singh's comments at the leadership summit were widely reported, but the left continued to resist. Former CNN consultant editor Ashis Ray comments, "Sonia was afraid the government would lose if a no-confidence vote was brought against it by opponents of the nuclear deal,"[4] which would lead to premature elections whose outcome was uncertain. But when the prime minister expressed his solid commitment to the deal, she came out in full support, showing that she was prepared to change her mind on occasion.

Like mother, like son. Rahul did not hesitate to add his imprimatur, a signal that was immediately picked up by doubters in the party who then threw their weight behind the prime minister. A vote on the issue was to be held in parliament on July 22, 2008. The left, with about 64 members in the lower house, decided to pull the ladder away from the United Progressive Alliance coalition over the upcoming motion. Concerned about the pullback, Sonia started to consider alliances that could replace the recalcitrant left. Bridges were built with the Samajwadi (Socialist) Party. Its spokesman and leading light was Amar Singh, the politician who had attacked her in 1999. To help him get to grips with the nuclear issue, he had a tutorial with rocket scientist and nuclear physicist, former Indian president Dr. Abdul Kalam,[5] who showed him that the deal would be good for the country. Amar Singh, a former Congress Party member, says that he and Sonia Gandhi met every couple of days during the time that the government was "in peril." Amar Singh shuttled back and forth, working on obtaining votes, not just the 39 or so from his party but from others as well, to make up the numbers for a majority.

Indian news channels spent most of their air time before and during the two-day debate predicting how the July 22 confidence vote would go; nearly everyone said it was too close to call. If the government did not command 272 votes out of 543, it could fall and the elections might have to be brought forward. The two days of debate saw scenes of histrionics with members throwing tantrums, rushing up to the speaker in an attempt to adjourn proceedings—daily drama, all on live television. Three BJP MPs theatrically cast 10 million rupees, worth around $200,000, onto the floor of the house, claiming they had been offered the money by Amar Singh to abstain from voting. Even before the trust vote took place, Amar Singh was accused by a left-wing party leader of horse-trading, a charge he vehemently denied.[6] (A parliamentary committee set up to examine the bribery charges would exonerate him five months later.[7])

Rahul Gandhi, taking part in the parliamentary debate, highlighted the need for energy security, linking it with poverty and growth. Calling the opposition's bluff, he said that it did not matter whether the government survived the trust vote; what mattered was India's position in the world. In the end, victory was secured by 276 votes to 265.

Four days after the vote, talking to students and academics about the agreement, Rahul said that "too much is said about short-term gains." Emphasizing that long-term gains mattered more to him than winning the next election, he reassured the audience that the deal gave India the chance to become a "global player in nuclear energy." He pointed out that Indian nuclear scientists "working with their hands tied to the back, and our nuclear establishments, painstakingly built over years, are choking because of lack of adequate fuel supplies and technology."[8]

The new UPA-Socialist party alliance would move the ruling coalition to the right, now that the left-leaning parties had deserted their former friends. According to Amar Singh, there were talks on developing the alliance, especially since Singh was strong in Uttar Pradesh, the state that had been a Congress heartland more than 20 years ago. Singh remembers a call from Sonia asking, "So will you work with me in UP or in the national context? Let us meet." He explains that the meaning of "work" in this context was "an electoral adjustment" between his party and the Congress group. Singh says he demurred. He claims, "She said, 'What shall we do?'" Singh replied by asking for her "confidence. I hope that it will be there?" Sonia did not reply, he remembers. Amar Singh says he took her silence for an implicit approval.[9] He may or may not have been right in his assumption—Sonia Gandhi's silences always leave people speculating.

With the confidence vote safely tucked away, the path was cleared for external affairs minister Pranab Mukherjee to sign a landmark treaty, the 123 Agreement, with US secretary of state Condoleezza Rice in Washington on October 11, 2008. Rice spoke of India and the United States standing "as equals, closer together than ever before." It had taken three years and much acrimony to make the 123 Agreement a reality; it is one of the defining international treaties of the United Progressive Alliance's first term. The nuclear agreement allows American companies to sell civilian nuclear reactors, fuel, and technology to India, and it allows India to reprocess US nuclear fuel within India itself.

Atomic power business with India was worth as much as $150 billion.[10] With the agreement issue resolved, India was in a position to develop nuclear energy relationships with countries like France and the Russian Federation, which were keen to sell their nuclear technology. In December 2008 Russian president Dmitry Medvedev, on a three-day visit to Delhi, agreed to build four nuclear power plants in India, adding to the two his country already had under construction in the south.

The Russian Federation is still India's largest arms supplier—India acquires around 70 percent of its military hardware from the RF and agreed to buy 80 military helicopters on this trip, as well as confirming Russian help in its program to send Indian astronauts into space. In 2009 officials from the two countries shook hands on a deal worth $700 million in which Moscow would supply uranium to Delhi. In March 2010 when Russian prime minister Vladimir Putin visited Delhi, more deals were agreed on: The number of nuclear reactor plants to be built rose to 16, and in the near future an additional 29 Russian fighter aircraft would be winging their way to India. These two countries have been allies since before the Cold War, and trade between them was worth $8 billion in 2010. In December 2010 when French president Nicolas Sarkozy visited for four days, it was announced that his country would build two nuclear power plants in India in a deal worth just over $9 billion.

On August 31, 2010, a Civil Liability for Nuclear Damage bill was passed by the upper house of parliament in Delhi, one week after it was approved by the House of the People. Compensation in the event of an accident was tripled,[11] which essentially limited the liability for private foreign firms wishing to build nuclear plants in India, in keeping with international standards.

27

INDIA'S 9/11

> I want to say very categorically here that those who perpetrate such attacks on our people and those who direct or support them cannot continue to take India for granted any longer. Our response has to be firm and effective.
>
> —*Sonia Gandhi*

On November 26, 2008, ten extremists with mass murder in mind arrived in Mumbai by boat. In this city of teeming millions, they were seeking out Americans, Britons, and Jews. Armed with assault weapons and grenades, they simultaneously attacked landmark luxury hotels—the Oberoi Trident and the Taj Mahal Palace—plus a railway station, a hospital, a cinema, and a Jewish center. They holed up overnight in the hotels, killing and injuring many of the terrified guests: 166 were killed,[1] and 305[2] were left injured. News teams delivered continuous coverage while, behind them, columns of dark gray smoke from the burning dome of the Taj Hotel appeared against a cloudy sky. Police, later supplemented by commandos, encircled the building. They could only play catch-up, searching the hotel floor by floor without maps and detailed knowledge of the buildings, while the attackers appeared to have prepared with surgical precision, even using a model of the Taj Hotel to plan their attack.[3] The same year, 130 people died in bomb attacks across various Indian cities. As in previous terrorist incidents—in 2006 multiple bombs were set off on trains and in railway stations across Mumbai, and in 2001 an attack on Parliament House in New Delhi had left 12 people dead—Islamic extremists were held accountable. The Lashkar-e-Taiba (LeT), in conjunction with another group,[4] was found in court to be responsible for the attack on parliament, and it was the LeT that was behind the 2008 Mumbai assaults, according to Ajmal Kasab, the only member of the 2008 killer squad captured alive, who was sentenced to death on five counts. Pakistan acknowledged that he was a national of its country. In early 2009, a Pakistani government official admitted, "Some part of the conspiracy" had taken place in his nation.[5] The Lashkar-e-Taiba that the group belonged to is a Pakistan-based militant organization classified as terrorist by India, the United States, the United Kingdom, and others. By targeting the city's most famous and most opulent hotels, LeT was striking at the most iconic Mumbai symbols of a resurgent India. By aiming for specific nationalities, they were sending a signal through the medium of murder—messages that they were against the policies of the countries of the slain. At the Oberoi and Taj hotels, the killers ordered receptionists to give them lists of room numbers and names of all British and American guests, and made their hostages declare their nationalities.[6] One of the scouts who had helped plan the attacks apparently dressed as a Jew to gain access to the Jewish center.[7] Because the extremists were instructed to kill as many as they could, most of the victims were Indian. As in the case of 9/11, the master handlers created such a situation of shock and panic that international attention was guaranteed, providing them with the oxygen of publicity for their cause.

Sonia Gandhi reacted immediately with a strong statement, calling the attack an act of cowardice. She said, "We shall not allow such incidents to deter our firm resolve to combat terror in all its manifestations. . . . India's one billion people have the strength and courage to defend themselves against the assault on its unity and secular fabric. . . . I urge the people of Mumbai to remain calm and firm in these testing times." She visited the wounded in Mumbai, and later, in March 2009, after Pakistan admitted that parts of the attack were planned on its soil, Sonia told a public rally ahead of the May general election, "We have the power and we could teach those antisocial forces a lesson. Our patience should not be treated as our weakness. . . . We will not tolerate any act against India."[8] There was an outcry from the media and the public over how all the outrages were allowed to happen. In response, the Union home minister was swiftly fired and replaced with Palaniappan Chidambaram, an accomplished lawyer and Harvard Business School MBA, who combines logic with intuition and is more assertive than his predecessor.

However, the combination of the attacks and the initial refusal by Pakistan to acknowledge that such terrorism could have emanated from its territory resulted in a spike in angry relations between the two countries.

November 26 reminded India of its vulnerability and the need for better intelligence systems, improved coordination between multiple agencies, more intensive training, and more efficient hardware for security personnel. Time and again it has been shown that the most serious threat to India and to its leadership emanates from *fedayeen*, attackers willing to die in the process of destroying their target(s), strapped with explosives, heavily armed with assault rifles and bombs, wearing bulletproof jackets, working in groups for maximum damage, and intent on instilling fear in order to obtain what they want.

India's homegrown insurgency, the Naxalites, or the Maoist movement, is seeded in swaths of the Indian tribal belt where lopsided economic development has led to ore-rich land being fought over by mining companies. What is known as the red corridor along central India is teeming with Naxals, hiding out in the region's thick forests, who have built cells of committed cadres and reject anything to do with parliamentary democracy. Founded on a sense of extreme injustice and a loss of control over land and projects, they believe in the use of force and are known for extortion.

Prime Minister Manmohan Singh has stated that the Naxalites are the country's largest internal security threat, and the Maoists have publicly declared that Sonia Gandhi and the prime minister are at the top of their hit list. But the modus operandi of this group tends to be well-organized hit-and-run guerrilla offensives rather than suicide attacks, which are more the hallmark of religious fundamentalist groups like the LeT. India has stated informally that any attack, be it another November 26 against buildings and civilians or on political leaders like the Gandhi family, will not go unanswered. That means retaliatory strikes and the potential for war.[9] An attack on Sonia, Rahul, or any other high-level target could have destabilizing consequences for the entire South Asian region.

The Indian capital of New Delhi has 18 million inhabitants. For its 80,000-strong police force the "superintending authority" is a lieutenant governor, Tejendra Khanna,[10] who describes three rings of security in the capital: The outer rings are covered by Delhi police; an inner ring is handled by the Special Duty Group; and the Special Protection Group (SPG), the executive protection agency of the government of India, provides continuous security around Sonia, her family, and other important personnel. The SPG is divided into house protection and close protection teams. Khanna has increased intelligence operations and the number of police stations in the city and engages with friendly countries like France, Germany, and Great Britain to borrow from their training methods.[11] Parliament House is now strictly protected with at least four checkpoints for entrants to pass through once inside the outer perimeter. The lieutenant governor's team liaises with the SPG to escort the Gandhis and other

VIPs for rapid movement around the city. Though Khanna is attempting to build a security firewall for Delhi, the city, with an area of just under 580 square miles, has highly porous perimeters, and it would be impossible to institute a complete lockdown.

The attacks of November 26, 2008, sharpened India's focus on its defense capability and security apparatus; in 2009 the government boosted its defense spending by 21 percent.[12] India's enemies still find ways of attacking vulnerable locations; second-tier cities, with their slightly lower profiles and reduced level of alertness, now seem to be popular targets. India is expected to spend $80 billion between 2012 and 2022 to upgrade its military, which includes $11 billion on 126 fighter jets and $4 billion on 200 helicopters.

But the threat can emanate from various sources. Even though the Tamil Tiger movement on Sri Lanka was decimated and its leader, Vellupilai Prabhakaran, was killed in a decisive, all-out war in 2009, the Gandhis continue to remain a target for remnants of the outlawed Liberation Tigers of Tamil Eelam, according to *India Today's* defense editor, Sandeep Unnithan. Rumors of surviving groups of Tamil Tigers trying to plot an assassination abounded as recently as the end of 2010. Fortunately, the Z-plus security is so heavy now that an assault by dozens of *fedayeen* would be stopped by the multiple rings of cover. The main focus of the protection around the Gandhis is on the prevention of assailants getting close to their intended target.

Sonia, Rahul, Priyanka, Manmohan Singh, and former prime ministers are in category Z, with maximum protection. The Janpath house has various checkpoints and metal detectors for visitors, with an SPG-manned barrier by the roadside. Today, no one gets to Sonia's home without being on cross-checked lists.

Once through the barrier, family, senior leaders, dignitaries, and visiting prime ministers drive straight to the front of the house and do not have to go through all the security checks. National secretary of the All India Congress Committee (AICC), Major Dalbir Singh, explains that close protection has been very carefully monitored and upgraded since the assassination of Rajiv Gandhi. A few roads away at the heavily fortified office-cum-home of Rahul Gandhi, which is more low-key, all visitors and those seeking appointments sign into a book or send emails to have their requests for appointments considered.

The Special Protection Group, or SPG, is an elite force of roughly 3,000, rigorously trained in procedures similar to that of the US Secret Service. Having spent a year training with the parent forces they are drawn from, SPG officers undergo a further intensive three months of stringent preparation.[13] The SPG has its own sprawling, self-contained complex with residences, shops, the largest gym in Asia, and an administration block providing logistical support at Dwarka, Delhi. The SPG head, appointed in 2004, is a Kashmiri who is "close to the Gandhi family and whose appointment is in keeping with the Gandhi family policy of rewarding loyalists."[14] Training is regularly upgraded and includes the Israeli Krav Maga, a powerful form of hand-to-hand combat. Communicating with other agencies, the SPG is constantly assessing threat perceptions to the leaders under its protection. Recruits are drawn from paramilitary forces and commando units; officers are mainly from the Indian police. They carry pistols, submachine guns, and assault rifles when traveling with Sonia and other family members, and officers manning stationary points carry submachine guns. A counterassault wing called the Special Intervention Unit has been added to the prime minister's SPG team, so that in the event of an attack, one group of officers will whisk the target away while the other will stand and fight. Close protection team officers always have their pistols or submachine guns fully loaded and ready to use. The SPG are around Sonia wherever, whenever, and however she goes—on foot, on the road, by rail, boat, or in the air. They are around her house, at her office, at public and private events. In four squads working six-hour shifts, they form ring-around teams, isolation cordons, sterile zones, and are on stage platforms with her, Rahul, or Priyanka, and they keep the public at bay.

Sonia sometimes walks to the AICC office, but when she goes by vehicle, a set of three Ambassador cars will be assembled for the very short journey. The SPG drill starts an hour and a half before her meeting, whereby agents carefully check rooms and all inanimate objects like flower pots. Sniffer dogs are deployed. One security officer is present throughout the process, and he drinks from the sealed water bottle placed on the table for Sonia before she takes a sip.[15] The compound is fully sanitized, and rooms adjoining anywhere Sonia, Rahul, or the prime minister will be are cleared of officials and workers. For longer journeys, in the constituencies or visiting other states, a set of bulletproof, customized, Tata Safari armored cars with upgraded engines and darkened windows are used. One of them, with antennae, contains remote-control jamming devices. Sonia and other principals are more vulnerable when the cars are traveling slowly, so for that purpose there are grab rails and steps for the SPG to leap and hold onto. A parliamentary security official, Ghanshyam Dutt Bhardwaj—the same one who confirms that neither Rahul nor Sonia wears a bulletproof vest—describes Sonia as usually sitting quietly in her vehicle and reading a newspaper or a magazine, not interacting much with security personnel.

The SPG drill changes daily for Sonia, and the family's travel plan details are not announced in advance. It is a far cry from the simpler days when she sat atop cars and open jeeps beside Rajiv.

For rallies, large barriers are erected, and the distance between Sonia, Rahul, Priyanka, and the audience is wide enough to keep any suicide bomber well out of range. Even in an intimate setting, such as a small meeting between Sonia and key Congress personnel at Fursatganj airport, often used by Sonia and her family when visiting their constituencies, a wooden-stick barrier was erected to keep at a distance a gathering of 15 or 20 people, including the author, as the SPG watched. Everyone had been security checked, cleared, and appeared on two lists of names. Sonia approached each of the gathered, but the group was more or less contained. No one was allowed to carry equipment or cameras. While for years there has been no major security incident involving the Gandhi family, they remain the most tempting targets for assassins. Priyanka's husband Robert, their son Raihan, and daughter Miraya are also covered by the SPG.

Unlike many older democracies, in India, politics is physical and emotional. The public needs to interact with its leaders. Sometimes the only way for a constituent to get a result is to stop their car. For the Gandhi family, the close protection can be suffocating, and Rahul often breaks the cordon, runs to the barrier to meet people, and sometimes even changes his planned route. Despite her experiences, Sonia has also started to occasionally break security detail. Although the Gandhis all appreciate that security has to be in place, they find ways to interact with local people and stay relevant. To be a part of the Indian people's lives, they have to work around the challenges that lie in the shadows and push forward.

28

GENERATION NEXT

> It is undemocratic that the Congress is still led by a Gandhi. But it's the reality. . . . My position gives me certain privileges. It is a fact of life in India that success in politics depends on who you know or are related to. I want to change the system.
>
> —*Rahul Gandhi*

It was just a short while before the election in 2004 that Rahul made the decision to move from a management environment to being out front on the political stage, contesting Amethi. At his first major press conference before his nomination was filed, on January 21, 2004, Priyanka was standing right next to him. Arvind Shukla, a reporter for India's largest-circulation Hindi daily, *Amar Ujala,* who also stood close to them, noticed Rahul trying to stay composed under the harsh glare of the media; and behind his back, Rahul's "slightly shaky hands were being held reassuringly by his sister's."[1]

The press was fierce, expecting Rahul to somehow already have acquired the magic, the oratorical skills, and the chutzpah of the entire clan of Nehru-Gandhis. He ignored the critics and continued fighting for votes. Priyanka managed his campaign in the constituency, introduced him at press conferences, and brother and sister soldiered on. Rahul cannot plunge into crowds the way Rajiv did in his last campaign. The Special Protection Group (SPG) presence, though necessary, can be an inhibitor: Shukla says that the SPG would never let him get as close to the son as he did to the father—though he did get an early interview with Rahul by holding onto the grab rails of his vehicle to ask him questions and committing his substantial answers to memory. The state of Uttar Pradesh was a Congress Party bastion in the days of Jawaharlal Nehru, Rahul's great-grandfather. With 80 lower house seats, it sends the largest number of members to parliament, but Congress Party dominance has been eroded by other parties over the years. In 2004, the party won only nine seats, though Rahul did get elected. From that moment on, Gandhi-hungry sycophants in the Congress Party started screaming for him to take on a larger public role. But Sonia is using a different induction method from the one Indira deployed for Sanjay. Sonia has not forced Rahul onto the national scene, an act that could alienate the electorate. She has often said that he needs to gain experience. In 2007 he was made a general secretary of the All India Congress Committee and given responsibility for two areas badly in need of rejuvenation. The first was the Indian Youth Congress (IYC), a training ground trodden by Rajiv, Sanjay, and many who went on to become ministers and leaders of the party. The second was the student wing of the party, the National Students Union of India (NSUI). If the IYC is like an elementary school, the NSUI is the kindergarten. Rahul has been very busy on these two fronts. With more than 75 percent of the population below the age of 35, the current Indian median age is around 24, which makes the youth vote an important constituency in Indian politics, especially at election time. If this demographic sweet spot is harnessed and converted into a productive work force, then the country has the potential to explode economically; if not, unemployment, insurgency, and social unrest could accrue.[2]

Rahul started off with some central thinking. A former Youth Congress general secretary describes three days of brainstorming in 2007, when Rahul told his executive that he wanted it to "work in a scientific manner"[3] to connect with the young so that they could see a future for themselves in the IYC, find their own leadership qualities, and perhaps enter politics one day. He repeats this message in student and youth arenas all over the country.

Rahul set about revolutionizing both organizations with a zeal and an energy that resulted in membership jumping from a few hundred thousands to millions. He's in his forties, but he has become the poster boy for Indian youth—natural in a country where the average age of the 2010 cabinet was 64. Inevitably as a Nehru-Gandhi, the press is interested in his every move and follows him wherever he goes. Frequently, images appear of the fair-skinned, photogenic Rahul Gandhi, in white handwoven cotton, in action—in a car, among crowds, on a train, talking to young audiences, in his constituency, meeting Youth Congress workers in different states. Rahul also gives occasional briefings to selected journalists at his combined office and home in New Delhi, particularly around election time. *India Today* senior editor Priya Sahgal has been to some of these and described them as "strictly business"—out on the grass in the summer heat, there are tables of coffee and brownies, but no chairs or social chat.

To help Rahul reorganize the youth and student wings of the party, he handpicked a team of educated, motivated young people as his mastermind group. Most of them are tech-savvy and umbilically attached to their cell phones, just like Rahul. Traditionally, officials of the youth wings were either politically connected or had a wealthy godfather; now they tend to be elected. In corporate style, Rahul introduced a system of transparency, accountability, and performance review for post-holders.

The general membership, too, is much more open than before, though people do have to be interviewed and those with criminal backgrounds are rejected. Like Sonia, he works in a collegial fashion, fostering discussion and brainstorming sessions although he remains a principal stakeholder and decision maker. To anyone who uses the dynastic adjective in an accusatory way, he responds, "Just because I am the outcome of a political system, it does not mean I can't change it. I consider it my duty to change the system of which I am a product."[4]

So far, Rahul has refused Congress Party calls for him to take a government position, preferring to follow a political apprenticeship. It allows him the freedom to do what he likes, and he seems to be enjoying the discovery process. In any case, he said when he was 40 that he did not think that he had enough experience to become prime minister then.[5] He calls meetings with experts, attends seminars, and travels continuously, visiting students all over the country as well as the homes of villagers, farmers, and untouchables. In 2005 food security and poverty expert Naresh C. Saxena was slightly surprised to find Rahul asking him for a meeting. Rahul was anxious to learn more about the main issues, needs, and potential solutions in Uttar Pradesh. He invited Saxena to a Youth Congress workshop to talk about the possible role of youth workers and the Congress Party in tackling development issues in the state and how the delivery of services could be improved. Saxena says that good governance is often missing in what he calls "rogue" states like Uttar Pradesh, which in turn affects life expectancy, health, and employment. He cites examples of children in Uttar Pradesh so hungry and so poor that they eat mud. He feels that there is a need for more teachers and doctors in rural areas to do their jobs conscientiously, for they have little incentive there.[6] Saxena describes conditions in Uttar Pradesh as being "very bad."

During his tours, Rahul often stops his convoy and steps into a field to tell some bewildered farmer about the workings of the National Rural

Employment Guarantee Act (NREGA) and asks him to spread the word. Rahul is a man of the people. Sonia, Manmohan Singh, and other Congress leaders have subtly increased mention of Rahul in their public speeches to sensitize the public to the idea that he may one day be standing on the most important platform in the country. Clearly being mentored, Rahul was part of Manmohan Singh's delegation to Afghanistan in August 2005. He accompanied Sonia to New York when she addressed a United Nations General Assembly Informal Plenary Meeting for the first international day of nonviolence on Mahatma Gandhi's birthday, October 2, 2007. He was also at her side in China that year. Priya Sahgal points out that Rahul Gandhi was projected as the man behind the announcement of an extension of the NREGA scheme to the national level from pilot projects.[7]

In the 2009 general election, Rahul was the party's star campaigner; steady in his sandals, he looked more confident and in command than in 2004. Standing squarely on the stage, relaxed, and engaging his audience, he addressed more public meetings than Sonia and Manmohan Singh put together. His work in Uttar Pradesh had paid off, for the seat tally rose to 21. Rahul's responsibility in the Youth Congress started with Uttar Pradesh and Bihar, the latter state sending the second highest number of lower house members to parliament. The path to Race Course Road, the home of the prime minister, is via Uttar Pradesh, so what happens in the state has become Rahul's litmus test.

During his trips, Rahul often dines with and stays the night in the homes of low-caste families, known as *dalits* or untouchables. The notion of an urban, educated member of India's most elite family camping out in villages (with security detail and armored SUVs discreetly on hand) has sent shock waves through Indian society. Understanding the power of the symbolic—as his mother, grandmother, and other family members have—in Uttar Pradesh he once stopped his car, which was being followed by his convoy of security and media, and got out to buy sugarcane from a roadside seller. The plight of sugarcane farmers not getting their fair prices was the subject of his first question in parliament. His grassroots concerns synchronize with his Rajiv Gandhi Foundation work; blending his great-grandfather's socialism with his father's promotion of liberalization, he explains that the extra resources that come from economic growth are what can be used for helping the poor. Some feel that he is closer to the Manmohan Singh school of economics than his mother is. While other politicians may talk about the need to provide sanitation, health care, and education to the poor, Rahul constantly refers to *actual* people he meets; he names examples, and because the public see him constantly out and about among the masses, they believe him. He consoles the widow of a farmer who has committed suicide one week, and the next time he is in parliament, he talks about her plight. The Indian media swarms over every place he visits, interrogating, cross-questioning, and turning the astonished common man or woman squatting on his or her haunches, blinking in the glare of flashbulbs, into an overnight sensation to find out if Rahul-*bheya* (brother) *really* sat on that floor, took his shoes off before entering, ate in that corner, slept on that rough charpoy—and discovers the story is true!

In February 2010 the Shiv Sena—a right-wing, Mumbai-located regional party—threatened to conduct a black-flag demonstration if he carried out a plan to meet with Youth Congress workers and students in India's financial hub. Ostensibly, they were protesting Rahul Gandhi's comment that Mumbai was for all Indians, a simple truth given that the city attracts workers from UP, Bihar, and all over the country, particularly in the unorganized sector.[8] The street equivalent of a political thumbs-down, black flags can indicate dislike or distaste for a person, idea, or party. Disregarding the threat, Rahul delivered his planned talk to college students, but instead of going to the airport for a helicopter ride to his next destination, he went to an ATM where he stood in a queue, withdrew some money, bought some train tickets, and was soon chatting away with amazed fellow commuter-train passengers (surrounded by his security detail). His train journey took him close to the Shiv Sena's headquarters. The *Times of India*'s consulting editor Dileep Padgaonkar suggests that sometimes what Rahul does, whether consciously or unconsciously, adds to the history of the family's courageous acts that acquire symbolic importance—like Indira Gandhi riding on an elephant through mud and rain to go to a village where hundreds had been massacred or sitting down in protest at the roadside after being arrested. The image of Rahul Gandhi waiting in line at an ATM—doing what ordinary city-dwellers do—is symbolic, like the Nano car or the mobile phone, of a resurgent India. According to Padgaonkar, Rahul used the ATM to show that he could connect with the average urbanite even in an environment made hostile by the Shiv Sena, "a party, like so many others that have mushroomed in India on the strength of exploiting religious or regional chauvinism, [that] contains in its ranks hoodlums by the score."[9] Padgaonkar says that while Rahul still has much to learn, he is "the most promising public figure that India has at the moment."

Television anchor Karan Thapar doesn't see Rahul's use of a Mumbai ATM as extraordinary. He feels that it is perfectly normal for politicians to go into areas to bolster and to rally support, but he adds that politicians matter *much more* in India than in the West because in India they are the instruments of change.[10]

Toward the end of October 2010, Rahul Gandhi again made a detour on the way back from an election rally. Hiring a car to take him and his security to the station—the driver was asked to switch off his mobile and, not recognizing his main passenger, asked if they were running away from the police[11]—Rahul spent roughly 30 hours on a sleeper-car train amongst many young people traveling from Uttar Pradesh to Mumbai in search of work, some of them for the first time. Keen to understand more about their motivation, he asked how much they expected to earn in each location.[12]

Sometimes he takes high-profile visitors into villages, again attracting media attention to the countryside. In May 2010 Rahul accompanied Bill Gates on a series of visits: first to a self-help training center for women Rahul helped set up, where they met around 300 participants, then to the only modern hospital in the region. In the evening, they went to two more low-caste villages, sat on charpoys, and, with Rahul interpreting, Gates asked about the quality of life for the villagers, their education, and salaries.[13] On the television program *Walk the Talk,* Gates said that Rahul wanted to show him what *was* and what was *not* working in his constituency. "I think that he and I share an interest that if we put the right things in place, 10 or 20 years ahead, you could make a big difference." What surprised Gates about Rahul Gandhi was that "he is very hands-on. He likes going into these villages but he doesn't come in and say that here I'm the big man with the answers. He is actually fairly quiet and really interested in what the people are saying."[14]

Rahul's visits into the countryside, of course, make for great photo-friendly news coverage: the good-looking man in the snow-white overshirt chatting seriously with farmers and their families in sunny fields. Priya Sahgal named these visits the "Discovery of India," a play on the book of the same name that his great-grandfather wrote. After seeing Rahul's ventures into the countryside, politicians across the board have started doing the same thing, sitting on the floor in the humble homes of startled villagers and sharing meals with them. "You can learn a lot just by listening to someone," Rahul said. "That is my job, to learn from them."[15] Rahul often asks those he meets in their huts about the quality of the food they eat and type of food they can buy; he takes notes and stores the information away for later use. Like his parents, he always asks for permission to enter before he goes into a home.

Rahul tries to avoid having senior politicians around him when he visits the dwelling of a tribal villager or ordinary party worker, and the media is regularly denied access to maintain the privacy of the families involved. He often asks his Youth Congress workers or a nongovernmental organization to quietly arrange the meeting so that it does not turn into a state visit with everyone jostling for a photograph.

Rahul may often fly into Uttar Pradesh to a local airport. Amethi can be reached from the state's capital city, Lucknow, by driving southeast along National Highway 56, an avenue lined with Indian rosewood trees and turning right at a little town called Jagdishpur for the road to the Nehru-Gandhi bastion.

In Amethi Sanjay Gandhi's belief in "each one, teach one" is being put into practice. Rahul was keen to tell a reporter in Amethi that Congress workers in the constituency were teaching children in their homes; 40,000 youngsters were already in the program. "Each one will teach one or two children," he said.[16] Rahul, it seems to one editor, embodies a combination of Rajiv's idealism and Sanjay's drive.[17]

Rahul is up against a dominant political force in Uttar Pradesh: a strong-willed representative of the lowest castes with a penchant for larger-than-life statues of herself and other prominent members of her caste. Her name is Mayawati, she is the state's chief minister, and her huge following won her an outright majority. She doesn't care about the press or the wider public outside her state. No matter how hard the "dimpled darling" (as one socialite described Rahul) works, Mayawati's followers are glad to have a so-called untouchable in a position of power. They are happy to have her create parks and statues in honor of herself and other low-caste leaders, as they enjoy seeing members of a group that was traditionally at the bottom of the heap being idolized like society's aristocratic icons. India waits to see if Rahul can capitalize on his work in Uttar Pradesh to puncture Mayawati's ego and massive vote base and eventually bring her down. However hard she is challenged, Mayawati is not going to buckle readily. When Rahul wanted to garland the statue of Dr. B. R. Ambedkar, the chief architect of the Indian constitution and a hero for many Indians, including untouchables, the same day as Mayawati was planning to, his team was told he could only do so after she did. He got around it by garlanding a photograph instead. Playing ball with appellations, in 2010 Mayawati's government changed the name of Rahul's constituency, Amethi, so synonymous with the Nehru-Gandhi family, to that of a former leader of the untouchable community.[18] Hardball tactics dog Rahul here and there; another state's chief minister decided Rahul could not proceed with a plan to talk to Youth Congress officials in a university auditorium, so his team simply moved the event to a hall used for weddings. Turf wars are rife. Some state authorities, particularly in Uttar Pradesh, complain that when he does something that isn't planned, they cannot guarantee his security.

Sonia and Rahul would probably like the Congress Party to reemerge as the single largest political entity one day. For that to happen, it needs a seat tally of 272 out of 543. Rahul is keen to strengthen the party so that, where possible, it does not have to make alliances—be they temporary or long-term—even if in the short term that means electoral losses in certain states.

The problem is that over the years at the local level, in many crucial areas the party has atrophied, relying in part on the magic Nehru-Gandhis to ensure victory in the important polls. Some local party workers feel that they do not have to work as hard—if at all—while they have a strong leader from the dynasty. This is dangerous now that the name competes with those of chief ministers who are committed to improving the infrastructure in their regions; ultimately all voters care about is what can improve their quality of life.

The National Students Union of India and the Indian Youth Congress buildings stand next to each other in Raisina Road in Delhi. The NSUI president, Hibi Eden, is from a Congress Party family but not a particularly privileged one. He speaks of the 25-year vision Rahul has for the student body, which has replaced the two- to three-year quick fixes of former days. Rahul's strategy evolved, Eden says, after discussions with previous office-holders and senior members. Within both the NSUI and the IYC, internal elections for officials take place state by state, and membership enrollment is subject to careful ID verification because voter fraud is a feature of Indian politics, even at the student level. Politics frequently plays a big part in the student world, and parties often target 10- to 15-year-olds, knowing that political affiliations made at a formative age can last for life. In many parts of India, whole villages marry and vote along political lines according to caste, religion, or historical allegiance.

Eden, handpicked by Rahul in 2008, observes that even within the NSUI there was some resistance to Rahul's idea of internal elections, with the old guard wanting to see their own nominees take positions. As the equivalent of a chief executive, Rahul will get his way at the NSUI level; whether he will be able to win if he wants to transform the organization of the parent body, the grand old party with its elderly retainers and fixed ideas, remains to be seen. Eden says that the move toward transparency in the NSUI should make the system stronger and healthier. It is crucial, he insists, to get students interested in politics. With the growing number of middle-class parents "designing their children's entire lives on a piece of paper"[19] even before they are born, students nowadays, often living in neo-nuclear families, have little time for social commitment and national action. Eden describes an overworked medical student, rushing to hospital to attend to his patients, ignoring an accident victim lying in a pool of blood on the roadside. The dream that Eden shares with Rahul is that the student of tomorrow will have the social conscience to want to stop and help anyone that they might see lying injured on the roadside. Rahul is working with purpose, for just as death stalked his father, the Gandhi heir-in-waiting is under no illusions about his own mortality. "I believe in building up a group of leaders because who knows when I [might] get killed," he said to writer Khushwant Singh.[20]

In the Youth Congress headquarters its president, Rajeev Satav, is often ensconced in quiet, serious meetings. Another of Rahul's close team members, Satav is charged with democratizing the IYC and transforming it from the bastion of nomination, influence, and power into a much wider pool from which may emerge future political leaders. Both the NSUI and the IYC now have databases, created in part by some of Rahul's team members. Apart from the ideology of secularism and nonviolence that Satav and Gandhi expect all those who join to follow, elected officeholders "have to perform."[21] The idea of monthly performance evaluations is well understood by the new breed of Youth Congress leaders but might cause the old boys of the grown-up party to go into paroxysms of shock if it were ever introduced there. So as well as political opponents, Rahul faces a cleaning out of the old guard within his own party, of men and women who are there simply because they have been close to, supported, or been a retainer of one of the Nehru-Gandhi family. Many of them know that Rahul has his own team of preferred aides and guides and feel insecure on account of it.

Rahul has grown much more comfortable in his public role. Like his mother, he encourages female empowerment and speaks at many girls-only higher education institutions. The female students greet him rapturously, and he appears to enjoy the attention. Smita Gupta, political editor with *The Hindu* group, notes acts of kindness by Rahul of the type mentioned by many others who have followed him professionally. She has seen him pull to safety a child who was about to be trampled by an overenthusiastic crowd. On one occasion, Rahul was sitting atop an SUV in his spotless white outfit when a throng threw red and green rose petals at him, splashing his clothes with color. "You'd have to be a saint not to enjoy that adulation," Gupta grins.[22] In the crush, an 18-mile drive took three hours to complete. At one point, Gupta's scarf came loose, and before it could be swept away, Rahul jumped up and caught it, asking to whom it belonged before returning it to her. Everyone describes him as well meaning and keen to be seen as on the side of the lower classes, not just in his adopted state of Uttar Pradesh but all over India. He is now masterful in press conferences, adroitly providing answers in the language of the questioner, Hindi or English, and often chairs these events.

Unlike his father, Rahul has the benefit of a long gestation period before he takes high office, even though his party is not nearly as strong as it was in

Rajiv's time. He reads voraciously but does not appear cerebral. He doesn't get unnerved at all now and sticks to his guns on the issues he believes in; his growing confidence can be seen in his readiness to answer questions. The change Rahul is effecting in the party in Amethi shows how he would like things to be at the center. Though he is a product of a dynastic system, he abhors the feet-touching and garlanding of the old India when leaders dispensed so much patronage. Democracy and the concept of working without reward are not credos espoused by many party seniors. The top leadership around Sonia has a vested interest in not wanting the system to change. In order to democratize the party, Rahul and his like-minded colleagues will have to redouble their efforts to win them over.

His message, expressed in a slightly different way but the same as that of his mother, is about the "two Indias"—the rich and the poor. One of the ways of reaching the masses is through a website set up by a dozen or so media professionals to dispense images, video footage, audio, and speech transcripts to press outlets that lack the resources to cover stories properly. The volunteer staff of Pressbrief all operate from their homes. The often underresourced regional media deep in state interiors have free access to its content, with material coming in from all over the country, wherever the Gandhis visit. It is a clever strategy to reach the common man who invariably reads the local press. In India there are more daily print newspapers bought than in any other country; it is one of the few nations where advertising in magazines and papers is growing apace.

In Uttar Pradesh alone, there are 1,400 Hindi papers; English language editions sell mainly in urban areas. A Pressbrief representative says, "The moment you leave Lucknow it is the village papers that sell; four more pages get added at each location, all catering to local needs." People in the countryside want to know what is happening locally; they are not so interested in picking up the *Times of India*. "We bridge that gap between the common man and the regional press, so that he knows what is going on."[23] English-language news channels, the Pressbrief worker says, reach only 7 or 8 percent of the total population. Rahul and his teams are placing resources on developing and energizing people outside the capital as well as in major cities; where the real, quiet India is located. Pressbrief has now developed into a site with current and past information on the Gandhi family, in Hindi, Urdu, and English. Since Rahul concentrates on mobilizing the young, there is, for example, a Pressbrief-linked presence on social media sites.

But the Indian press demands instant results. This is difficult, especially in states where the Congress Party lost its way decades ago. In Bihar, which went to the polls toward the end of 2010 and where both Rahul and Sonia campaigned vigorously, the infrastructure on the ground was not strong enough to translate the excitement around Rahul into votes. The press and the opposition lost no time in raising questions over "the Rahul magic," but he doesn't care. He is playing the long game and he knows it will take time.

Priyanka admires this in him. "He doesn't have this thing that he absolutely has to succeed every time, and he's very good with things in which perhaps maybe in the short term he won't succeed, but he can see that there is a long-term success. He will work through that short-term failure."[24] "I don't focus on elections," Rahul has commented. "I focus on thoughts and on bringing the youth into politics. . . . My aim is to provide the state a new type of politics and thinking."[25]

Rahul has a political advantage over his mother in that he is Indian-born and so his loyalty to either the country or his heritage is not such an easy target for opponents. Aside from having to defend charges of dynastic rule, he should not suffer as much bad press as Sonia did in the early days of her political career. And his team, those around him in parliament and who manage his organizations, share his passion for change. They are uniformly polite and businesslike, and they avoid the media, preferring to concentrate on their work. The era of the personality cult, in their eyes, is knocking at death's door. Rahul and his cohort are *generation next.*

29

DEAREST MOTHER

> I do not believe in anger, hatred and violence. It was my way of coming to peace with the violence and loss that I experienced. Meeting Nalini was my personal initiative. I would be grateful if it's respected.
>
> —*Priyanka Gandhi*

Even as they mourned Rajiv together, each of the three Nehru-Gandhis had their own ways of coming to terms with their loss. Priyanka's anger dissipated to the extent that in 2008 she decided she wanted to meet with one of the death squad, Nalini Sriharan, who was in jail in the southern state of Tamil Nadu. Sriharan now had a daughter by one of her co-conspirators, also behind bars. Sonia had not wanted the child to be left an orphan, so she had asked the Indian president for Nalini's death sentence to be commuted to life imprisonment in 1999. Priyanka explained years later in an interview that her mother's compassion was "because you've been through it. . . . Something has happened to you that made you feel awful. Something has happened that crushed you inside. So how can you want that to happen to someone else? An innocent child, what has that child got to do with anything?"[1] The little girl was being brought up in Sri Lanka by her paternal grandmother, and although Nalini was aching to see her, the authorities forbade it.

In 2005, after Sonia received through an intermediary a letter from Sriharan that began "Dearest Mother," it was reported that Sonia "stepped in" to have the 14-year-old brought to India to be reunited with her mother and father. Since then, the girl has lived with Nalini's parents in Tamil Nadu.[2] In 2007 Nalini Sriharan sent to the intermediary and to Sonia copies of a letter she wrote to the Union home minister, asking to be let out of prison as she had served 14 years of her sentence.[3] Priyanka traveled south the following year for a private meeting with Nalini, expecting to forgive the woman who had been an integral part of the squad that murdered her father. She found that forgiveness was no longer appropriate, for she felt that Nalini too had suffered. According to Sriharan's counsel, both the women cried during the hour-long meeting—Priyanka breaking first. She asked Nalini why her father had been killed and about Nalini's role in the murder.[4] Priyanka said that her father had been "a good person" and that the grievance could have been resolved through talks. She wanted to know who was responsible, if Nalini saw Rajiv when the bomb went off, and if the Liberation Tigers of Tamil Eelam were behind the blast. Word got out about the visit (through a lawyer who used the Right to Information Act),[5] and the media pounced on the story. Priyanka issued a short statement for the press. Rahul, when later asked about Priyanka's meeting, replied that he and his sister "have been taught not to carry hatred with us . . . we don't carry anger." When asked what was the aim of the exercise, Rahul replied, "It's not an exercise . . . she felt that she wanted to go and see the person . . . she's been feeling that for some time."[6]

Priyanka's independent streak led her to do the unexpected—as far as the public is concerned—and seize her right to support her young family as she sees fit. Though a primary member of the party, she chose to concentrate on raising her children while supporting her brother and mother during election campaigns. She did say in a 2009 interview that her husband and children often accompany her because she wanted her children to get "used to the fact that their family is involved in this thing. They'll see crowds. I don't want them to . . . when they're 14 or 15, be intimidated or to suddenly think they're great shakes because people are running around them."[7] Her son, Raihan, and daughter, Miraya, accompany their parents for the ritual visits to family cremation sites too. In raising her own children, Priyanka emulates Sonia's style: "She is an extremely involved mother and everything I have learned about parenting is from my parents. The way I am as a parent to my children is exactly like her: She was always there for us."[8] Priyanka has said that the one woman in the world she admires is her mother.[9]

Though an editor told Priyanka that one day her destiny would drag her into politics, "kicking and screaming,"[10] she has so far resisted the call.

Priyanka holds a master's degree in Buddhist studies and says that she now likes "to be left alone to be an ordinary person. I like my ordinary life. . . . On a typical day [I] get up . . . get my children ready, and take them to school . . .

sometimes I make the children . . . something nice to eat—they like cupcakes, so I often make them."[11] The family discreetly participates in cultural and spiritual events; in 2010, Priyanka, Rahul, and Robert attended sessions in Delhi led by Zen master Thich Nhat Hahn, a Vietnamese Buddhist monk.

Having been a trustee of the Rajiv Gandhi Foundation since its 1991 inception, by 2010 Priyanka had become its executive trustee. She goes to the foundation office on a regular basis and is overseeing a new direction for the organization. Dr. V. Krishnamurthy, long-time member of the executive committee and the board of trustees, says that while previously the work of the foundation was quite varied—"we were batting all around the wicket"—the foundation now seeks to focus on specific areas, namely education and training. Sonia, still chairperson, has "given the lead" to Priyanka and Rahul. Krishnamurthy says that the board always wanted the younger generation of Gandhis to get more involved because "it would do them good." Rahul is focusing on training the young, and Priyanka's priorities are women's development and the disabled. Sonia mentors her children in meetings, encouraging them to take more initiative and make more decisions: Krishnamurthy observes that "where they suggest drastic remedies, she cautions them, is able to temper them, and sees that they don't go too fast."[12]

For the 2009 general election, Priyanka campaigned hard for her mother and her brother, appearing on the stump, tall and graceful, sometimes a hand on her hip, smiling and relaxed. The Congress Party does not normally announce its candidate for prime minister in advance, but at the launch of its manifesto, Sonia was asked who it would be. Dr. Manmohan Singh was sitting next to her. She picked up a copy of the party manifesto and indicated the gentle technocrat in his trademark sky-blue turban, saying that it would be him. In 2009 Sonia also began moving Rahul to center stage.

One of Sonia's main themes, particularly in the wake of the 2008 Mumbai attacks, was firm action against terrorism. The terrorist threat was being made much of by the opposition parties. The Congress campaign also highlighted various social bills, including ones on education and midday meals for children, the Right to Information and the National Rural Employment Guarantee Acts, and a loan waiver for farmers it had introduced. A public relations consultant involved with the 2009 campaign said that while in 2004 the party was the champion of the underdog and the savior of the common man, in 2009 it sent an added signal: There was unfinished work and a larger agenda that needed time to complete.

May 2009 saw international commentators hedging their bets on the likely election outcome. In Uttar Pradesh the popularity of Mayawati and her larger-than-life personality fooled many into believing that she could even become prime minister. As author and columnist M. J. Akbar says, "Anyone who predicts the future in Indian politics should be sent to a mental asylum."[13]

No one could guess the makeup or the strength of the winning coalition. As the votes and seat numbers were counted, it was clear that the United Progressive Alliance (UPA), the umbrella group that the Congress Party leads, had done better than anyone dared hope. It won 261 seats, and Congress, with an improved tally of its own, 206,[14] did not even need the hefty left numbers this time, as the UPA was only nine seats short of the majority 272 in the lower house. In the event it gained much more; the generally held view is that voters, especially among the middle and upper classes, felt that the combination of Manmohan Singh, Sonia, and the rising star, Rahul, made a neat ticket, and they were voting for stability. Strategic alliances helped. Asked afterward if she had expected to win, Sonia said that she had no doubt that Congress would be the single largest party but had not expected such a large margin.[15]

Sonia immediately moved to continue her agenda to promote women's rights whenever possible. On June 4, 2009, India elected its first female speaker of the parliament, Meira Kumar, a former Union minister, a diplomat whose postings included London and whose hobby is rifle-shooting. The team Sonia put in place has led India to be a major voice in the G20; and the nation is courted by other countries that are amazed at the nation's ability to withstand economic downturns and experience nearly double-digit growth rates. Sonia and Rahul both have a strong sense of Indian honor and pride, and both are internationalists keen to engage with the rest of the world—but only on what they consider equal terms.[16]

In the second half of 2010, five permanent members of the United Nations Security Council, three of which had been hit by economic crises in their countries, visited India. There is an international fascination with the 50 million or so in the Indian middle class, which is predicted to leapfrog by a factor of 10 by 2025.[17] UK prime minister David Cameron visited with the largest-ever British delegation in July, aiming to boost bilateral trade to double its current strength of just under $12 billion. In early November 2010 American president Barack Obama arrived with his wife, met with Sonia as well as other leaders, and shared a formal dinner, which Rahul attended. When Secretary of State Hillary Clinton visited, Rahul met with her too. Obama, it was said, wanted to double India-US trade, taking it to $75 billion.[18] French president Nicolas Sarkozy arrived with his wife in early December to sign agreements. Chinese premier Wen Jiabao arrived in mid-December with the largest-ever Chinese delegation, of 400, for a three-day visit. One of the formal functions was a private dinner hosted by the prime minister at Race Course Road. Sonia was, of course, invited. When the road was blocked due to a heavy cavalcade of vehicles, instead of waiting in traffic, the famously punctual UPA chairperson simply got out of her car and walked less than half a mile to the house, surrounded by her security. Sonia's position as head of the United Progressive Alliance places her in the forefront of powerful international leaders; China worked out that it ranks her equivalent to the Chinese president Hu Jintao in protocol and senior to Wen. It was therefore agreed that the formal direct interaction between the two of them would be described as a "meeting," and, as the *Indian Express* put it, "Wen would walk the extra distance" to visit Sonia at the Janpath home.[19] In New Delhi, visiting heads of government call on her, whereas Sonia Gandhi calls on heads of state.[20]

India remains on good terms with Russia, its historically close ally. Prior to President Dmitry Medvedev's arrival just before Christmas 2010, the Russian ambassador to Delhi noted that his country looked on India as a "beautiful radiant bride" surrounded by many grooms in the form of the various world leaders courting India, but that since Russia also saw India as its sister, it would like her to find a "very good match." His country was not "jealous" of India's improving relations with the United States.[21] Medvedev, as well as Prime Minister Vladimir Putin, has met with Sonia on several occasions, and the ties between the two countries remain strong.

Sonia Gandhi is at ease with other leaders on the international stage; her attitude to the subject of politics that she once, by her own admission, detested, has reversed. Perhaps this is because of the undoubted difference she has been able to make to her party and the Indian polity. In the 2007 *Hindustan Times* leadership summit, she told the audience that being in politics is not as "bad," not as "dark and slimy"[22] as she thought it would be. In fact, she exhorted the elite audience of business leaders and thinkers to "engage and involve themselves more directly in politics . . . and I am sure you will make a difference for the better."[23] These days she is so comfortable in public that, whereas once Vir Sanghvi noted how she would always answer each question fully and frankly, now she is not only smarter in her responses, but the lady once dubbed the "sphinx" intervenes with aplomb. At the 2008 *Hindustan Times* summit,[24] she commented during a vote of thanks Vir Sanghvi was giving her so many times that he jovially asked if she and he might have a conversation instead. In March 2011 she atypically interrupted an opposition speaker in the lower house with a one-liner that drew cheers and clapping from her own party and its allies. Some opposition members smiled, too, and gesticulated in genuine astonished pleasure and joined in the applause.

EPILOGUE

JANPATH

> My journey from the placid backwaters of a contented domestic life to the maelstrom of public life has not been an easy one. Yet, despite its sorrows and difficulties, I have found in my new existence both fulfillment and a larger sense of purpose.
>
> —*Sonia Gandhi*

Sonia disliked the sycophantic behavior of courtiers she observed around Indira at the time when she was prime minister. That is why in her own regime, her court is smaller though the deference in the DNA of Congress Party workers is still in evidence. She does not maintain the kitchen cabinet that Indira did; those upon whom she relies politically have institutional roles. Her personal staff has little authority.

By watching those who came, betrayed, and went in Indira's life, she also learned the importance of trust, a trait Sonia values. In her governments, she often includes erstwhile enemies and detractors as a way of reaching out to other factions of her country's society; she will work with them, but she may not fully trust them.[1]

Sonia has built a reliable core group of people around her. Ahmed Patel is her right-hand man and political secretary. Low-key, he avoids the media and is one of the most powerful men in the party. Engineer and economist Jairam Ramesh is one of those who writes Sonia's English speeches and policy documents for the party and is the United Progressive Alliance's environment minister. Unlike many of the current guard, he could transfer smoothly to the next generation taking power. Ramesh has what the *Times of India* describes as "the language, the flair and the gizmo-friendly brain to connect with Rahul Gandhi."[2] With flowing hair and rolled-up sleeves, his awareness of twenty-first-century concerns endears him to Rahul. Finance minister Pranab Mukherjee is Sonia's trouble-shooter. Thus most of the central players, like defense minister A. K. Anthony, come from the Congress Working Committee (CWC). Along with Sonia, Rahul, Manmohan Singh, and key members of the cabinet, says one journalist, these are "the guys who run India."[3] And the guys who run India need expert spokesmen to deal with the constant demands of India's media. One of these representatives, member of the lower house Manish Tewari, says that the party president gives him "a large and substantive degree of autonomy to really say things the way you feel, that within the broad policy framework of the party need to be articulated." He finds that when "her intervention is required, she is always available," and that on current political or governance issues, "her perspective can be very incisive."[4]

The CWC comes up with ideas that are taken forward once it has determined which leaders will support them. Sonia, with her capacity for creating allies, manages a national array of competing egos and factions very well. CWC members are increasingly trusted, articulate, educated party stalwarts. The party constitution allows for 12 members of the CWC to be elected and 11 to be nominated by the Congress Party president—both Sonia and the prime minister are ex-officio members. There has been no election contest for the CWC ever since Sonia took over the party presidency in 1998. Everyone in the party's nerve center is handpicked by Sonia, which means that there is no challenger to her position. Moreover, everyone chosen to be in the CWC is naturally beholden to her; she holds the keys to their political survival. Running the party and the coalition and leaving the government to Manmohan Singh has worked well. Remaining cautious, looking to the Nehru-Gandhi forebears, and thinking about what they would have done has guided her. Some commentators believe that with her emphasis on social reform and women's empowerment, she has moved closer to the Mahatma Gandhi model than anyone else from the Nehru family.

Sonia's induction of Rahul into the mainstream of politics has been gentle. Though many critics are unhappy with the concept of dynastic leadership, it is a worldwide phenomenon, and dynastic heirs are deeply conscious of the preservation of values as assets. Priyanka and Rahul often say that whatever the background, voters still rule, and that can be seen from the reaction to the family after the Emergency and the 1989 election. While the Congress Party wants Rahul to be the next prime minister, Rahul appears happy with his allotted tasks. "I will continue to work for the youth unless I am forced [to do otherwise] by the prime minister and my boss, which they can do," he has said.[5] As he accompanies Sonia on the public stage, gradually Indian voters see the two of them as sharing a metaphorical throne.

Rahul is coping well with the clamor from Congress members for him to move to the front. At a Delhi stadium in early November 2010, Sonia had just finished speaking at a meeting of the All India Congress Committee when the audience shouted for Rahul to address them. He was not on the schedule, but after exchanging pieces of paper with his mother, he reluctantly agreed, amid wild applause and cheering. He easily extemporizes now and went straight into his pet theme of there being two Indias, "one that is moving forward fast and the other that is for the poor, which is full of energy and potential but is in crisis. We have to work to connect and unite the two," he said.[6]

For a larger December plenary meeting of the party, which celebrated its hundred-twenty-fifth anniversary in 2010, the choreography for the speakers was more scripted than at the previous month's meeting. While Sonia's image remains squeaky clean, practically every month a story of corruption is highlighted by some news channel or magazine to a weary audience. The level of rottenness, bribery, and dishonesty does not abate, and it is pretty evenly spread across the political spectrum. A spate of corruption scandals almost paralyzed a whole winter session of parliament. In 2010 the media comments on the putrefaction of the standards of public figures increased, and it was impatient for Sonia to denounce the gangrene. In response, at the plenary session, Sonia called for anticorruption measures, transparency, and accountability at all levels and outlined a blueprint for dealing with the problems.

Rahul has also railed against corruption, and his signature speech on the same Delhi platform will likely be remembered as one of his most significant. Defining his own take on India, the summary of his various discovery tours, and his hopes for the future of the country, he said that the common man, "The *aam admi* in India is that person who does not have a connection to the system . . . a population unconnected to the growth engine of our economy is a wasted and unproductive resource." To illustrate, Rahul described an array of people—someone from a northern hill station who gets top marks but cannot get a job because he does not have the right connections; a tribal boy suddenly ejected from his land without judicial recourse; a young professional in a southern IT hub who cannot place her child in a decent school; a bureaucrat who will not be promoted because he will not compromise; a worker who helps build an underground tube system but will never be acknowledged.[7] Presenting the unique face of the unlinked person earned him plaudits at the plenary but also demonstrated how far he has come; his forays into far-flung India have taught him a great deal, and his mother's careful positioning of him gives the fledgling leader an aura of readiness. One minister sighed nostalgically, "If you closed your eyes and listened to the voice, one could hear echoes of Rajiv speaking 25 years ago."[8]

Devoid of demagoguery, Sonia, Rahul, and Priyanka (even though she took a back seat) are the main assets of the Congress Party. Sonia has brought allies and foes together into a cohesive alliance; she has strengthened and energized her party's base. As long as she enjoys a reputation as a winner, the Indian political class—described by the *Times of India* consulting editor as "having the backbone of an eel"[9]—will stay with her. The veneration of the elderly in a country where a mother past middle age occupies an exalted position, her widowhood lending even greater depth, means that the mother-son and mother-daughter combinations are playing to great effect. She has inherited the mantle of the matriarch and wears it well. Rahul, on the other hand, representing the politics of hope, is taking the young demographic by storm.

While Rahul frequently answers questions, Sonia's silence on many issues is both a strength and a weakness. Some would like her to be more accessible to the media, but, unlike her son, she rarely gives press conferences. Though much more relaxed in an interview than ever before, she is still careful about whom she speaks to from the media. One journalist says, "We know more about Rahul than we do about Sonia!" and adds, "She just tells you what she wants you to know."[10] Though confident now in public and with a set of well-wishers who carefully guard her privacy, she learned from Indira that no one, apart from her children, can be her total confidant, and that in her position she *is* alone—so she understands how to shed her friends. One editor feels that is the reason she is ambitious for Rahul: "In India, you don't trust anybody, and she needs someone because she's all alone."[11]

There are no signs that Sonia is going to stop being Congress Party president any time soon. Senior and junior leaders alike know she has unified a party full of competing egos and factions and that there is probably no one else who can perform that function. An excellent manager, she brought it back from the brink of destruction; so long as Congress can continue to win national elections under her leadership, it will support her. In fact, it has accommodated itself to ensure that power rests with her and that she is comfortably able to carry on for as long as she wishes. Unopposed in September 2010, Sonia was reelected party president for the fourth consecutive time, setting a record (12 years) for the longest serving incumbent ever of the oldest political party in India. At the December 2010 plenary session on the outskirts of Delhi, a resolution was passed that amended the party's constitution to extend the party president's term from three to five years. Sonia's position is not in peril. No one would dare to contest her, even though the rules permit it, and it appears that the political will among the senior leadership is not there anyway. Compared to when she first entered politics, her approval rating is extremely high.

The little girl who grew up in a protective family and the loving shelter of the Salesian sisterhood in a small Italian town is now leading the coalition running a country of more than a billion people, halfway around the world from her place of birth. It was not ambition that paved her path to power but circumstance and tragedy. Sonia's story represents the greatest transformational journey made by any world leader of the last four decades. She has been faithful to her adopted country and to the memory of her husband. "[Rajiv and Sonia] were the eternal teen lovers . . . whatever Sonia Gandhi is today is what a woman can be if she finds true love,"[12] one movie star noted. She has never wavered in her sense of duty, showing a determination to keep going under the most trying of circumstances.

Sonia has seen the gap between India's rich and poor widen and its underprivileged classes enlarge. Her concern for the deprived and marginalized is one of the most significant aspects of her political personality. She is determined to have that class, which *is* India, helped and uplifted. The legislation that she has pushed for is all to that end. Sonia is holding the torch high, waiting for the next generation of Gandhis to take it up.

NOTES

All extracts from the *Hindustan Times* are from the New Delhi edition of the newspaper. Positions and titles of persons quoted in articles and interviews, where identified, were current at the time the book went to press.

PROLOGUE THE TIGERS' REVENGE

1. Sonia Gandhi, *Rajiv* (New Delhi: Viking, 1992), 9.
2. Sonia Gandhi, *Rajiv,* 13.
3. Hon. Sonia Gandhi, interviewed by Vir Sanghvi for *Star Talk* on Star Plus Television, 1999.
4. Sonia Gandhi, *Rajiv,* 9.
5. Hon. Sonia Gandhi, interview by Shekhar Gupta, editor in chief, *Indian Express,* on *Walk the Talk,* NDTV, May 15, 2004.
6. The Tamil Tigers is the short form; the full name of this group is the Liberation Tigers of Tamil Eelam (LTTE).
7. Mark Tully, former BBC Delhi bureau chief, author's interview, New Delhi. The interview was conducted in two parts over several months; the first of these took place in March 2010.
8. Dr. Rema Devi, medical practitioner and assassination eyewitness, telephone interview by author, May 2010.
9. V. Jayanth, M. Prakash, T. S. Subramanian, "The Gory End," *Frontline,* June 8, 1991, 11.
10. "Many Rajiv Organs Damaged," *Hindustan Times,* May 30, 1991, 3.
11. Dr. Rema Devi, telephone interview by author, May 2010.
12. Sonia Gandhi, interviewed on *Star Talk,* 1999.
13. Jayanti Narayan was one of those looking after the coffin.
14. Jad Adams and Phillip Whitehead, *The Dynasty* (London: Penguin Books, 1997), 363.
15. Footage from *The Dynasty,* a four-part series aired on BBC-TV, 1997.
16. Ashok Kalkur, *Frontline,* June 8, 1991, 124.
17. "The Last Post," *Frontline,* June 8, 1991, 125.

CHAPTER 1 FROM ITALY TO BRITAIN

1. Encyclopedia Britannica Online, s.v. "Sonia Gandhi (Indian politician)," http://www.britannica.com/EBchecked/topic/225270/Sonia-Gandhi, accessed March 6, 2011.
2. Rasheed Kidwai, *Sonia* (New Delhi: Viking, 2009), 1.
3. Ibid. The information about the children's names has not been challenged to date. The author verified this detail again in 2010 with Sonia Gandhi biographer Rasheed Kidwai, who said that he had various sources for the story, including former minister of state Natwar Singh.
4. Sister Maria Angela Gribaudo, author's telephone interviews and author's email correspondence, Turin, Italy, August 2010.
5. All education information here and below from separate email interviews by the author with the Sisters Domenica Macario, Maura Reissent, and "one of her school friends," translated for the author by Sister Maria Angela Gribaudo, from Turin, August 2010.
6. Ibid.

7. Ibid. A *novena* is a nine-day prayer during which people, usually together, ask for something important for a person or situation they care for. The prayers, culminating in May, were "to the young St. Dominic Savio," said Sister Maria Gribaudo.
8. Sonia Gandhi, interview, "In Our House We Only Speak in Hindi," by Pushpa Bharati, first carried in now-defunct Hindi magazine *Dharamyug,* 1985; reprinted in *The (Chandigarh, India) Tribune,* May 1, 1991.
9. Hon. Sonia Gandhi, interviewed by Vir Sanghvi, *One on One,* NDTV, 2006.
10. Sonia Gandhi, *Living Politics* (Tilburg: Nexus Institute, 2007), 16.
11. "Detailed Profile: Smt. Sonia Gandhi," India.gov.in, April 3, 2011, http://india.gov.in/govt/loksabhampbiodata.php?mpcode=130.
12. The exams offered were for the Cambridge First Certificate and the Certificate of Proficiency. Sonia Gandhi's detailed Lok Sabha profile shows that she finished her certificate in English exams in 1965.
13. Sonia Gandhi, *Rajiv* (New Delhi: Viking, 1992), 1.
14. The Right Honorable Kenneth Clarke, British Lord Chancellor, author's interview, London, September 21, 2010.
15. Sonia Gandhi, *Rajiv,* 1.
16. Ibid.
17. Cherry Topden (Yorke), telephone interview by author, June 2010.
18. There are several different versions of the spelling of this name—Puccina, Piccina (affectionate nicknames), and Peccina—even among interviewees.
19. Karma Topden, former ambassador and upper house member of parliament, author's interview, New Delhi, April 2010.
20. Ibid.
21. From a Cambridge contemporary of Rajiv Gandhi.
22. There is little accurate data on this time, and family names of all tenants are now difficult to trace.
23. Hans Loeser's recollections in this chapter are from author's telephone interview, August 2010. Loeser became a scientific adviser to the German government. Thilo Dilthey's recollections are also from this interview.
24. Tahir Jahangir, contemporary of Rajiv Gandhi at Cambridge, telephone conversation with author, February 2011.
25. Amorey Gethin, former director, Lennox Cook School, author's telephone interview, November 2010.
26. Sonia Gandhi, *Rajiv,* 58.
27. Ibid., 2.
28. Sonia Gandhi, interview, "In Our House We Only Speak in Hindi."

CHAPTER 2 SAFDARJANG ROAD

1. Quotes from Sonia Gandhi, interview, "In Our House We Only Speak Hindi," by Pushpa Bharati, first carried in now-defunct Hindi magazine *Dharamyug,* 1985; reprinted in *The (Chandigarh, India) Tribune,* May 1, 1991.
2. Hon. Sonia Gandhi, interview by Shekhar Gupta, editor in chief, *Indian Express,* on *Walk the Talk,* NDTV, May 15, 2004.
3. Indira Gandhi was information minister from 1964 to 1966, then became prime minister in 1966 after the death of the previous incumbent.
4. Malvika Singh, author of *Delhi: India in One City,* author's interview, New Delhi, March 2010. Singh is a publisher and has written books on the architecture and design of buildings in Delhi.
5. Ibid.
6. Sonia Gandhi, interview, "In Our House We Only Speak Hindi."
7. "Onlooker: PM at Mehndi Ceremony," *Hindustan Times,* February 25, 1968, 11.
8. Malvika Singh, author's interview, New Delhi, March 2010.
9. "Shenai, Shlokas at Rajiv-Sonia Wedding," *Hindustan Times,* February 26, 1968.
10. "Wedding Scene Turbans, Tailors, and Fireworks," *Hindustan Times,* February 26, 1968, 55.
11. Sonia Gandhi, interview, "In Our House We Only Speak Hindi."
12. Hon. Sonia Gandhi, interview on *Walk the Talk,* May 15, 2004.
13. Ibid.
14. Sonia Gandhi, interview, "In Our House We Only Speak Hindi."

15. Salesian Sister Domenica Macario, author's email interview, Turin, August 2010.
16. Katherine Frank, *Indira* (London: Harper Perennial, 2005), 310.
17. Hon. Sonia Gandhi, interview on *Walk the Talk,* May 15, 2004.
18. Sonia Gandhi, interview, "In Our House We Only Speak Hindi."
19. M. L. Fotedar, former minister, author's interview, Gurgaon, April 2010.
20. Vinod Mehta, editor in chief, *Outlook* magazine group, author's interview, New Delhi, April 2010.
21. Frank Christopher, director, Parliament Library, author's interview, New Delhi. The interview was conducted in two parts over two months; the first of these took place in April 2010.
22. Inder Malhotra, former *Guardian* correspondent and former editor, *Times of India,* author's interview, New Delhi. The interview was conducted in three parts over several months; the first of these took place in March 2010.
23. Sonia Gandhi, *Living Politics* (Tilburg: Nexus Institute, 2007), 17.
24. Mushirul Hasan, historian, author's interview, New Delhi, April 2010.
25. *India's Rajiv,* Siga Arts International, April 1, 1989. The 5,000-rupee-a-month figure is from the documentary. It is not known exactly when during Rajiv's flying career he earned this salary, so it is difficult to convert, even approximately, as the rates would vary enormously. But as a rough guide, in 1980 5,000 rupees was perhaps worth over $600.
26. Sonia Gandhi, *Rajiv* (New Delhi: Viking, 1992), 67.
27. Ibid.
28. Sonia Gandhi, interview, "In Our House We Only Speak in Hindi."
29. From author's email interview with Sister Maria Gribaudo, and author's telephone interview with Sister Agnes, Istituto Magistrale Sant'Anna Turin, March 2011.
30. This and other photographs can be seen in the book catalog called "Rajiv Gandhi: An Intimate Vision," produced to accompany a 1997 same-name exhibition of Rajiv Gandhi's work.
31. Natwar Singh, former minister of state, author's interview, New Delhi. The interview was conducted in three parts; the first of these took place in February 2010.
32. Commander-in-chief Sam Manekshaw prepared his army thoroughly but cautioned against all-out action before the end of the rainy season. Inder Malhotra, *Indira Gandhi* (London: Coronet Books, 1991), 134; Jad Adams and Phillip Whitehead, *The Dynasty* (London: Penguin Books, 1997), 235.
33. "Nixon's Dislike of 'Witch' Indira," BBC News, June 29, 2005, http://news.bbc.co.uk/2/hi/4633263.stm.
34. The Sikh army officer was General Shahbeg. Malhotra, *Indira Gandhi,* 135; Mark Tully and Satish Jacob, *Amritsar* (New Delhi: Rupa, 1985), 126.
35. The Indian Ministry of Defense defines the Bangladesh war as lasting 14 days, according to a brochure published by the directorate of public relations, Ministry of Defense, 1972. Documentary evidence provided to author in January 2011 by Sandeep Unnithan, defense editor of *India Today.*
36. His Excellency Tariq Karim, author's interview, New Delhi, April 2010.
37. Mushirul Hasan, historian, author's interview, New Delhi, April 2010.
38. Hon. Sonia Gandhi, interview on *Walk the Talk,* May 15, 2004.
39. Sonia Gandhi, *Living Politics,* 17.

CHAPTER 3 NOT JUST BRINGING UP BABIES

1. Jad Adams and Phillip Whitehead, *The Dynasty* (London: Penguin Books, 1997), 156.
2. J. Radhakrishnan, "You Always Win!" *Hindustan Times,* June 24, 1980.
3. Pupul Jayakar, *Indira Gandhi* (New Delhi: Penguin Books, 1995), 420.
4. Mrs. Hemant Pasrich, director, the Study, author's interview, New Delhi, March 2010. All of Pasrich's recollections in the chapter are from this interview.
5. Jyoti Aluwalia, teacher, the Study, author's interview, New Delhi, March 2010.
6. Vinod Mehta, editor in chief, the *Outlook* magazine group, author's interview, New Delhi, April 2010.
7. Ibid.
8. Jayakar, *Indira Gandhi,* 231.
9. Dileep Padgaonkar, consulting editor, *Times of India,* author's interview, New Delhi. The interview was conducted in three parts over the course of several months; the first of these took place in February 2010.
10. Natwar Singh, former minister of state, author's interview, New Delhi. The interview was conducted in three parts over several months; the first of these took place in February 2010.

11. Hon. Dr. Sanjay Sinh, member of the lower house, author's interview, New Delhi, April 2010.
12. Priyanka Gandhi, interview with Barkha Dutt, NDTV, April 25, 2009.
13. Sunita Chauhan, former education minister and former member of the Uttar Pradesh state legislative assembly, author's interview, Lucknow, March 2010.
14. Inder Malhotra, *Indira Gandhi* (London: Coronet Books, 1991), 183.
15. Priyanka Gandhi, interview with Barkha Dutt, April 25, 2009.
16. Sonia Gandhi, *Living Politics* (Tilburg: Nexus Institute, 2007), 18.
17. Hon. Sonia Gandhi, interview by Shekhar Gupta, editor in chief, *Indian Express,* on *Walk the Talk,* NDTV, May 15, 2004.
18. Hon. Maneka Gandhi, member of lower house of parliament, BJP, author's interview, New Delhi, March 2010.
19. Adams and Whitehead, *The Dynasty,* 245.
20. Hon. Maneka Gandhi, author's interview, New Delhi, March 2010.
21. Najma Heptulla, vice-chair, BJP, author's interview, New Delhi, April 2010.

CHAPTER 4 THE EMERGENCY

1. Different sources give different figures for the attendance.
2. Katherine Frank, *Indira* (London: Harper Perennial, 2005), 373.
3. Jad Adams and Phillip Whitehead, *The Dynasty* (London: Penguin Books, 1997), 248.
4. Ibid., 249.
5. Inder Malhotra, *Indira Gandhi* (London: Coronet Books, 1991), 168.
6. Pupul Jayakar, *Indira Gandhi* (New Delhi: Penguin Books, 1995), 277.
7. Siddhartha Shankar Ray.
8. Frank, *Indira,* 374.
9. "To Our Readers," *Hindustan Times,* June 28, 1975, front page.
10. Malhotra, *Indira Gandhi,* 173.
11. "No Grounds Necessary for MISA Detention," *Hindustan Times,* July 1, 1975, front page.
12. Mark Tully, former chief of bureau, BBC, New Delhi, author's interview, New Delhi. The interview was conducted in two parts; the first of these took place in March 2010.
13. Kuldip Nayar, former member of upper house, author, and human rights activist, author's interview, New Delhi and London. The interview was conducted in two parts; the first of these took place in March 2010.
14. Malhotra, *Indira Gandhi,* 177.
15. Frank, *Indira,* 391.
16. Ibid., 396.
17. Ibid., 404.
18. Malhotra, *Indira Gandhi,* 177.
19. Inder Malhotra, former *Guardian* correspondent and former editor, *Times of India,* author's interview, New Delhi. The interview was conducted in three parts; the first of these took place in March 2010.
20. Hon. Sonia Gandhi, interview by Shekhar Gupta, editor in chief, *Indian Express,* on *Walk the Talk,* NDTV, May 15, 2004.
21. Najma Heptulla, vice-chair, BJP, author's interview, New Delhi, April 2010.
22. Frank, *Indira,* 403.
23. Mark Tully, author's interview, 2010.
24. H. E. Tariq Karim, High Commissioner to Bangladesh, author's interview, New Delhi, April 2010.
25. Swraj Paul, businessman, author's interview, London, September 2010.
26. Hon. Sonia Gandhi, interview on *Walk the Talk,* May 15, 2004.
27. Jayakar, *Indira Gandhi,* 320.
28. Ibid., 318.
29. Ibid., 321.
30. Shekhar Gupta, editor in chief, *Indian Express,* author's interview, New Delhi, March 2010.

CHAPTER 5 WILLINGDON CRESCENT

1. Sunita Kohli, architectural restorer and interior designer, author's telephone interview, May 2010.
2. Pupul Jayakar, *Indira Gandhi* (New Delhi: Penguin Books, 1995), 335.

3. Hon. Maneka Gandhi, member of lower house of parliament, BJP, author's interview, New Delhi, March 2010.
4. "Icon Curry," extracted quote from *Truth, Love and a Little Malice* by Khushwant Singh, *Outlook*, February 11, 2002, http://www.outlookindia.com/article.aspx?214503.
5. Hon. Maneka Gandhi, author's interview, March 2010.
6. Sonia Gandhi, *Rajiv* (New Delhi: Viking, 1992), 76.
7. Ibid.
8. Hon. Dr. Sanjay Sinh, Congress member of lower house of parliament, author's interview, New Delhi, April 2010.
9. M. J. Akbar, *Nehru: The Making of India* (London: Viking Penguin, 1998), 349.
10. Jad Adams and Phillip Whitehead, *The Dynasty* (London: Penguin Books, 1997), 276.
11. Inder Malhotra, former *Guardian* correspondent and former editor, *Times of India*, author's interview, New Delhi. The interview was conducted in three parts over several months; the first of these took place in March 2010.
12. *India's Rajiv*, Siga Arts International, April 1, 1989.
13. Jayakar, *Indira Gandhi*, 375.
14. Inder Malhotra, author's interview, New Delhi, March 2010.
15. Jayakar, *Indira Gandhi*, 375.
16. Hon. Dr. Sanjay Sinh, author's interview, New Delhi, April 2010.
17. Adams and Whitehead, *The Dynasty*, 279.
18. Katherine Frank, *Indira* (London: Harper Perennial, 2005), 437.
19. Jayakar, *Indira Gandhi*, 356, 380.
20. Ibid., 355.
21. Ibid.
22. Hon. Maneka Gandhi, author's interview, New Delhi, March 2010.
23. Adams and Whitehead, *The Dynasty*, 284.
24. Jayakar, *Indira Gandhi*, 402.
25. Najma Heptulla, vice-chair, BJP, author's interview, New Delhi, April 2010.
26. Sonia Gandhi, *Rajiv*, 76.
27. Inder Malhotra, *Indira Gandhi* (London: Coronet Books, 1991), 183.
28. Hemant Pasrich, director, the Study, author's interview, New Delhi, March 2010.

CHAPTER 6 ANYONE BUT SANJAY

1. Sonia Gandhi, *Rajiv* (New Delhi: Viking, 1992), 40.
2. Katherine Frank, *Indira* (London: Harper Perennial, 2005), 445.
3. Najma Heptulla, vice-chair, BJP, author's interview, New Delhi, April 2010.
4. *India's Rajiv*, Siga Arts International, April 1, 1989.
5. *Hindustan Times*, June 24, 1980. Unless otherwise noted, all quotes in this chapter relating to Sanjay's crash are taken from that issue's stories.
6. Ibid.
7. Hon. Maneka Gandhi, member of the lower house of parliament, BJP, author's interview, New Delhi, March 2010.
8. Frank, *Indira*, 445.
9. Pupul Jayakar, *Indira Gandhi* (New Delhi: Penguin Books, 1995), 411; *Hindustan Times*, June 24, 1980.
10. *Hindustan Times*, June 24, 1980. Unless otherwise noted, all quotes in this chapter relating to Sanjay's crash are taken from that issue's stories.
11. Jayakar, *Indira Gandhi*, 413.
12. Ibid.
13. Hon. Maneka Gandhi, author's interview, New Delhi, March 2010.
14. "Sanjay Gandhi Cremated at Shantivana," *Hindustan Times*, June 25, 1980, front page.
15. Vijayalaxmi Pandit was the sister of Jawaharlal Nehru. This is the spelling Sonia Gandhi uses, though the first name can be spelled in other ways.
16. Mark Tully, former chief of bureau, BBC, New Delhi, author's interview, New Delhi. The interview was conducted in two parts over several months; the first of these was in March 2010.
17. Footage from *The Dynasty*, a four-part series aired on BBC-TV, 1997.

18. Jayakar, *Indira Gandhi,* 417.
19. Natwar Singh, former minister of state, author's interview, New Delhi. The interview was conducted in three parts over several months; the first of these was in February 2010.

CHAPTER 7 THEIR TOUGHEST DECISION

1. Sonia Gandhi, *Rajiv* (New Delhi: Viking, 1992), 6.
2. Ibid.
3. Ibid., 7.
4. *India's Rajiv,* Siga Arts International, April 1, 1989.
5. Natwar Singh, former minister of state, author's interview, New Delhi. The interview was conducted in three parts over several months; the first of these took place in February 2010.
6. Sonia Gandhi, *Rajiv,* 7.
7. Jad Adams and Phillip Whitehead, *The Dynasty* (London: Penguin Books, 1997), 295.
8. Footage from *The Dynasty,* a four-part series aired on BBC-TV, 1997.
9. M. L. Fotedar, former minister, author's interview, Gurgaon, April 2010.
10. Sonia Gandhi, *Rajiv.* 7.
11. The population stands at over 199 million.
12. Ram Sewak, member of Legislative Assembly, author's interview, Jagdishpur, March 2010.
13. Ram Sewak and Rakesh Singh, author's interview, Jagdishpur, March 2010.
14. Ibid.
15. Rakesh Singh, author's interview, Jagdishpur, March 2010.
16. Verified by Rakesh Singh and Ram Sewak, author's interview, Jagdishpur, March 2010.
17. Natwar Singh, author's interview, February 2010.
18. Sunita Kohli, architectural restorer and interior designer, telephone interview with author, New Delhi, May 2010.
19. Sonia Gandhi, *Rajiv,* 7.
20. Dalip Mehta, author's interview, New Delhi, March 2010.
21. Frank Christopher's certificate was awarded January 9, 1984.
22. Frank Christopher, former director, Lok Sabha Secretariat, author's interview, New Delhi. The interview was conducted in two parts over two months; the first of these took place in April 2010.
23. Sonia Gandhi, *Rajiv,* 7.

CHAPTER 8 ENEMIES WITHOUT AND TENSIONS WITHIN

1. Pupul Jayakar, *Indira Gandhi* (New Delhi: Penguin Books, 1995), 420.
2. Katherine Frank, *Indira* (London: Harper Perennial, 2005), 452.
3. Ibid.
4. Pupul Jayakar, in *The Dynasty,* a four-part series aired on BBC-TV, 1997.
5. Jayakar, *Indira Gandhi,* 420.
6. Ibid., 421.
7. Frank, *Indira,* 457.
8. Jad Adams and Phillip Whitehead, *The Dynasty* (London: Penguin Books, 1997), 294.
9. Jayakar, *Indira Gandhi,* 422.
10. Inder Malhotra, former *Guardian* correspondent and former *Times of India* editor, author's interview, New Delhi. The interview was conducted in three parts over the course of several months; the first of these took place in March 2010.
11. *The Dynasty,* BBC-TV series, 1997.
12. Adams and Whitehead, *The Dynasty,* 303.
13. Inder Malhotra, *Indira Gandhi* (London: Coronet Books, 1991), 240.
14. Pupul Jayakar, *The Dynasty,* BBC-TV series, 1997.
15. Hon. Maneka Gandhi, member of lower house of parliament, BJP, author's interview, New Delhi, 2010.
16. Sonia Gandhi, *Rajiv,* 88.
17. Hon. Maneka Gandhi, author's interview, New Delhi, 2010.
18. According to journalist Rasheed Kidwai, they both attended Junior Modern School before boarding school.
19. Swraj Paul, author's interview, London, September 2010.
20. Mrs. Hemant Pasrich, director, the Study, author's interview, New Delhi, March 2010.

21. Vikram Lal, Doon School board member, author's interview, New Delhi, April 2010.
22. Mark Tully and Satish Jacob, *Amritsar* (New Delhi: Rupa and Co., 1985), 141.
23. Mark Tully, former chief of bureau, BBC, New Delhi, author's interview, New Delhi. This interview was conducted in two parts over several months; the first of these took place in March 2010.
24. Col. M. P. Choudhary, author's interview, New Delhi, April 2010.
25. Sonia Gandhi, *Rajiv*, 8.

CHAPTER 9 EVERY DROP OF MY BLOOD

1. Sandeep Unnithan, defense editor, *India Today*, author's interview, New Delhi, April 2010.
2. Sonia Gandhi, *Rajiv* (New Delhi: Viking, 1992), 8.
3. Katherine Frank, *Indira* (London: Harper Perennial, 2005), 487.
4. Sandeep Unnithan, author's interview, April 2010.
5. Sonia Gandhi, *Rajiv*, 8.
6. Ibid., 9.
7. Mark Tully and Satish Jacob, *Amritsar* (New Delhi: Rupa and Co., 1985), 2.
8. Sonia Gandhi, *Rajiv*, 8.
9. Ibid., 8.
10. Tully and Jacob, *Amritsar*, 10.
11. Frank, *Indira*, 492.
12. Jad Adams and Phillip Whitehead, *The Dynasty* (London: Penguin Books, 1997), 314.
13. Frank, *Indira*, 492.
14. Adams and Whitehead, *The Dynasty*, 314.
15. Sonia Gandhi, *Rajiv*, 9.
16. Frank, *Indira*, 493.
17. Tully and Jacob, *Amritsar*, 2.
18. "Gunshots Broke the Still," *Hindustan Times*, November 1, 1984.
19. Frank, *Indira*, 493.
20. Sonia Gandhi, television interview with Vir Sanghvi, *Star Talk* on Star Plus Television, 1999.
21. "Gunshots Broke the Still," *Hindustan Times*, November 1, 1984.
22. "Many Questions Still Unanswered," *Hindustan Times*, November 1, 1984.
23. Ibid.
24. "Milling Crowds at AIIMS," *Hindustan Times*, November 1, 1984.
25. Tully and Jacob, *Amritsar*, 3.
26. Pupul Jayakar, *Indira Gandhi* (New Delhi: Penguin Books, 1995), 486.
27. Ibid., 486-487.
28. Adams and Whitehead, *The Dynasty*, 315.
29. Jayakar, *Indira Gandhi*, 487.
30. Ibid., 488.
31. Ibid.
32. P. C. Alexander, in *The Dynasty*, a four-part series aired on BBC-TV, 1997.
33. Ibid.
34. Ibid.
35. Natwar Singh, former minister of state for external affairs, author's interview, New Delhi. The interview was conducted in three parts over several months; the first of these was in February 2010.
36. This is the actual time of the start of the swearing-in ceremony of Rajiv Gandhi, from authentic records—sources give different versions.
37. This is the actual swearing in-time, from authentic records—sources give different versions.
38. Hon. Dr. Sanjay Sinh, member of the lower house of parliament, author's interview, New Delhi, April 2010.
39. Frank, *Indira*, 499.
40. Shekhar Gupta, editor in chief, *Indian Express* group, author's interview, New Delhi, March 2010.
41. "Lakhș Pay Homage at Teen Murti," *Hindustan Times*, November 2, 1984.
42. "A Moving Scene," *Hindustan Times*, November 3, 1984.

CHAPTER 10 RACE COURSE ROAD

1. From official photographs of the funeral, Photo Division, Ministry of Information and Broadcasting, New Delhi.

2. Jad Adams and Phillip Whitehead, *The Dynasty* (London: Penguin Books, 1997), 321.
3. Devender Khanna, friend of Rajiv Gandhi, author's interview, New Delhi, March 2010.
4. *India's Rajiv,* Siga Arts International, April 1, 1989.
5. Debatosh Sengupta, the official stills photographer in October 1984.
6. Dr. Rita Bahuguna Joshi, president, Uttar Pradesh Congress Committee, author's interview, Lucknow, March 2010.
7. Col. M. P. Choudhary, former Special Group Commander, author's interview, April 2010.
8. The Border Guarding Force is known as the Sashastra Seema Bal.
9. *India's Rajiv,* Siga Arts International, April 1, 1989.
10. Ibid.
11. Adams and Whitehead, *The Dynasty,* 329.
12. Natwar Singh, former minister of state for external affairs, author's interview, New Delhi. The interview was conducted in three parts over the course of several months; the first of these took place in February 2010.
13. *India's Rajiv.*
14. Sonia Gandhi, television interview with Vir Sanghvi, *Star Talk* for Star Plus, 1999.
15. *India's Rajiv.*
16. Rajiv Gandhi, interviewed for *India's Rajiv.*
17. Ibid.
18. Ibid.
19. Hon. Dr. Sanjay Sinh, member of lower house of parliament, author's interview, New Delhi, April 2010.
20. Ram Sewak, author's interview, Jagdishpur, March 2010.
21. Devender Khanna, author's interview, New Delhi, March 2010.
22. Sunita Kohli, architectural restorer and interior designer, author's telephone interview, New Delhi, May 2010. All Kohli quotations this chapter are from this interview.
23. Natwar Singh, author's interview, February 2010.
24. "Dear Reader, A Handsel," January 12, 2009, http://www.outlookindia.com/article.aspx?239443.
25. The Communist Party of India's Sitaram Yechury was the gift-giver, according to Smita Gupta, political editor of the *Hindu* group. Author's interview, Delhi, March 2010.
26. Mark Tully, former BBC Delhi bureau chief, author's interview, Delhi. The interview was conducted in two parts over the course of several months; the first of these took place in March 2010.
27. Rajiv Gandhi, in *The Dynasty,* a four-part series aired on BBC-TV, 1997.

CHAPTER 11 REMEMBERING INDIRA

1. Sonia Gandhi interview, "In Our House We Only Speak in Hindi," by Pushpa Bharati, first carried in now-defunct Hindi magazine *Dharamyug,* 1985; reprinted in *The (Chandigarh, India) Tribune,* May 1, 1991.
2. Sonia Gandhi, *Living Politics* (Tilburg: Nexus Institute, 2007), 20.
3. Ibid.
4. Ibid.
5. Nandini Mehta, former editor with Penguin Books, author's interview, New Delhi, March 2010.
6. *India's Rajiv,* Siga Arts International, April 1, 1989.
7. Sonia Gandhi, *Rajiv* (New Delhi: Viking, 1992), 10.
8. Population figures from the Registrar General and Census Commissioner of India, for the latest census data, see http://www.censusindia.gov.in/2011-prov-results/indiaatglance.html; http://www.countrystudies.us/india/.
9. Karma Topden joined the Indian Administrative Service, became an ambassador, a member of the upper house of parliament and Sikkim Congress committee president. Author's interview, New Delhi, April 2010.
10. Sonia Gandhi, *Rajiv,* 11.
11. Dr. Rita Bahuguna Joshi, president, Uttar Pradesh Congress Committee, author's interview, Lucknow, March 2010.

CHAPTER 12 GLIMPSES OF FREEDOM

1. Wajahat Habibullah, chairperson, National Commission for Minorities, author's interview, New Delhi. The interview was conducted in two parts over two months; the first of these took place in March 2010.

2. Ibid.
3. Shahila Habibullah, author's interview, New Delhi, March 2010.
4. Ibid.
5. Sonia Gandhi, "In Our House We Only Speak in Hindi," interview by Pushpa Bharati, *Dharamyug*, 1985, reprinted in *The (Chandigarh, India) Tribune*, May 1, 1991.
6. The wars were in 1948 and 1965; another took place in 1999.
7. Figure from Sandeep Unnithan, defense editor, *India Today*, January 2011.
8. Hon. Sonia Gandhi, address to a meeting of the All India Congress Committee, "Give Peace a Chance, says Sonia Gandhi to Kashmiris," *The Hindu*, November 2, 2010, http://www.thehindu.com/news/national/article864877.ece.
9. Author Sadia Dehlvi, author's interview, New Delhi, March 2010. The Shama group was the biggest set of Urdu publications at the time.
10. Dileep Padgaonkar, former *Times of India* editor and author, author's interview, New Delhi. The interview was conducted in three parts over the course of several months; the first of these took place in February 2010.
11. Dalip Mehta, former joint secretary with the Indian Foreign Service, author's interview, New Delhi, March 2010.
12. Sonia Gandhi, *Rajiv* (New Delhi: Viking, 1992), 106.
13. Dalip Mehta, author's interview, March 2010.
14. Satish Jacob, former deputy chief, BBC Delhi bureau, author's interview, New Delhi, April 2010.

CHAPTER 13 THE PREMIER'S WIFE

1. Sunita Kohli, architectural restorer and interior designer, telephone interview with author, New Delhi, May 2010.
2. Vir Sanghvi, author and columnist, quoted Simi Garewal, formerly a Bollywood actress who produced the documentary *India's Rajiv*. Author's interview, New Delhi, April 2010.
3. The Right Honorable Kenneth Clarke, British secretary of state, author's interview, London, September 2010.
4. Hon. Sonia Gandhi, at exhibition for sculptor Anish Kapoor, *Daily News & Analysis*, November 28, 2010, http://www.dnaindia.com/india/report_art-opens-mind-frees-it-of-prejudice-narrowness-sonia-gandhi_1473180.
5. Katherine Frank, *Indira* (Great Britain: Harper Perennial, 2005), 460.
6. Dalip Mehta, former joint secretary with the Indian Foreign Service, author's interview, New Delhi, March 2010.
7. Mrs. I. P. Singh, wife of late High Commissioner I. P. Singh and her daughter, Sujata Singh, author's interview, New Delhi, May 2010. The sari was made of *Jamawar* silk brocade.
8. Sonia Gandhi, *Rajiv* (New Delhi: Viking, 1992), 99.
9. Bassam Abu Sharif, *Arafat and the Dream of Palestine* (New York: Palgrave Macmillan, 2009), 136.
10. Sonia Gandhi, *Rajiv*, 123.

CHAPTER 14 SHADOW OF DEATH

1. "60 Minutes at Rajghat," *Hindustan Times*, October 3, 1986.
2. "Man in Army Uniform Fires Thrice, Arrested," *Hindustan Times*, October 3, 1986, front page.
3. Interview: "The Man Who Tried to Gun Down Rajiv Gandhi," Sify.com, April 8, 2009, http://www.sify.com/news/interview-the-man-who-tried-to-gun-down-rajiv-gandhi-news-columns-jeivEKheefj.html.
4. Sonia Gandhi, *Rajiv* (New Delhi: Viking, 1992), 119.
5. "The Man Who Tried to Gun Down Rajiv Gandhi." The article states that while Karamjit Singh was on remand, Rajiv Gandhi visited him twice, offering a pardon in return for an apology, which the unrepentant Sikh refused to give. The would-be assassin was convicted and jailed for 14 years. He contested the 2009 elections as an independent, during which time he gave this interview.
6. Sonia Gandhi, *Rajiv* (New Delhi: Viking, 1992), 119.
7. Ibid.
8. Jad Adams and Phillip Whitehead, *The Dynasty* (London: Penguin Books, 1997), 336.
9. The president's name is also sometimes spelled Jayewardane.
10. "Rajiv Hurt in Rifle-butt Attack by Lanka Sailor," *Hindustan Times*, July 31, 1987, front page.
11. Author's description of a photograph in Sonia Gandhi, *Rajiv*, 125.
12. Footage from *The Dynasty*, a four-part series aired on BBC-TV, 1997.

13. Sonia Gandhi, *Rajiv,* 125.
14. "Indian Troops Reach Lanka, *Hindustan Times,* July 31, 1987, front page.
15. Adams and Whitehead, *The Dynasty,* 344.
16. "Rajiv Gandhi Cleared over Bribery," BBC News, February 4, 2004, http://news.bbc.co.uk/2/hi/south_asia/3458319.stm.
17. Adams and Whitehead, *The Dynasty,* 350.
18. Sonia Gandhi, *Rajiv,* 14.
19. "Rajiv Files Nomination," *Hindustan Times,* April 25, 1991.
20. Sonia Gandhi, interview by Barkha Dutt, *Indian of the Year,* NDTV, 2006.
21. V. Jayanth, M. Prakash, T. S. Subramanian, "The Gory End," *Frontline,* June 8, 1991, 17.
22. Sonia Gandhi, interview by Vir Sanghvi, *One on One,* NDTV, 2006.
23. Author's description of a photograph in Sonia Gandhi, *Rajiv,* 153.
24. Arvind Shukla, journalist with Hindi daily *Amar Ujala,* author's interview, Amethi, March 2010.
25. Sonia Gandhi, *Rajiv,* 15.
26. Ibid., 15.

CHAPTER 15 THE LAST POST

1. "'Sivarajan' and Co. at V. P. Singh Rally," *Frontline,* August 3, 1991, 32.
2. "Sivarajan at Jayalalitha's Meeting," *Frontline,* July 20, 1991, 129.
3. V. Jayanth, M. Prakash, T. S. Subramanian, "The Gory End," *Frontline,* June 8, 1991, 11.
4. "Rajiv's Last Moments," *Frontline,* June 22, 1991, 70.
5. Wajahat Habibullah, chairperson, National Commission for Minorities, author's interview, New Delhi. The interview was conducted in two parts over two months; the first of these took place in March 2010.
6. Ibid.
7. Sunil Nehru's grandfather, Brij Lal Nehru, and Jawaharlal Nehru were first cousins; *their* fathers were brothers. Sunil was a senior company executive in Max India Ltd.
8. Sunil Nehru, former senior company executive in Max India Ltd., email interview by author, July-August 2010.
9. "Mourners Throng Funeral Route," *Hindustan Times,* May 25, 1991.
10. "Hysterical Crowds Mob Sonia, Amitabh's Car," *Hindustan Times,* May 25, 1991, 3.
11. Ibid.
12. Dalip Mehta, author's interview, New Delhi, March 2010.
13. Ibid.
14. "World Leaders Express Shock," *Hindustan Times,* May 23, 1991.
15. His Excellency Tariq Karim, Bangladesh High Commissioner to Delhi from 2009, author's interview, New Delhi April 2010.
16. Sonia Gandhi, *Rajiv* (New Delhi: Viking, 1992), 9.
17. Wajahat Habibullah, author's interview, March 2010.

CHAPTER 16 DEFYING THE PARTY

1. "Acting Cong-I Chief Mooted to Avert Rift," *Hindustan Times,* May 25, 1991, front page. All the reports of the Congress Party's discussion are from this edition of the daily newspaper.
2. "Congress Leaders May Approach RV," *Hindustan Times,* May 25, 1991, 10.
3. Hon. Sonia Gandhi, interview with Vir Sanghvi, *One on One,* NDTV, 2006.
4. Natwar Singh, former minister of state for external affairs, author's interview, New Delhi, 2010. The interview was conducted in three parts over several months; the first of these took place in February 2010.
5. Professor Pamela Price, "Personal Rule, Honor and Sonia Gandhi's Political Ascent," March 29, 2011, http://www.uio.no/?vrtx=searchuio&query=sonia+gandhi.
6. Ram Sewak and Rakesh Singh, author's interview, Jagdishpur, March 2010.
7. "Opinion Divided on Sonia Gandhi," *Hindustan Times,* New Delhi edition, May 25, 1991, 7. Though 2 of the 27 nonpolitical interviewees in the small survey in one town supported Sonia at this stage, an anti-Sonia feeling lasted in some quarters for several years.
8. Ibid.
9. "Sonia to Retain Janpath Bungalow," *Hindustan Times,* New Delhi edition, May 30, 1991.
10. "Ashes to Be Taken to Allahabad Today," *Hindustan Times,* May 27, 1991, front page.

11. Ibid.
12. Author's description from photographs appearing in the *Hindustan Times,* May 27, 1991, 5.
13. Gargi Parsai, "Rajiv's Ashes Immersed at Sangam," *Hindustan Times,* May 29, 1991, 1.
14. Sonia Gandhi, *Rajiv* (New Delhi: Viking, 1992), 9.
15. Rupa Chatterjee, *Sonia Gandhi: The Lady in Shad*ow (New Delhi: Butala Publications, 1998), 130.

CHAPTER 17 PRESERVING RAJIV'S LEGACY

1. Priyanka Gandhi Vadra, interview by Barkha Dutt, NDTV, April 25, 2009.
2. "Sonia Agrees to Meet MPs," *Hindustan Times,* June 19, 1991.
3. Inder Malhotra, former *Guardian* correspondent and former *Times of India* editor, author's interview, New Delhi. The interview was conducted in three parts over several months; the first of these took place in March 2010. What Malhotra said was corroborated by Natwar Singh in author's three-part interview, February 2010.
4. Sonia Gandhi, *Living Politics: What India Has Taught Me* (Tilburg: Nexus Institute, 2007), 21.
5. Cherry Yorke (Topden), telephone interview with author, June 2010. Karma Topden became president of the Sikkim state Congress committee, a member of parliament and ambassador to Mongolia.
6. Katherine Frank, *Indira* (London: Harper Perennial, 2005), 301.
7. Pupul Jayakar, *Indira Gandhi* (New Delhi: Penguin Books, 1995), 437.
8. Malvika Singh, publisher and author, author's interview, New Delhi, March 2010.
9. Later an archive would be added, to be looked after by the very professional Saurabh Dubey, RGF archivist, author's interview, New Delhi, April 2010.
10. Sunil Nehru, email interview by author, July-August 2010.
11. Rajiv Gandhi Foundation, Deed of Declaration, June 21, 1991.
12. Wajahat Habibullah, chairperson, National Commission for Minorities and member of World Bank Access to Information Appeals Board, author's interview, New Delhi. The interview was conducted in two parts over two months; the first of these took place in March 2010.
13. Ibid.
14. Sunil Nehru, nephew of B. K. Nehru, original RGF trustee, email interview with author, July-August 2010.
15. V. Krishnamurthy, chairman, National Manufacturing Competitiveness Council, author's interview, New Delhi. The interview was conducted in two parts; the first of these took place in April 2010.
16. Ibid.
17. Wajahat Habibullah, author's interview, March 2010.
18. Ibid.
19. Ibid.
20. Ibid.
21. V. Krishnamurthy, author's interview, New Delhi. The interview was conducted in two parts; the first of these took place in April 2010.
22. Wajahat Habibullah, author's interview, March 2010.
23. Ibid.
24. V. Krishnamurthy, author's interview, April 2010.
25. "Family Planning Needs People's Involvement," *RGF Newsletter,* Rajiv Gandhi Foundation, October 1997, 2.
26. "Era of Coalition Govts. Still Away," *RGF Newsletter,* Rajiv Gandhi Foundation, October 1997, 4.
27. V. Krishnamurthy, author's interview, April 2010.
28. With Mrs. Sonia Gandhi, the widow of the late Indian prime minister, Rajiv Gandhi, from documentary records of meetings between President Ikeda and Sonia Gandhi, held at Soka Gakkai International office, New Delhi.
29. Akash Ouchi, author's interview, New Delhi, April 2010.
30. The exhibition was called "Rajiv Gandhi: An Intimate Vision." Sonia's two photo-memoirs, *Rajiv* and *Rajiv's World,* were published in 1982 and 1996.
31. Soka Gakkai International Newsletter, "Recollections of My Meetings with Leading World Figures—Sonia Gandhi, Wife of Late Former Indian Prime Minister Rajiv Gandhi," September 1996, 83.

CHAPTER 18 NOT JUST TEARS

1. "1992: Mob Rips Apart Mosque in Ayodhya," BBC News, December 6, 1992, http://news.bbc.co.uk/onthisday/hi/dates/stories/december/6/newsid_3712000/3712777.stm.

2. Mobasshar Javed Akbar, author's interview, New Delhi, April 2010. All quotes attributed to Akbar in this chapter are from this interview. M. J. Akbar is the editorial director of *India Today,* TV channel Headlines Today, and the editor in chief of the *Sunday Guardian.*
3. Ibid.
4. Hon. Sonia Gandhi, interview by Shekhar Gupta, editor in chief, *Indian Express,* on *Walk the Talk,* NDTV, May 15, 2004.
5. Resolution from executive committee meeting, "Sankalp," *RGF Newsletter,* January 1993.
6. Hon. Sonia Gandhi, interview on *Walk the Talk,* May 15, 2004.
7. Sadia Dehlvi, author, author's interview, New Delhi, March 2010.
8. Wajahat Habibullah, chairperson, National Commission for Minorities, author's interview, New Delhi. The interview was conducted in two parts over two months; the first of these took place in March 2010. All anecdotes and quotes attributed to Wajahat Habibullah in this chapter are from this interview.
9. See Pranay Gupte, "Sonia Gandhi Comes into Her Own," first published in *The Straits Times,* PranayGupte.com, July 5, 2004, http://www.pranaygupte.com/article.php?index=96.
10. Information is from Varsha Das, director, National Gandhi Museum, who worked on the projects, author's interview, New Delhi, April 2010.
11. "Employment Opportunities for People with Disabilities," *RGF Newsletter,* July 1999, 6.
12. V. Krishnamurthy, chairman, National Manufacturing Competitiveness Council, author's interview, New Delhi. The interview was conducted in two parts; the first of these took place in April 2010.

CHAPTER 19 UNDERSTAND MY ANGUISH

1. Rasheed Kidwai, political journalist and Sonia Gandhi biographer, telephone and email interview by author, August 2010 to March 2011.
2. Inder Malhotra, *Dynasties of India and Beyond* (New Delhi: Harper Collins, 2003), 158.
3. Yusuf Ansari, *Triumph of Will* (New Delhi: India Research Press, 2006), 80.
4. Sutapa Mukherjee, "On Popular Demand," *Outlook,* August 4, 2003.
5. Dr. Rita Bahuguna Joshi, president, Uttar Pradesh Congress Committee, author's interview, Lucknow, Uttar Pradesh, March 2010.
6. Ansari, *Triumph of Will,* 116.
7. Hon. Sonia Gandhi, interview by Shekhar Gupta, editor in chief, *Indian Express,* on *Walk the Talk,* NDTV, May 15, 2004.
8. Priyanka Gandhi, interview with Barkha Dutt, NDTV, April 25, 2009.
9. Malhotra, *Dynasties of India and Beyond,* 170.
10. Hon. Sonia Gandhi, address at Bangalore, January 15, 1998, www.aicc.org.in/new/president-speech-detail.php?id=1.
11. Ibid.
12. Priyanka Gandhi, interview with Barkha Dutt, NDTV, April 25, 2009.
13. Ansari, *Triumph of Will,* 117.
14. Major Dalbir Singh, AICC national secretary, author's interview, New Delhi. The interview was conducted in three parts over several months; the first of these took place in March 2010.
15. Ibid.
16. Smita Gupta, political editor the *Hindu* group, author's interview, New Delhi, March 2010.
17. Inaugural Address of the Congress President, Pachmarhi camp, September 14, 1998, www.congresssandesh.net.
18. Ibid.
19. Shekhar Gupta, editor in chief, *India Express,* author's interview, New Delhi, March 2010.
20. Natwar Singh, former foreign minister, author's interview, New Delhi. The interview was conducted in three parts over three months; the first of these took place in February 2010.
21. Inaugural Address of the Congress President, Pachmarhi camp, September 14, 1998, www.congresssandesh.net.
22. On population control, Congress Party office-bearers and candidates would be disqualified if they parented more than two children after 2000.
23. Dr. V. Krishnamurthy, chairman, National Manufacturing Competitiveness Council, author's interview, New Delhi. The interview was conducted in two parts; the first of these took place in April 2010.

Chapter 20 Akbar Road

1. Sheela Reddy, "A Nose for Politics," *Outlook,* May 11, 2009, 46.
2. Information provided directly to author from British School Director Graham Ranger, 2010.
3. Ibid.
4. Promila Kalhan, "A Most Relaxed Evening at 10, Janpath," Rediff.com, February 19, 1997, http://www.rediff.com/news/feb/19wed.htm.
5. Sheela Reddy, "I Met Robert When I Was Just 13," *Outlook,* May 11, 2009, 46.
6. Priyanka Gandhi Vadra, interviewed by Barkha Dutt, NDTV, April 25, 2009.
7. Major Dalbir Singh, AICC national secretary, author's interview, New Delhi. All anecdotes and quotes from Major Singh are from this interview, conducted in three parts; the first of these took place in March 2010.
8. Dr. Rita Bahuguna Joshi, president, Uttar Pradesh Congress Committee, author's interview, Lucknow, March 2010.
9. Ibid.
10. Ibid.
11. Najma Heptulla, vice-chair, BJP, author's interview, New Delhi, April 2010.
12. Smita Gupta, political editor, *Hindu* group, author's interview, New Delhi, March 2010.
13. Vir Sanghvi, author and columnist and adviser to the *Hindustan Times,* author's interview, New Delhi, April 2010.
14. Natwar Singh, former minister of state, author's interview, New Delhi. The interview was conducted in three parts over several months; the first of these took place in February 2010.

Chapter 21 This Is My Land

1. Yousuf Ansari, *Triumph of Will* (New Delhi: India Research Press, 2006), 149.
2. "I Didn't Join Politics to Become PM, Says Sonia," interview with Vir Sanghvi, *Hindustan Times,* April 17, 2004.
3. Hon. Sonia Gandhi, interview with Vir Sanghvi, *One on One,* NDTV, 2006.
4. Dileep Padgaonkar, author and consulting editor of the *Times of India,* author's interview, New Delhi. The interview was conducted in three parts over several months; the first of these took place in February 2010.
5. Inder Malhotra, former *Guardian* correspondent and former editor, *Times of India,* author's interview, New Delhi. The interview was conducted in three parts over several months; the first of these took place in March 2010.
6. Vir Sanghvi, author and columnist and adviser to the *Hindustan Times,* author's interview, New Delhi, April 2010.
7. Priyanka Gandhi, interview by Barkha Dutt, NDTV, April 25, 2009.
8. Tarun Tejpal, editor in chief, *Tehelka* group, author's interview, New Delhi, April 2010.
9. Kuldip Nayar, author, human rights activist, author's interview, New Delhi and London. This interview was conducted in two parts over several months; the first of these took place in March 2010.
10. Hon. Amar Singh, member upper house of parliament, author's interview, New Delhi, April 2010.
11. Sumit Mitra, "Amar Singh: The Network Neta," October 25, 1999, http://www.india-today.com/itoday/19991025/profile.html.
12. Tarun Tejpal, author's interview, New Delhi, April 2010.
13. Lal Krishna Advani was home minister and then deputy prime minister in the Vajpayee government 1999-2004, now a senior BJP leader.
14. Amar Singh, author's interview, New Delhi, April 2010.
15. "Mahajan and Monica," *Indian Express,* August 30, 1999, http://www.expressindia.com/ie/daily/19990830/iex30042.html.
16. Murali Krishnan, "Many Jackals on the Prowl," *Outlook,* May 31, 2004.
17. Hon. Sonia Gandhi, interview with Vir Sanghvi, *Star Plus* on Star Talk Television, 1999.
18. Sunita Kohli, architectural restorer and interior designer, telephone interview by author, New Delhi, May 2010.
19. Tarun Tejpal, author's interview, April 2010.
20. Yousuf Ansari, *Triumph of Will* (New Delhi: India Research Press, 2006), 159.
21. Sonia Gandhi, Resignation Letter, CongressSandesh.com, May 15, 1999, http://www.congresssandesh.com/speaches/resignation_letter.htm.

22. Hon. Sonia Gandhi, Withdrawal of Resignation, translated speech in English at Talkotara Stadium, May 25, 1999.
23. Ibid.
24. Tarun Tejpal, author's interview, April 2010.
25. Major Dalbir Singh, All India Congress Committee national secretary, author's interview, New Delhi. All anecdotes and quotes are from this interview, conducted in three parts over several months; the first of these took place in March 2010.

CHAPTER 22 THE PEACE DIVIDEND

1. Author's description of photograph of Sonia Gandhi from Yousuf Ansari, *Triumph of Will* (New Delhi: India Research Press, 2006).
2. Accurate date is scarce. Official figures put the final death toll of Muslims at 1,000. "Gujarat Riot Muslims Eliminated," BBC News, April 14, 2005, http://news.bbc.co.uk/2/hi/south_asia/4445107.stm. Human rights groups estimate at least double that number.
3. Hon. Sonia Gandhi, interview by Shekhar Gupta, editor in chief, *Indian Express*, on *Walk the Talk*, NDTV, May 15, 2004.
4. News report, TV Today News Network, "Election Battle," December 4, 2007.
5. Nandini Mehta, editor and writer, author's interview, New Delhi, March 2010.
6. Jason Burke, "Ayodhya Verdict: Indian Security Forces Braced for Court Decision," *The Guardian*, September 30, 2010, http://www.guardian.co.uk/world/2010/sep/30/ayodhya-verdict-india-security-braced.
7. Liz Matthews, "Sonia Gandhi Appeals for Peace Citing the Ayodhya Verdict," LiveMint.com, September 29, 2010, http://www.livemint.com/2010/09/29142406/Sonia-Gandhi-appeals-for-peace.html.
8. Burke, "Ayodhya Verdict."
9. Figures from Shobhana Bhartia's Foreword, *The Peace Dividend* (New Delhi: Lotus Collection, 2004), xv.
10. Ibid., 37. "India's Roadmap for Peace," 36–41. All of Sonia Gandhi's quotes are from her speech and Q&A, which appear in *The Peace Dividend.*
11. Vinci is the married family name of Sonia's elder sister, Anouchka Maino Vinci.
12. Smita Gupta, Hindu group political editor, author's interview, New Delhi, March 2010. Gupta was told the contents of the conversation between Sonia Gandhi and Ram Vilas Paswan by Paswan.
13. Major Dalbir Singh, All India Congress Committee national secretary, author's interview, New Delhi, 2010. The interview was conducted in three parts over several months; the first of these took place in March 2010.
14. Neerja Chowdhury, political columnist, author's interview, New Delhi, April 2010.

CHAPTER 23 AGAINST THE ODDS

1. "Confidence in Motion, but Is She Ready?" *Outlook*, cover story, September 1, 2003.
2. The 2004 general election was the first in which electronic voting machines were used all over the country.
3. In addition to Sharad Pawar, who had formed a National Congress Party, also present at the 2003 dinner were Mulayam Singh Yadav, three-time chief minister of the state of Uttar Pradesh and founder of the Socialist Party, Lalu Prasad Yadav, who was strong in the state of Bihar and ran a political party, plus former prime ministers Chandra Shekhar and Deve Gowda, who had their own followings. "Bloom, Leading from the Front," *Outlook*, May 24, 2004, 37.
4. Sachin Pilot, minister of state for communications and IT, author's interview, New Delhi, February 2010.
5. Ibid.
6. Naveen Jindal, member of the lower house of parliament, author's interview, New Delhi, February 2010.
7. Major Dalbir Singh, All India Congress Committee national secretary, author's interview, New Delhi. The interview was conducted in three parts over several months; the first of these took place in March 2010.
8. Ibid. The war room was largely manned by Ahmed Patel, Ambiha Soni, Jairam Ramesh, and Dalbir Singh to formulate day-to-day strategy.

9. Ibid.
10. Parvez Hashmi, upper house parliament member and AICC secretary, author's interview, New Delhi, 2010.
11. Dr. Rita Bahuguna Joshi, president, Uttar Pradesh Congress Committee, author's interview, Lucknow, March 2010.
12. Sadia Dehlvi, writer, author's interview, New Delhi, March 2010; Tarun Tejpal, editor in chief of the *Tehelka* group, author's interview, New Delhi, April 2010.
13. Hon. Sonia Gandhi, interview by Vir Sanghvi, *Hindustan Times,* April 17, 2004.
14. Major Dalbir Singh, author's interview, March 2010.
15. Hon. Sonia Gandhi, interview by Vir Sanghvi, *One on One,* NDTV, 2006.
16. Breakdown of seats: 145 Congress, 72 from allies, and 61 from the Left Front.
17. Rahul Gandhi, "My Mother Won against All Odds: Rahul," ExpressIndia.com, May 13, 2004, http://www.expressindia.com/news/fullstory.php?newsid=31412.
18. *Hindustan Times* Leadership Initiative conclave, "India and the World," 2004.

CHAPTER 24 MY INNER VOICE

1. Priyanka Gandhi, interview by Barkha Dutt, NDTV, April 25, 2009.
2. News report, TV Today Network, May 18, 2004.
3. Neerja Chowdhury, political columnist, author's interview, New Delhi, April 2010.
4. The Intelligence Bureau is responsible for domestic intelligence and security matters within India.
5. Murali Krishnan, "Many Jackals on the Prowl," *Outlook,* May 31, 2004, 32.
6. Ghanshyam Dutt Bhardwaj, parliamentary security assistant, confirmed that Sonia and Rahul Gandhi do not wear bulletproof vests. Author's telephone interview, October 2010.
7. Tarun Tejpal, editor in chief, *Tehelka* group, author's interview, New Delhi, April 2010.
8. Priyanka Gandhi, interview by Barkha Dutt, April 25, 2009.
9. Major Dalbir Singh, All India Congress Committee national secretary, author's interview, New Delhi. The interview was conducted in three parts over several months; the first of these took place in March 2010.
10. Ibid.
11. All Sonia Gandhi quotes, asides, and descriptions of the meetings are taken from live Doordarshan television coverage of the May 18, 2004, events. Her speech is extracted, not quoted in full.
12. Ibid.
13. Ibid.
14. Ibid.
15. Ibid.
16. Priya Sahgal, senior editor, *India Today,* author's interview, New Delhi, 2010.
17. From live Doordarshan television coverage of the May 18, 2004, meeting.
18. Dr. Rita Bahuguna Joshi, president, Uttar Pradesh Congress committee, author's interview, Lucknow, Uttar Pradesh, March 2010.
19. Sonia Gandhi, *Democracy and Progress, India and the World,* ed. Namita Bhandare (New Delhi: Lotus Collection, 2005), 36.
20. Hon. Sushma Swaraj, leader of the opposition, author's interview, New Delhi, March 2010.
21. News report, TV Today Network, May 19, 2004.
22. Author Sadia Dehlvi, author's interview, New Delhi, March 2010.
23. Tarun Tejpal, author's interview, New Delhi, April 2010.
24. Hon. Sonia Gandhi, interview by Vir Sanghvi, *One on One,* NDTV, 2006.
25. Indira Gandhi biographer Inder Malhotra uses the phrase for those appointed by the Nehru-Gandhis to a high position who then maintain power unto themselves, setting up a rival court.
26. Priya Sahgal, author's interview, New Delhi, April 2010.
27. Dileep Padgaonkar, author, consulting editor with the *Times of India,* author's interview, New Delhi. The interview was conducted in three parts over several months; the first of these took place in February 2010.

CHAPTER 25 I AM HAPPY

1. Sonia Gandhi, *The Government and Civil Society: A Partnership for Sustainable Growth, Building a Better Future,* ed. Nandita Sengupta (New Delhi: Lotus Collection, 2006), 28.
2. Tarun Tejpal, editor in chief of *Tehelka* group, author's interview, New Delhi, April 2010.

3. According to the Multidimensional Poverty Index, applied by the Oxford Poverty and Human Development Initiative, 2010; "8 Indian States Have More Poor than 26 Poorest African Nations," *Times of India,* July 12, 2010, http://articles.timesofindia.indiatimes.com/2010-07-12/india/28276383_1_measure-ophi-multidimensional-poverty-index.
4. Arjun Sengupta, "Report on Conditions of Work and Promotions of Livelihood in the Unorganized Sector," National Commission for Enterprises in the Unorganized Sector, Government of India, August 2007, http://nceuis.nic.in/Condition_of_workers_sep_2007.pdf.
5. "India Still Home to Largest Illiterate Population: UNESCO," article quoting "The Education for All Global Monitoring Report," ExpressIndia.com, January 20, 2010, http://www.expressindia.com/latest-news/India-still-home-to-largest-illiterate-population-UNESCO/569609/.
6. Palagummi is Sainath's family name, placed first according to regional custom.
7. P. Sainath, rural affairs editor, *The Hindu,* telephone interview by author, December 2010.
8. Harsh Mander, National Advisory Council member, author's interview, New Delhi. The interview was conducted in two parts over several months; the first of these took place in February 2010.
9. M. J. Akbar, editorial director, *India Today,* author's interview, New Delhi, April 2010.
10. N. C. Saxena, National Advisory Council member, author's interview, New Delhi, April 2010.
11. Ibid.
12. Ibid.
13. Section 19, 1A, of India's constitution covers the right to freedom of speech and expression.
14. Wajahat Habibullah, former chief information commissioner, author's interview, New Delhi. The interview was conducted in two parts over two months; the first of these took place in March 2010.
15. Ibid.
16. Ibid.
17. Ibid. All opinion in this paragraph is from this interview.
18. Ibid.
19. Data provided by P. Sainath, compiled from National Crime Records Bureau, author's telephone interview, December 2010.
20. In August 2010 farmers from Jharkand wrote to the president that drought had destroyed their livelihoods for two years running, and if something could not be done for their families, they would kill themselves.
21. *Nero's Guests,* Mistral Movies, November 2009.
22. The name has now been changed to the Mahatma Gandhi National Rural Employment Guarantee Act, and the accompanying schemes are called the Mahatma Gandhi National Rural Employment Guarantee Schemes.
23. P. Sainath, author's telephone interview, December 2010.
24. Put as "eight crore" by Dr. C. P. Joshi, then minister of rural development, author's interview, New Delhi, February 2010.
25. Wajahat Habibullah, author's interview, New Delhi, March 2010.
26. Hon. Maneka Gandhi, member of the lower house of parliament, BJP, author's interview, New Delhi, March 2010.
27. "Office of Profit, Sonia Resigns from LS, to Contest Again from Rae Bareli," *Outlook India,* March 23, 2006, http://news.outlookindia.com/item.aspx?372254.
28. Hon. Sonia Gandhi, interview by Vir Sanghvi, *One on One,* NDTV, 2006.
29. Hon. Manish Tewari, MP and Congress party spokesman, author's interview, New Delhi, March 2010.
30. For instance, Hon. Agatha Sangma, Congress member of lower house of parliament elected in 2009, is the daughter of former speaker of the lower house, P. A. Sangma.
31. Her Excellency President Pratibha Devisingh Patil, author's interview, President's Palace, New Delhi, March 2010. The president of India serves a five-year term.
32. Dileep Padgaonkar, consulting editor, *Times of India,* author's interview, New Delhi. The interview was conducted in three parts over several months; the first of these took place in February 2010.
33. Hon. Brinda Karat, Communist Party of India (Marxist) Polit Bureau, member of upper house, author's interview, New Delhi, March 2010.
34. Hon. Sonia Gandhi, interview by Barkha Dutt on Women's Bill, NDTV, March 9, 2010.
35. Dileep Padgaonkar, author's interview, February 2010.

CHAPTER 26 THE NUCLEAR ISSUE

1. Brinda Karat, Polit Bureau member, Communist Party of India (Marxist) central committee, member of upper house of parliament, author's interview, New Delhi, March 2010.

2. Y. P. Rajesh, "India's Gandhi Backs Nuclear Deal," Reuters, August 14, 2007, http://www.reuters.com/article/2007/08/14/us-india-usa-nuclear-idUSDEL32177320070814.
3. Namita Bhandare, "In Conversation," *Imagine the India that Can Be* (Delhi: Lotus Collection, 2008), 41.
4. Ashis Ray, author's interview, London, October 2010.
5. Dr. Abdul Kalam played a pivotal role in India's 1998 nuclear test, Pokhran II, the first since Pokhran I, sanctioned by Indira Gandhi in 1974.
6. "SP Offering Crucial Support to the UPA Government, Refutes Horse-trading Charges," *ThaIndian News,* July 15, 2008, http://www.thaindian.com/newsportal/world-news/sp-offering-crucial-support-to-the-upa-government-refutes-horse-trading-charges_10071887.html.
7. "Amar Singh Gets Clean Chit in Cash-for-Vote Scam," CNN-IBN, December 15, 2008, http://ibnlive.in.com/news/amar-singh-gets-clean-chit-in-cashforvote-scam/80587-37.html.
8. "N-Deal More Important than Winning Lok Sabha Poll: Rahul Gandhi," Press Trust India, July 27, 2008, http://ibnlive.in.com/news/ndeal-to-be-pushed-even-at-the-cost-of-polls-rahul/69666-3.html.
9. Amar Singh, member of the upper house of parliament, author's interview, New Delhi, April 2010.
10. "Dollar amount estimate from US-India Business Council.
11. Compensation was raised to $320 million.

CHAPTER 27 INDIA'S 9/11

1. Figures verified by Major Dalbir Singh.
2. From Indian government dossier to Pakistan.
3. David Headley, a Lashkar-e-Taiba member, provided this information to Indian authorities.
4. The other group was the Jaish-e-Mohammad.
5. "Pakistan Admits India Attack Link," BBC News, February 12, 2009, http://news.bbc.co.uk/2/hi/south_asia/7885261.stm.
6. Gordon Rayner and Damien McElroy, "Mumbai Attacks: Indian Troops Storm Jewish Centre," *The Telegraph,* November 28, 2008, http://www.telegraph.co.uk/news/worldnews/asia/india/3532446/Mumbai-attacks-Indian-troops-storm-Jewish-centre-as-hotel-hostage-flee-Bombay-India.html.
7. Jonathan Miller, "David Headley: Stranger than Fiction," Channel4 News, January 21, 2010, http://www.channel4.com/news/articles/world/asia_pacific/david+headley+stranger+than+fiction/3511057.html.
8. "Terrorism Is a Deterrent to Growth: Sonia Gandhi," *ThaIndian,* March 1, 2009, http://www.thaindian.com/newsportal/politics/terrorism-is-a-deterrent-to-growth-sonia-gandhi_100161383.html.
9. Sandeep Unnithan, defense editor of *India Today,* author's interview, New Delhi, April 2010.
10. As described by Ranjan Mukherjee, officer on special duty to LG Tejendra Khanna, author's interview, March 2010. Khanna was appointed to the post in 2007; as this book went to press, he still held the position.
11. Lieutenant governor Tejendra Khanna, author's interview, New Delhi, March 2010.
12. Adrian Croft, "China, India Boost Defence as Crisis Takes Toll on West," *Reuters,* London, February 3, 2010, quoting *The Military Balance,* the annual report of the International Institute for Strategic Studies.
13. The SPG training includes jungle warfare, explosives, and five-day sleep deprivation.
14. Sandeep Unnithan, defense editor of *India Today,* author's interview, New Delhi, April 2010. In 2011, the SPG special director was Bharat Vir Wanchoo, installed in 2004 when the UPA came to power.
15. AICC security information is from Major Dalbir Singh, AICC national secretary, author's interview, New Delhi. The interview was conducted in three parts over several months; the first of these took place in March 2010.

CHAPTER 28 GENERATION NEXT

1. Arvind Shukla, reporter for India's largest Hindi daily *Amar Ujala,* author's interview, Amethi, March 2010.
2. From author's interview with journalist Aniruddha Bahal, New Delhi, February 2010.
3. Vikram Malhotra, Indian Youth Congress foreign affairs, former IYC general secretary, author's interview, New Delhi, February 2010.
4. Rahul Gandhi, "Rahul Unplugged," article by Priya Sahgal, *India Today,* January 4, 2010, 26.
5. Ibid.
6. N. C. Saxena, National Advisory Council member, author's interview, New Delhi, April 2010.

7. Priya Sahgal, senior editor, *India Today,* author's interview, New Delhi, April 2010.
8. The Shiv Sena also objected to Rahul Gandhi's indication that commandos fighting the *fedayeen* on November 26, 2008, in Mumbai consisted of Indians from the north as well as Mumbai.
9. Dileep Padgaonkar, consulting editor of *Times of India,* author's interview, New Delhi. The interview was conducted in three parts over several months; the first of these took place in February 2010.
10. Karan Thapar, television anchor, president, Infotainment Television, and columnist, author's interview, New Delhi, April 2010.
11. "Rahul Travels Like *aam admi* Again," *Deccan Herald,* October 29, 2010, http://www.deccanherald.com/content/108856/rahul-travels-like-aam-admi.html.
12. Piyush Srivastava, "Rahul Gandhi Travels Sleeper Class from Gorakhpur to Mumbai," *India Today,* October 29, 2010, http://indiatoday.intoday.in/site/story/rahul-gandhi-travels-sleeper-class-from-gorakhpur-to-mumbai/1/118161.html.
13. "Bill Gates' Amethi Visit a Hush-hush Affair," Rediff.com, May 12, 2010, http://news.rediff.com/report/2010/may/11/bill-gates-amethi-visit-a-hush-hush-affair.htm.
14. Bill Gates, interview by Shekhar Gupta, *Walk the Talk,* NDTV, May 2010.
15. Rahul Gandhi, quoted in "Rahul Unplugged," article by Priya Sahgal, *India Today,* January 4, 2010, 26.
16. Vijay Simha, "Rahul Gandhi Unravels Himself," Tehelka.com, September 24, 2005, http://www.tehelka.com/story_main14.asp?filename=Ne092405_I_could_CS.asp.
17. Priya Sahgal, "The RG File," *India Today,* January 4, 2010, 28.
18. Amethi has been changed to Chattrapati Shahuji Maharaj Nagar.
19. Hibi Eden, president, National Students Union of India, author's interview, New Delhi, February 2010. In 2011 Eden was elected a member of a legislative assembly.
20. Sheela Reddy, "A Nice Boy to Know (Really)," *Outlook,* June 1, 2009, 43.
21. Rajeev Satav, president, Indian Youth Congress, author's interview, New Delhi, February 2010.
22. Smita Gupta, political editor, *The Hindu* group, author's interview, New Delhi, March 2010.
23. Press brief spokesman, author's interview, New Delhi, April 2010.
24. Priyanka Gandhi, interview by Barkha Dutt, NDTV, April 25, 2009.
25. Priya Sahgal, "Rahul Unplugged," *India Today,* January 4, 2010, 26.

CHAPTER 29 DEAREST MOTHER

1. Priyanka Gandhi, interview by Barkha Dutt, NDTV, April 25, 2009.
2. Arati Jerath, "The Assassin Letters," *Times of India,* April 10, 2010, http://articles.timesofindia.indiatimes.com/2010-04-10/india/28125698_1_nalini-plea-for-early-release-life-imprisonment.
3. Ibid.
4. News report, TV Today Network, April 30, 2008.
5. "Yes, I Met My Dad's Killer: Priyanka," Rediff.com, April 15, 2008, http://www.rediff.com/news/2008/apr/15rajiv.htm.
6. News footage from TV Today Network, April 15, 2008.
7. Priyanka Gandhi Vadra, interview with Barkha Dutt, NDTV, April 25, 2009.
8. Priyanka Gandhi, interview by Sheela Reddy, "A Nose for Politics," *Outlook,* May 11, 2009, 47.
9. Priyanka Gandhi Vadra, interview by Barkha Dutt, NDTV, April 25, 2009.
10. Tarun Tejpal, *Tehelka* group editor in chief, author's interview, New Delhi, April 2010.
11. Priyanka Gandhi, interview by Sheela Reddy, "A Nose for Politics."
12. V. Krishnamurthy, chairman, National Manufacturing Competitiveness Council, author's interview, New Delhi. The interview was conducted in two parts in April 2010.
13. M. J. Akbar, editorial director, *India Today, Headlines Today,* and editor in chief of *Sunday Guardian,* author's interview, New Delhi, April 2010.
14. Congress gained 206 seats in 2009—up 61 from 2004.
15. Priya Sahgal, senior editor, *India Today,* author's interview, New Delhi, April 2010.
16. Vir Sanghvi, author and columnist and adviser to the *Hindustan Times,* believes the key relationship will be with the United States. Author's interview, New Delhi, April 2010.
17. According to the MacKinsey Global Institute. Brian Bremner, "Coming Soon to India: Middle Class Money," *BusinessWeek,* http://images.businessweek.com/ss/07/06/0601_india_middleclass/source/1.htm.
18. "The Big Five in India: Did India Gain?" *India Today,* http://indiatoday.intoday.in/site/gallery/the-big-five-in-india.-did-india-gain/3/4008.html.

19. "Sonia Senior to Wen in Protocol," *India Express,* December 20, 2010, http://www.indianexpress.com/news/sonia-senior-to-wen-in-protocol/726959/.
20. Protocol information from the Hon. Dr. Karan Singh, member of upper house of parliament and chairman of foreign affairs department at the Indian National Congress, in answer to author's question at roundtable session for Indian journalists, London, May 13, 2011.
21. "Grooms Aplenty, 'Bride' India Should Pick Right Match: Russia," *Times of India,* December 17, 2010, http://articles.timesofindia.indiatimes.com/2010-12-17/india/28241277_1_india-us-ties-grooms-russian-ambassador.
22. Namita Bhandare, "In Conversation," *Imagine the India that Can Be* (Delhi: Lotus Collection, 2008), 32–33; footage of the 2007 Leadership Summit.
23. Ibid.
24. From footage of the 2008 *Hindustan Times* Leadership Summit.

EPILOGUE JANPATH

1. Priya Sahgal, senior editor, *India Today,* author's interview, New Delhi, April 2010.
2. Subodh Ghildiyal, "What Makes It So Difficult to Box Jairam Ramesh?" *Times of India,* August 28, 2010, http://articles.timesofindia.indiatimes.com/2010-08-28/india/28286823_1_jairam-ramesh-congress-upa-2.
3. Priya Sahgal, author's interview, April 2010.
4. Hon. Manish Tewari, member of lower house of parliament, Congress party spokesman, author's interview, New Delhi, March 2010.
5. Smita Gupta, "A Question of the Heir and Now," *Outlook,* June 1, 2009, 32.
6. Naqshbandi Aurangzeb, "Rahul's Impromptu Act," *Hindustan Times,* November 3, 2010, http://www.hindustantimes.com/Rahul-s-impromptu-act/Article1-621455.aspx.
7. Bhaskar Roy, "Common Man Yet to Be Connected to System: Rahul," *Times of India,* December 20, 2010, http://articles.timesofindia.indiatimes.com/2010-12-20/india/28246046_1_aam-admi-common-man-university-topper; "Rahul Gandhi's Prescription for Defining 'Aam Aadmi'," December 24, 2010, http://www.pressbrief.in/index.php?option=com_content&task=view&id=947&Itemid=51.
8. "Close Your Eyes, Listen to Rahul, You Hear Rajiv: P.C.," *Indian Express,* December 21, 2010, http://www.indianexpress.com/news/close-your-eyes-listen-to-rahul-you-hear-r/727337/.
9. Dileep Padgaonkar, consulting editor of *Times of India,* author's interview, New Delhi. The interview was conducted in three parts over the course of several months; the first of these took place in February 2010.
10. Priya Sahgal, author's interview, April 2010.
11. Vinod Mehta, editor in chief, *Outlook* group, author's interview, New Delhi, April 2010.
12. Interview with Rekha, *Eastern Eye,* November 29, 2002, 5.

INDEX